LESSER LIVING CREATURES OF THE RENAISSANCE

ANIMALIBUS
OF ANIMALS AND CULTURES

Nigel Rothfels, General Editor

ADVISORY BOARD:
Steve Baker (University of Central Lancashire)
Garry Marvin (Roehampton University)
Susan McHugh (University of New England)
Kari Weil (Wesleyan University)

Books in the Animalibus series share a fascination with the status and the role of animals in human life. Crossing the humanities and the social sciences to include work in history, anthropology, social and cultural geography, environmental studies, and literary and art criticism, these books ask what thinking about nonhuman animals can teach us about human cultures, about what it means to be human, and about how that meaning might shift across times and places.

OTHER TITLES IN THE SERIES:

Rachel Poliquin, *The Breathless Zoo: Taxidermy and the Cultures of Longing*

Joan B. Landes, Paula Young Lee, and Paul Youngquist, eds., *Gorgeous Beasts: Animal Bodies in Historical Perspective*

Liv Emma Thorsen, Karen A. Rader, and Adam Dodd, eds., *Animals on Display: The Creaturely in Museums, Zoos, and Natural History*

Ann-Janine Morey, *Picturing Dogs, Seeing Ourselves: Vintage American Photographs*

Mary Sanders Pollock, *Storytelling Apes: Primatology Narratives Past and Future*

Ingrid H. Tague, *Animal Companions: Pets and Social Change in Eighteenth-Century Britain*

Dick Blau and Nigel Rothfels, *Elephant House*

Marcus Baynes-Rock, *Among the Bone Eaters: Encounters with Hyenas in Harar*

Monica Mattfeld, *Becoming Centaur: Eighteenth-Century Masculinity and English Horsemanship*

Heather Swan, *Where Honeybees Thrive: Stories from the Field*

Karen Raber and Monica Mattfeld, eds., *Performing Animals: History, Agency, Theater*

J. Keri Cronin, *Art for Animals: Visual Culture and Animal Advocacy, 1870–1914*

Elizabeth Marshall Thomas, *The Hidden Life of Life: A Walk Through the Reaches of Time*

Elizabeth Young, *Pet Projects: Animal Fiction and Taxidermy in the Nineteenth-Century Archive*

Marcus Baynes-Rock, *Crocodile Undone: The Domestication of Australia's Fauna*

Deborah Nadal, *Rabies in the Streets: Interspecies Camaraderie in Urban India*

Mustafa Haikal, translated by Thomas Dunlap, *Master Pongo: A Gorilla Conquers Europe*

Austin McQuinn, *Becoming Audible: Sounding Animality in Performance*

Karalyn Kendall-Morwick, *Canis Modernis: Human/Dog Coevolution in Modernist Literature*

LESSER LIVING CREATURES OF THE RENAISSANCE

Volume 2: Concepts

EDITED BY KEITH BOTELHO AND JOSEPH CAMPANA

THE PENNSYLVANIA STATE UNIVERSITY PRESS
UNIVERSITY PARK, PENNSYLVANIA

Library of Congress Cataloging-in-Publication Data

Names: Botelho, Keith M., editor. | Campana, Joseph, editor.
Title: Lesser living creatures of the Renaissance / edited by Keith Botelho and Joseph Campana.
Other titles: Animalibus.
Description: University Park, Pennsylvania : The Pennsylvania State University Press, [2023] | Series: Animalibus : of animals and cultures | Includes bibliographical references and index. | Contents: v. 1. Insects—v. 2. Concepts.
Summary: "Explores the prominence of insects in the literal and symbolic economies of early modern England. Examines concepts cutting across species (insect and otherwise) and draws attention to the work of early modern natural historians"—Provided by publisher.
Identifiers: LCCN 2022037304 | ISBN 9780271094465 (v. 1 ; hardback) | ISBN 9780271094489 (v. 2 ; hardback) | ISBN 9780271094472 (v. 1 ; paper) | ISBN 9780271094496 (v. 2 ; paper)
Subjects: LCSH: English literature—Early modern, 1500-1700—History and criticism. | Insects in literature. | LCGFT: Essays.
Classification: LCC PR408.I58 L47 2023 | DDC 820.9/36257—dc23/eng/20221011
LC record available at https://lccn.loc.gov/2022037304

Copyright © 2023 The Pennsylvania State University Press
All rights reserved
Printed in the United States of America
Published by The Pennsylvania State University Press,
University Park, PA 16802-1003

The Pennsylvania State University Press is a member of the Association of University Presses.

It is the policy of The Pennsylvania State University Press to use acid-free paper. Publications on uncoated stock satisfy the minimum requirements of American National Standard for Information Sciences—Permanence of Paper for Printed Library Material, ANSI Z39.48–1992.

*For all creatures
great and small*

CONTENTS

List of Illustrations (ix)
Acknowledgments (xi)

Introduction Concepts (1)
JOSEPH CAMPANA

1 *Sting* Stinging like a Bee in Early Modern England (13)
JULIAN YATES

2 *Scale* Lesser Living in the Renaissance (29)
JOSEPH CAMPANA

3 *Pest* Environmental Justice and the (Early Modern) Rhetoric of Pest Control (49)
JENNIFER MUNROE AND REBECCA LAROCHE

4 *Infestation* Out of Africa: Locust Infestation, Universal History, and the Early Modern Theological Imaginary (62)
LUCINDA COLE

5 *Habitat and Politics* "Regardles of his gouernaunce": Exploring Human Sovereignty and Political Formation in Early Modern Insect Habitats (83)
ANDREW FLECK

6 *Consume* Consuming Insects (104)
AMY L. TIGNER

7 *Decompose* Worm Work (122)
FRANCES E. DOLAN

8 *Locomotion* Creeping and Crawling (132)
KEITH BOTELHO

9 *Communication* Tettix (141)
LOWELL DUCKERT

10 *Swarm* Song of the Swarm (160)
DEREK WOODS

11 *Illumination* "Living Lamps" (180)
JESSICA LYNN WOLFE

Epilogue Concepts (197)
KEITH BOTELHO

List of Contributors (201)
Index (205)

ILLUSTRATIONS

2.1.1   Robert Hooke, *Micrographia: or, Some Physiological Descriptions of Minute Bodies Made by Magnifying Glasses.* 21
2.2.1   Francesco Stelluti and Federigo Cesi, *Apiarium.* 40
2.2.2   Francesco Stelluti and Federigo Cesi, *Melissographia.* 41
2.2.3   Francesco Stelluti, *Persio.* 41
2.2.4   Francesco Stelluti, *Persio.* 42
2.2.5   Francesco Stelluti, *Persio.* 43
2.9.1   From Thomas Moffett, *Insectorum sive Minimorum Animalium Theatrum.* 148
2.11.1 Richard Waller, "Observations on the Cicindela Volans, or Flying Glow-Worm. 185
2.11.2 Ulisse Aldrovandi, *De Animalibus Insectis Libri Septem.* 187

ACKNOWLEDGMENTS

A decade ago, we first met in a seminar at the Shakespeare Association of America and there discovered a shared scholarly interest in bees. In 2013, we organized a panel, Lesser Living Creatures of the Renaissance, at the Arizona Center for Medieval and Renaissance Studies Conference, and over the next few years we developed the outline of a collection on insects in the early modern world.

Thank you to Penn State University Press and editor-in-chief Kendra Boileau for offering us an advance contract, and to Nigel Rothfels, general editor of the series Animalibus: Of Animals and Cultures, who was an early advocate for the collection.

The comments and feedback on our manuscript from Erica Fudge and an anonymous reader were pivotal in the early stages of revision. Thank you especially to Erica for her enthusiasm and encouragement.

Along the way, our editorial assistants—including Evan Choate, Brooke Payne, and Amanda Kruger—worked diligently on the project, and to them we are grateful.

We thank the librarians and staff at the Folger Shakespeare Library and the John and Mary Nichols Rare Books Library at the University of Oklahoma.

Thank you to the Norman J. Radow College of Humanities and Social Sciences and the English Department at Kennesaw State University for support and release time to work on this collection, and to the School of Humanities, Humanities Research Center, and Department of English at Rice University for their support.

To our network of friends and colleagues who supported this massive undertaking in both big and small ways, thank you. Thank you as well to our twenty-four contributors who exhibited remarkable patience during this very long process.

Keith Botelho thanks his son, Ethan, and daughter, Julia, for their unfailing love and support and for filling his life with sweetness and light.

Joseph Campana thanks both his hive-mate, Theodore Bale, and his teacher, Nolan Marciniec, expert in poems and bees, for the buzz of conversation over the years: all sweet, no sting.

INTRODUCTION
CONCEPTS

Joseph Campana

Creatures conjure worlds, whole logics around them. Take, for instance, John Yianni's award-winning tabletop game Hive, which Gen42 Games launched in 2001 to much acclaim.[1] Described as an abstract strategy game, Hive requires two players to face off with a series of hexagonal tiles, each with a different insect blazoned on it: beetle, soldier ant, spider, grasshopper, and queen bee. Each player places a tile next to another and tries to encircle the opponent's queen bee. The process of playing requires the creation of a hive-like architecture made of opposing pieces. But each tile implies a different strategy. The queen bee moves slowly, one space at a time, as the beetle does, but the latter possesses a special capacity to climb vertically on top of an adjacent tile, thus adding a new dimension of travel and immobilizing an opponent's tile. Spiders can move three spaces around the circumference of the hive layout, as do the soldier ants, though their movement is unlimited. Not surprisingly, the grasshopper can leap over pieces but only in a straight line. Just as each of these strategic creatures in Hive implies a different strategy, vector, and style of movement, so too does each concept invoked here offer a singular view of the architecture of the living. It also speaks to a larger world of lesser living creatures, not isolated in their individual species worlds but complexly interacting—even if improbably—under the parameters of a tabletop strategy game.

Locomotion, particularly of insects, is just one of many vectors of experience that might encourage us to reconsider our interpretive practices precisely because it redirects our attention from the totality of a creature to other considerations, like habit or morphology. And, indeed, a common taxonomy for early modern creatures combined both habitat and locomotion in considering whether creatures tended to crawl or creep on or in the earth, to fly in the air, or to swim through water. This very way of indexing insects animates Samuel Purchas's 1657 *A Theatre of Politicall Flying-Insects*, the exquisite title of which sends a series of conceptual signals. Like Thomas Moffett's *Theater of Insects*, Purchas's text used the common master metaphor of the theater to invoke breadth of worldly scope (as in "this wide and universal theater") and seriousness of scientific importance (as in the theaters of anatomy and war increasingly referenced in the period). These creatures offer insights into group psychology—they are political creatures whose social grouping yields useful insights into both insects and humans—as debated in a lineage dating back at least to Aristotle. They are creatures of the air—flying insects—as opposed to insects that crawl or burrow and perhaps more like other creatures of the air, like birds. Purchas does not encompass, then, the encyclopedic array of Moffett, but he does address a lesser multitude of creatures, including several varieties of bees, along with wasps, hornets, and grasshoppers.

If *A Theatre of Politicall Flying-Insects* was typical in its invocation of categories and capacities that cut across life-forms, it quickly falls prey to the specific gravity of the creature. It will be no surprise that a singular creature rises up: the charismatic bee. Indeed, the very title of the work describes the book as one "where in especially the Nature, the Worth, the Work, the Wonder, and the manner of Right-ordering of the BEE is discovered and described" and with the word *BEE* appearing in the largest letters on the title page. Purchas promises further a mix of "discourses, historical, and observations physical," as well as "meditations, and observations *Theological* and *Moral*, in Three *Centuries* upon that Subject." All of these additions pertain solely to the bee, which occupies twenty-six of thirty-two chapters, with three of the remaining six chapters varying from *Apis mellifera* to address wild bees, humble-bees, and American bees. Purchas casts his net wide in the dedication to the book, identifying "creatures [as] the Book of Nature" and claiming "the world is Gods library," but the excellency of bees, which Purchas considers "a little neglected creature," grabs the lion's share of the spotlight. Indeed, he identifies the bees as "so curious in Architecture, and in the fabrick of her hexangle Combs," marveling that bees "should observe as just proportions as the best Geometrician."[2] No effusions of wonder emerge for other feats of insect architecture and geometry, such as webs. Once he begins, Purchas has eyes only for bees, and the dedicatory poems confirm as much. One poem is titled "To the Author on his Physio-theological History of Bees," and another is an "Elaborate Treatise of BEES." These descriptive tags recur in the other poems, nearly all of which flag the bee, along with complimentary notice of the author's industry in this "Bee-like laborious treatise." Quite consistently, then, Purchas's fascinating cross-categorical thinking ("physio-theological") collides with the irresistible allure of singularity of creaturely reference. Even social insects can appear to offer the prospect of individuation or even personhood assimilable to the human. Insects can appear to be all too human, with the long-standing mimetic dynamic between human and bee resolving too easily in favor of anthropocentrism. Bees were, as indicated in volume 1, the most charismatic of insects, to be sure. But inclinations dating back far earlier than Purchas threaten to domesticate the strangeness of the insect world.

While the first volume of *Lesser Living Creatures of the Renaissance* seeks to conjure and capture the charisma of *creatures*, this one directs its attention to the *concepts* elicited by insect life. It does so at a moment, of course, of what we might call the maximum exposure of the keyword. In 1976, Raymond Williams articulated his task in the first edition of *Keywords* as producing "the record of an inquiry into a vocabulary: a shared body of words and meanings in our most general discussions, in English, of the practices and institutions which we group as *culture* and *society*."

Keywords were, then, "significant binding words in certain activities and their interpretation" and "significant, indicative words in certain forms of thought" that ultimately offer "a way of recording, investigating and presenting problems of meaning in the area in which the meanings of *culture* and *society* have formed."[3] In a revised edition of *Keywords* published in 1983, Williams added more words to the mix, and did so more recently in a "new" edition in 2015. The intervening decades witnessed an explosion of keywords. Could Williams have predicted how dominant this interpretive strategy would become? In 2009,

New Keywords: A Revised Vocabulary of Culture and Society promised an updated, multiauthor strategy, as does the more recent *Keywords for Today: A 21st Century Vocabulary*. John Patrick Leahy's 2019 *Keywords: The New Language of Capitalism*, which directs its attention to terms of economic import, is one of many such keyword books calibrating itself to more specific vocabularies. New York University Press features a "Keywords" series, with volumes treating a range of subjects (e.g., *Keywords for African-American Studies*, *Keywords for Disability Studies*, *Keywords for Media Studies*). More particular instances from within early modern studies become visible of late as well. Roland Greene's *Five Words: Critical Semantics in the Age of Shakespeare and Cervantes* advocates for a "critical semantics" that obeys the dictum that "words precede everything" and attends to five particular "protagonist words, complex words, keywords, and, not least, everyday words" whose complex transformations between early modernity and the present offer insights into the transformation of worldviews.[4]

Certainly the logic of the keyword relies on, even as it differentiates itself from, earlier interpretive strategies in dictionaries and encyclopedias. Of course, the omnipresence of search strategies plays as potent a role in the dominance of keywords. Whether one traces a lineage to Williams or acquiesces to the latest trends in digital search technologies, it is hard not to feel keyworded to death. In one sense, then, *Lesser Living Creatures* joins an onslaught of new dictionaries, encyclopedias, and keyword-oriented publishing series across interest, discipline, and period. And yet the hope here is to find unexpected connections and revelatory moments in turning to conceptual nodes that might otherwise be obscured by creature logic. The word *insect* derives from the Latin *insectare*, which means "to cut into." These concepts represent not an anatomization of the insect but rather the exposure of modular qualities that stretch across insect species and even beyond the insect world, reminding us of Eric C. Brown's description of "segmentation" as "the most important identifying characteristic of the insect."[5]

Concepts enable, then, a kind of modular thinking, a thinking across categories that even the rich natural-historical materials of the era may at times prevent. The charisma of the creaturely form can easily draw us into predictable emotional patterns, which is no doubt why historians and theorists of nonhuman life seem to be so consistently attracted to either strange and terrifying creatures that provoke awe (monsters or rare exotics) or the familiar and even domestic creatures that promise obedient intimacy (pets and livestock). Insects may provoke this familiar range of emotions—wonder and horror, fascination and disgust. And yet they participate in a kind of ordinary ubiquity that, no matter how wondrous or repellent insects may still prove to be, prevents them from serving as what we might call affective storehouses for humans to the same degree as other creatures. This tendency makes visible a series of other patterns, those not necessarily dictated by creature comforts, by which I mean the comfort of certain familiar feelings in response to the most charismatic of other-than-human creatures.

Indeed, the logic of the creature, which is not unlike the logic of objects or persons, conjures a kind of integrity: the singular insect compelling and on its own terms, however partial that singularity may be. But one of the guiding premises of *Lesser Living Creatures* is also that to consider creaturely life from the point of view of insects is not only to understand the strange proximities between divergent creatures (such as humans and flies) but also to understand insects as a spur to a conversation about the concepts and operations that govern forms of life. How do insects move, swarm, and infest? How do they fly, sting, and devour? How do they sing, glow, and work? How do they scale? And how do they grow both pestilence and polities around them?

Of the many qualities connecting across, like runners or tethers, the myriad forms of insect life, scale may be one of the most primary and primal. I explore the *lesser* of the lesser living creatures on offer in Moffett's *Theater of Insects* and more broadly represented by early modern insectophilia. It seems of late that scale becomes more important only across a wide range of disciplines and subjects. Given that scale is a core comparative and evaluative impulse that works through forms of speculative modeling, the reach of notions of scale should be no surprise. In "Lesser Living in the Renaissance," after surveying the various uses of scale, which most often refer to great sweeps of distance and time, I explore the importance of relative magnitude, from scales of measure that evoke the heft and importance of objects to broad shifts in size, from microscopic to macroscopic. In so doing, I consider the frequent articulation of a *diminutive sublime*, from Moffett to Robert Hooke, expressed in the celebration of the wonders of small things that serves to stabilize disorienting sweeps of scale that not only upend the centrality of the human but also, more importantly, call into question the certainty of measure and consequently fuel a longing for ever more powerful and stabilizing technologies of measure and magnification.

Ever since Aristotle introduced the notion of the political animal, he left open the question of what creatures might qualify. And while "human" has always been the most common answer, several insect species have been claimants to the title. Andrew Fleck's "'Regardles of his gouernaunce': Exploring Human Sovereignty and Political Formation in Early Modern Insect Habitats" ties these ancient questions of creaturely polity and community to early modern reflections on habitat. "Peering into the dwellings of insects to find examples of the supposedly natural order of society," he argues, "early modern thinkers imported their own prejudices into their artificial imaginings of these habitats, confirming their own sense of what makes it possible for individuals to live in harmonious, efficient community." More particularly, Fleck considers "the early modern politicization of the spider web and the butterfly's garden field" from John Heywood's *Spider and the Flie* to Edmund Spenser's *Muiopotmos*. And in this fascinating journey from web to garden, Fleck exposes forms of insect-inflected thought about liberty and jurisdiction.

To be "Consuming Insects" with Amy L. Tigner is to consider one of the more prominent, if less often discussed, aspects of natural history. Since the whole world of creation existed for the benefit of humankind, that benefit stretched from education to alimentation, explaining why so many natural history texts include the manifold medicinal uses of the bodies of animals and insects. For cultures unaccustomed to eating insects, it requires some reminding that "bees, flies, worms and beetles occur regularly as ingredients in household recipes." This causes a radical revaluation of what might otherwise be nuisance species, since "within the household kitchen these minute nonhumans were highly esteemed for their particular culinary, medicinal, and even aesthetic value." Tigner's study of early modern recipe books reveals what she calls "the pragmatic intimacy of consumption" whereby the utility of insects in early modern food and medicine implies a kind of mutual incorporation "between human body and insect body, manifesting as a kind of circular table—each acting in turn as eater and eaten." And by highlighting the importance of the culinary theater to the theater of insects, Tigner also emphasizes the importance of women to how we understand insect life, which was by no means merely the province of men of science.

If for Tigner the perhaps to some grotesque intimacy with insects reveals a culture of mutual benefit, Lucinda Cole's "Out of Africa: Locust Infestation, Universal History, and the Early Modern Theological Imaginary" builds powerfully on her award-winning monograph, *Imperfect Creatures: Vermin, Literature, and the Sciences of Life, 1550–1750*, to consider the terrifying and literally border-crossing nature of swarms. A series of insect events in the era "kept the problem of transnational infestation at the forefront of a wide range of discussions about the typological meanings of, and remedies for, swarming things that threatened the ecological and sociopolitical stability of the state." Cole reveals just how fascinating these terrifying events were inasmuch as they connected a range of early modern discourses, from ethnography to natural history. Moffett's *Theater of Insects* should be read not only in light of early modern scientific discourse but also in light of universal history and theodicy. As such, "infestation reappears as a form of personal and political infection, in contrast to Judeo-Christian agricultural practices that supposedly offer a real but always precarious protection." Consequently, attention to insect infestations, especially locusts, fueled burgeoning colonial impulses: "God instructs Christians to rid Africa and India of the insects that serve as both evidence of these regions' need for colonial intervention and signs of their sins in resisting a different and divinely sanctioned regime." The consequence of this stunning analysis is to widen the geography of an early modern theater of insects while understanding these lesser living creatures to be "deeply entangled in theologically inflected arguments about punishment and mercy, diet and disease, self and other."

Swarms terrified and destroyed, but could they also sing? Bees were not the only mellifluous insect, but the sound Derek Woods listens for in "Song of the Swarm" is "the relation between the concepts of swarming and communication—among humans, among bees and other social insects, and between humans and bees." The concept of the swarm, from early modern insect lore to contemporary computing technologies, considers "the paradox of swarming," which concerns a "distinction between control by a subject and order that emerges from interaction among simple elements." Moving deftly between "bee song in works of Renaissance natural history" and "Karl von Frisch's famous work... on the bee dance language," Woods finds the connection between seemingly disparate centuries in information theory. How, then, to reconcile the logic of sovereignty associated with hives and "decentered communication" typical of the swarm? Perhaps there is no such reconciliation. But rather than understanding the long transit of thinking about swarm from a sovereignty-inflected early modernity to a decentered postmodernity, Woods tracks a much more complicated dance. In so doing, he suggests the importance of the "life-form topos," a way of recognizing how "life-forms come into being as material-semiotic entities that occupy a level of partial abstraction between concrete species and individual, on the one hand, and metaphysical distinctions such as human/animal, on the other." These topoi, Woods argues, "are an expansive subject for those interested in studying the relatively deep historical timescales of literature and culture."

If for Tigner the pestilence associated with insects belies their medicinal value in the home economics of early modernity, for Jennifer Munroe and Rebecca Laroche, the moniker *pest* assiduously denies what they call "our shared susceptibilities with creeping things and with each other." In "Environmental Justice and the (Early Modern) Rhetoric of Pest Control," Munroe and Laroche examine the gendered, militaristic language used to "keep" not only insects "at bay" but any sense of common vulnerability. In this chapter, as in several others in this volume, Munroe and Laroche move deftly between early modern and present-day concerns, showing how these long-standing languages of pest control precondition our own responses to insects and also in ways that "pertain to twenty-first-century environmental justice as well." From this point of view, the most common early modern invaders relevant to this rubric were the omnipresent ants and lice, which align in battalions, seeking vulnerable homes, gardens, and bodies. Husbandry manuals and natural history texts alike would construe insects as brute assailants and gardens as tender victims. Insects were, by nature, resistant to borders, and as such it was that tendency toward "boundlessness" that provoked anxieties and enhanced "an imperative for protection." Munroe and Laroche identify the insidious "mobility of such creatures and the ambiguous boundaries they traverse . . . their blurring of 'here' and 'there.'" In the masculinist language of pest control, two contradictory impulses coexisted: the necessary intimacy with the insect world and the consequent (and unrealizable) desire to reject and exclude such intimacy.

As is the case for Woods, communication is at the heart of Lowell Duckert's searching "Tettix," an essay in its etymological sense, that seeks, in six sections corresponding to the six-legged cicada, to understand the root of communication that concerns what is held in common and therefore related to ideas of community. His approach is not to query the capacities of insects, comparing them to capacities purportedly only humans enjoy in a game of comparative valuation. Rather, Duckert's goal is to ask, "not *whether* insects *can* speak but *why* they have been prevented from doing so, and, more important, *what* they would say *when* asked the 'right' questions." In a wide-ranging journey from the "cicada mania" of twenty-first-century West Virginia back to Ben Jonson's dismissal of "screaming grasshoppers," Duckert asks whether insects have gotten lost in a pernicious signal-noise distinction as creatures presumed to produce noise only because "language, however conceived, detrimentally dominates our questions of communication; logos has been the loudest speech impediment historically." Unlike Jonson, Moffett found the grasshopper sweet, encouraging his reader to "hearken" unto the mellifluous creature. Grasshoppers are not the only such singers, as attested to by bees, hornets, and other lesser living creatures. This intense and open act of listening pays dividends. Moffett "has been permitted to speak—theatricalize, that is—by his insect subjects," thus demanding we pay "greater attention to the speech-enabling parasitism of lesser things in stature, [thus troubling] anthro- and logo-centric dictation." One might say that Duckert, along with a few other contributors to this volume, might well add "grasshopper" or "bee" to the voluminous list of contributors to Moffett's *Theater of Insects*, a text that has neither a single author nor a single species behind it.

The drone was the exception that proved the rule of the bee's legendary work ethic. Ants too soldiered, literally and figuratively, for the common benefit. But these were not the only industrious ones among the lesser living creatures, as Frances E. Dolan's "Worm Work" clarifies. Her chapter takes up the fascinating dialectic of the earthworm and the silkworm, "one maligned as a consumer and destroyer and the other idealized as a paragon of both industry and artistry." Both creatures offer a window into the agricultural ambitions of the era in "the revival of soil amendment and composting and the attempt to establish a silk industry in colonial Virginia." Despite great interest in these apparently opposed worms, from Gervase Markham to Samuel Hartlib, a set of misperceptions prevailed in both the failure to recognize how beneficial earthworms are for soil and in the unrealizable fantasies about the lucrative productivity of silkworms. As Dolan puts it, "However invested in soil amendment early moderns were, their quest to improve their soils was hampered by what they not only did not yet know but by the ways that their cultural associations with the earthworm impeded their knowledge and their observation, making it impossible to imagine the lowly and dirty worm as a central agent in creating fertile soils." Thus, although today's readers of such husbandry and natural history manuals are left to marvel at how much early modern writers were able to figure out about lesser living creatures without the aid of more recent technologies, there were also notable and impactful errors.

In the case of motion, or as Keith Botelho styles it in "Creeping and Crawling," recent technologies, at least of the past few decades, turn to the movements of insects with fascination and with the hope of utility. What if our technologies might deploy insect mobility and morphology to human advantage? And yet in the age of Moffett, insectoid motions like creeping and crawling may have indicated a creature's habitation as a denizen of the earth, but they also became the basis of a sense of human character anchored in creaturely choreography, which no doubt is why the likes of Marlowe, Shakespeare, and Donne anchored surreptitious, venomous, and other vile inclinations in patterns of movement that would at best indicate a descent from human up- and forthrightness. The norm for worms proves insidious in persons making earthly locomotion the inverse of a core principle of so much early modern entomology. The bee, which flits airborne from flower to flower gathering sweets and which mastered the architecture of rule in the infrastructure of the hive, served as a great mirror for human conduct. The creeping, crawling, slime-tracking creatures of the world offered primarily negative exempla, their utility residing not in technological but in moral realms. Not all insects creep or crawl; indeed, flight may represent a major and underexplored entomological division in early modernity. And yet those words bear a potent visceral trace of the insect world that so captivated Moffett, as if behind each is visible a track of slime or as if to invoke them is to burrow in the fecund earth.

Death may lack its sting in the wake of the beneficence of Christ, but insects did not. Julian Yates's "Stinging like a Bee in Early Modern England" considers that iconic, if not universal, feature of insect life. To be sure, not all insects possessed a sting, and indeed there was some debate about whether all bees, say, had a sting. But in Yates's chapter, a sting is not the differentiating feature of one species but a kind of nexus or an incitement to sting effects that draw a range of creatures and objects into odd alignments and assemblages. Thus, the real subject of the chapter is "how the action of a bee sting on human skin was understood in Tudor England." The fascinating story of that trace follows Thomas Penny and Moffett back to the early modern home of physicians and natural historians, Lime Street, "a node or hub that concentrated multiple orders of expertise, technical know-how, and forms of evidence, and which, accordingly, was able to produce significant orders of knowledge and expertise." Moffett and Penny's conjectures, their attempt to write the story of "sting," was in fact a way of being written as they tried to understand the implications of sting not just for animal anatomy but for political sovereignty. The series of interchanges enabled by the sting indicates that "the emerging discourses of sixteenth-century England as a field science that necessarily functions also as a conceptual trading zone between natural history and political economy."

Some insects burrow, some bite, some swoop, some sting. Sometimes they even glow. Even as natural history tried to decipher the book of nature, many of its passages would not yet be cracked. Reproduction, for instance, drove various authors to flights of imaginative speculation. As Jessica Lynn Wolfe indicates in her wide-ranging "Living Lamps," "bioluminescence was poorly understood during the Renaissance, but no less compelling for its mysteriousness." Certainly authorities of the era like Ulisse Aldrovandi, Robert Boyle, Robert Plot, and Thomas Bartholin attempted to delve into the mysteries of these living lamps, and as Wolfe also indicates, their interest "was almost certainly sparked by various reports of luminous insects in the new world." Whatever the source, the consequences of that fascination were myriad. For Thomas Browne, living lamps suggested something he called "'vivency,' the conditions and requisites for the maintenance of life." For Thomas Heyrick, it was the insect's "capacity to elucidate, in miniature form, the macrocosmic processes at work in the sky." And for the Royal Society? The secrets of oxygen itself.

To open the book of nature to the chapters on lesser living creatures is to consider the revelatory capacities of tiny lives flickering in and out of perception, capturing our attention, and lighting the way to mysteries wondrous to behold.

Notes

1. Hive is available at https://gen42.com/games/hive.
2. Purchas, *Theatre of Politicall Flying-Insects*, sig. A3.
3. Williams, *Keywords*, xxvii.
4. Greene, *Five Words*, 1. For an extension of this method, see the special online colloquy "Critical Semantics."
5. Brown, *Insect Poetics*, 29.

Bibliography

Brown, Eric C., ed. *Insect Poetics*. Minneapolis: University of Minnesota Press, 2006.

Cole, Lucinda. *Imperfect Creatures: Vermin, Literature, and the Sciences of Life, 1550–1750*. Ann Arbor: University of Michigan Press, 2016.

"Critical Semantics: New Transnational Keywords." *Arcade: Literature, the Humanities, and the World*, curated by Anston Bosman. Stanford University, 2020. https://arcade.stanford.edu/colloquies/critical-semantics-new-transnational-keywords.

Greene, Roland. *Five Words: Critical Semantics in the Age of Shakespeare and Cervantes*. Chicago: University of Chicago Press, 2013.

Heywood, John. *The Spider and the Flie*. Edited by A. W. Ward. London: Spenser Society; New York: Burt Franklin, 1967. First published 1894.

Moffet, Thomas. *The Theater of Insects: or, Lesser Living Creatures*. In *The Historie of Four-Footed Beasts*, by Edward Topsell. London, 1658.

Spenser, Edmund. "Muiopotmos: or The Fate of the Butterfly." In *The Shorter Poems*, edited by Richard McCabe. New York: Penguin, 1999.

Purchas, Samuel. *A Theatre of Politicall Flying-Insects*. London, 1657.

Williams, Raymond. *Keywords: A Vocabulary of Culture and Society*. Oxford: Oxford University Press, 2014.

CHAPTER 1
STING
Stinging like a Bee in Early Modern England

Julian Yates

Is not this a lamentable thing, that of the skin of an innocent lamb should be made parchment; that parchment, being scribbled o'er, should undo a man? Some say the bee stings, but I say, 'tis the bee's wax; for I did but seal once to a thing, and I was never mine own man since. How now? Who's there?
—WILLIAM SHAKESPEARE, *Henry VI, Part 2*

Admittedly, the use of the word *sting* is metaphorical. Admittedly, rebel leader Jack Cade is not really talking about bees or insects exactly. Instead, he is out to decode the efficacy of legal writing in the period, backed as it was by a world of parchments, of sheepskin writing authorized into law by the impress of a metallic seal on wax. "How, rhetorically," he seems to ask, "do you manage to make sensible the way a whole infrastructure of writing systematically parcels out privilege and pain?" "How is it that a supposedly Christian universalism creates such a differentiated flock of haves and have-nots?" It's quite a challenging exercise in *ethopoeia*, which is to say, of capturing the essence of a thing that allows the listener to feel that essence. The answer Jack comes up with is inspired, even if it challenges the limits of the rhetorical exercise and the limits of what we count as ethos—less a character now than parchment itself as a constellation of animal and mineral beings.[1]

Recalling the moment at which he signed his life away, though as we learn later he probably did not sign but made his mark—"like an honest plain-dealing man"—Jack reaches into the world of those lesser creatures named insects in order to register the deprivation he now feels—the "sting" that touching parchment gives him.[2] "Some say the bee stings," he says, only to correct this commonsense observation by offering that experience has taught him that "'tis the bee's wax; for I did but seal once to a thing, and I was never mine own man since" (4.2.72–76). The efficacy of this sting migrates from a bee to its wax. Or, to be more precise, this sting migrates to the efficacy of the writing on this tooled skin of a lamb, authorized into law by the wax that bears the impress of a metallic seal. Jack reverses the mode of production that creates the world of parchments. He reanimates the lamb or lambs and so also the bees, whose bodies and products provide the "raw" materials "cooked" into parchment. His performance momentarily unfolds the folding together of different beings that make up the world of parchment (sheepskin tooled into a writing surface; wax harvested from the bee hive or skep; metal mined and smelted into a seal; ink confected from soot, iron gall, and alum). Focusing on the "innocent lamb" that recalls the Agnus Dei, Jack laments on its behalf. And this innocent lamb's death comes to stand in approximate relation to the deprivation he now feels and registers before the law. Likewise, the bees that might once have defended their hive with their stings find themselves deprived of their stingers, their means of defense, robbed also of the labor that went into making all that wax, to say nothing of their honey. Perhaps beyond Jack's own lamentation, then, which alliteratively recalls the sound we use to name the lamb, we can hear the faint buzzing of those bees and, beyond that, even the eerie quiet of unmined mineral ores.

Elsewhere, I have argued that Jack's open-ended question concerning parchment represents one moment in *Henry VI, Part 2*'s minimal conservation of insurgent writing in the period, attempts by differently literate social groups in Tudor England's recent past to intervene in the writing technologies of their present by way of carefully orchestrated attacks on specific forms of writing.[3] In this chapter, I am interested in something more visceral and immediate: the order and quality of the pain Jack seeks to evoke by his recruitment of bees and their stingers to his rhetorical gambit. The transfer of the bee's sting to the parchment as the effect of its gathering of animal, vegetable, and mineral remainders and investment of labor seeks to make knowable the uncanny, encrypted organization of resources on which the routines of a built world depend. Such routines fragment, combine, and rezone all manner of entities, animal, vegetable, and mineral, but something of their origins remains as they are manufactured and put to use. It is that residue that Jack renders sensible as his skin touches the skin of the lamb that was, and his words register the literal and metaphorical "sting" of this multispecies skin on skin contact.[4] Here differences in scale between sheep, bees, and humans quite literally matter. Bees, we know, were lauded in the period for their sociality, their industriousness, and their sense of order. They were regarded as their own autonomous polity. Bees had sovereignty. But there remained something of a mystery to their mode of order, government, and the mechanism of their stinger. Jack deploys this apian sovereignty, the efficacy of their sting, and the displacement of their labor in his metaphorical troping of parchment to render the deprivations it causes palpable. The mysterious mobility of the pain he says he feels erupts with the shock of a bee sting gone mobile, deterritorialized from the bee (to which it belongs) and now grafted in translated form to the manufactured skin of a lamb. Jack's appeal to a sheepy Christian universalism betrayed by the world of parchment laws depends on the salutary surprise generated by touching the remains of a lamb that now stings like a bee.[5]

In what follows, I elaborate on Jack's zoomorphic ethopoeia by inquiring further into how the action of a bee sting on human skin was understood in Tudor England. What was the status of this only partially visible sting? Why were bees understood to sting? And what, for that matter, was their stinger thought to be? Ultimately I am interested in something that Jack's synesthesia and multispecies modeling of parchment takes as a given, and that the ontological or multispecies "turn" in anthropology and the humanities today seeks to own, once again: that what we apprehend as individual kinds of animals derive from the stacking or enfolding of different states of being (animal, vegetable, and mineral) to produce differing forms of life. Tracing the mobility of the "sting" Jack feels back to the bee he evokes enables us to make out the coextensive anthropomorphism/zoomorphism that shaped the lives of creatures we now name "human," along with the so-called lesser creatures of Renaissance England. In order to begin, however, we leave

Shakespeare's theater, cross the Thames, and head north into one of London's quieter and rather better neighborhoods.

Lime Street

Thomas Penny (1530–1588) and Thomas Moffett (1553–1604) may no longer walk down Lime Street, but between 1585 and 1590, the two friends and physicians lived on Lime Street and played their parts as core members in an "important community interested in natural history with links to other naturalists in England and on the European continent."[6] With its apothecary shops, physicians, surgeons, large houses, and walled gardens; the comings and goings of its international visitors; the amassing of books and manuscripts; illustrations; all manner of flora and fauna, in its gardens, living and "dry" (Penny had an extensive *Hortus siccus*); and its cabinets of curiosities, Lime Street was home to a group of humanist-trained thinkers committed to collecting animal and plant specimens as well as other curiosities; to firsthand observation and exploration; to collating and classifying their findings; and to publishing the results. Apprehended systematically, as Jack's modeling of parchment invites us to do, Lime Street aspired to be what a historian or sociologist of science would call a "center of calculation," a node or hub that concentrated multiple orders of expertise, technical knowhow, and forms of evidence and that, accordingly, was able to produce significant orders of knowledge and expertise.[7]

The two most avid entomologists of the group were Penny and Moffett. Penny had studied with Conrad Gessner in Zurich and then at the University of Montpellier and served as a conduit for medical, zoological, and botanical information from abroad. As Deborah Harkness tells us, it was he who introduced the younger Moffett to the community on Lime Street. After Penny's death, Moffett set about gathering up "all his friend's manuscripts on insects and compiled them with his own observations into [the] monumental work of more than 1200 pages" that would be published posthumously as the *Insectorum sive Minimorum Animalium Theatrum* (1634) and then in English as *The Theater of Insects* in volume 2 of Edward Topsell's *The Historie of Four-Footed Beasts and Serpents* (1658).[8] Both men enjoyed their fieldwork and travel—as ends in themselves and because they "carefully distinguished between the natural objects they witnessed and those they knew only secondhand from manuscripts, books, illustrations, and conversation."[9] Firsthand observation was a powerful technique for corroboration and contradiction. Both men were committed, then, to fieldwork as a way of establishing the status of the "epistemic things" they collected: accounts (ancient and modern) of insects and their behavior; illustrations of insects from books and manuscripts of varying quality; and the host of ephemera from all over the world that Lime Street drew to itself.[10] While, as Harkness offers, "natural objects led double lives... [as] both subjects of study and inquiry and artifacts cherished for their rarity and beauty," those lives and so the status of the objects themselves were transformed by the results of Penny and Moffett's direct observations.[11]

Moffett, in particular, was committed to this idea of fieldwork and remained "undaunted [even] by the prospect of studying an insect that could hurt him."[12] Indeed, he seems to have taken a particular interest in stinging insects and went to great lengths to test the conclusions about their anatomy and behavior he found in the works of the ancients—Aristotle and Pliny especially. Synthesizing current knowledge of the "Politick, Ethick, and Oeconomick virtues of Bees," in *The Theater of Insects*, for example, Moffett offers that "bees are swayed by soverainty, not tyranny," so much so that their monarch is selected not by "succession or by lot, but by due advice, and circumspect choice." And, "though they willingly submit to regall authority," he continues, "they do in a principal manner love" their king.[13] This being the case, "some have thought that the King is without a sting," for "their law is the law of nature, not written but imprinted in their manners." Theory had it that all the bees, drones and workers, play their parts within the hive out of the love and devotion they naturally feel for their king. Hence there is no need for the differential lawmaking and enforcing violence of the world of parchment whose sting Jack registers when he touches parchment in *Henry VI, Part 2*.[14] Perfect polity that they are, bees apparently know no internal struggles and swarm only when their king is dead. Similarly, it was a subject of debate as to whether female insects had stingers as well as the males—a confusion that speaks to the translational difficulties posed by representing the organization of the hive or nest within the lexicon afforded by the gender system of Penny and Moffett's day, which rendered the bee's queen a "king."[15]

Penny and Moffett were not deaf to such translational static. On the contrary, for the Lime Street community, the evidentiary "noise" produced by dissonant or incompatible accounts and observations signaled the fault line for their investigations of natural objects and their fieldwork. Theories, no matter how ancient or revered their authorities, needed testing or proving. Moffett went on his field trips armed with a series of questions or epistemic queries tuned to this "noise." His observations of insect anatomy and behavior in *The Theater of Insects* come primed by his reading and the natural objects available to him back on Lime Street. In the chapters on bees and wasps, for example, he takes it upon himself to establish once and for all if it is true that certain kinds of these insects do not in fact have stings. The descriptive cast to the chapters, punctuated as they are by seemingly anecdotal remembrances of details gleaned from particular observations while in the field, speak to the way Moffett combines his differently timed fieldwork experiences into an anthology or compilation of details that speak back to either confirm or contest current thinking. The chapters collate fieldwork notes from different times and places, which they juxtapose with his knowledge of contemporary entomologists elsewhere in Europe and the ancients. Of course, it is in the nature of fieldwork also to go wrong—or to go right by going wrong in very particular ways—which is all to say that in the process, Moffett manages to get himself and his companions right royally stung.

In the chapter on wasps, Moffett explicitly puts Aristotle's contention that there are "but two kindes of wasps, one milde, the other fierce . . . having a stronger stinger" (924) to the test. He recalls a trip to the "top of *Chartmell* hills" in 1582, where "amongst the stones I saw two sorts of Wasps very eagerly fighting with one another," but he could discern "no difference . . . but in bigness" (924). And then, another time, "in a [different, undated] wood in *Essex*," he came across "these two kindes" again and

> not without great peril of my life, at such time as by chance I carelesly wandered here and there a simpling, with my friend *Penny* and one servant attending us. I would needs be prying into their nest: with which they being offended, all the swarm flusht out upon us with all the force they had, and but (as God would have it) we had carried in our hands some sprigs of Broom, (with which we used to catch those Insects) for our safeguard and defence, we had payed for our folly, not only with the hazzard of safety but of our lives; for the[y] followed

hard to the very middle of the wood, and a great while it was before they would leave pursuing us. (924)

In 1587, Moffett found "an entire wasp's nest" in "Hanes, a village town in the West" (921). Taking no chances this time, "I poured hot water over all the females and killed them," he writes, "and yet could finde none that had not a sting, either within their bodies, or sticking out," which put paid to the contention that some authors made that "their females are without stings." The authorities were wrong. All bees and wasps, so he and his companions discover only too painfully, have stings.

This finding raises two important but differently immediate questions. First, if all wasps have stings, even the females, and the king bee has a sting also, regardless of the natural love felt for him by his drones, "to what purpose is (will you say) that sting, against whose poyson and venome *Pliny* himself knew no remedy?" (906–7). And, second, what should you do if after your fieldwork, and despite your precautionary broom and the providential grace of the divine, you find yourself very badly stung? What, indeed, should you do, if "there arise pain, perturbation, swelling, redness, heat, nauseousness, and thirst; and not long after swooning" from the sting or stings you have received?

The second question Moffett answers quickly and concisely. "Physicians," he writes, "have found out a preservative and remedy whereby to repell their stings and easily cure them." Citing Pliny's *Natural History*, Moffett recommends "the virtue of Mallowes, and Marsh-mallowes ... against the stinging of Wasps," adding that "thus the most soft and supple herb becomes a remedy against the most warlike and injurious creature, with whose juice and a little oyl mingled with it, and the part anointed, doth either mitigate the rage of the Wasp, or doth not suffer the sting to enter, *Plin. l. 22. c. 179*" (924–25). Both cure and preventative, mallow, mint, rue, and bay or laurel were regarded as highly effective remedies—something corroborated by sometime Lime Street visitor John Gerard in his *Herball* (1597).[16]

The answer to the first question proves rather more involved and so requires more extensive treatment and elaboration in a new section. But it is worth pointing out the way both questions—the personal and the natural-philosophical—signal the way Moffett and Penny's fieldwork and their extrapolations from it localize a series of differently scaled biopolitical questions. The mishaps of fieldwork lead to an urgent and immediate question about regimes of health and the maintenance and well-being of the city-dwelling, Christian, humanist bodies that venture out into the field, about which remedies are best for the sting of a wasp or the sting of a bee. But these same mishaps yield the discovery that all bees and wasps appear to have stings, including their "king," which raises a series of further questions about behavior, the nature of apian sovereignty, and so the metaphorical relations mediated between human creatures and their bees as differently scaled but otherwise fellow political animals.

What, then, is the function and status of a bee's sting?

Politics, Ethics, Economics

While for Penny and Moffett the exact nature of the bee's sting remained a matter of some conjecture, the publication of Robert Hooke's *Micrographia: or, Some Physiological Descriptions of Minute Bodies Made by Magnifying Glasses* in 1665, which included plates, or as he named them, "schema" or visual dissections of all manner of "lesser creatures" such as flies, fleas, and bees (figure 2.1.1), seemed to settle the matter. For Hooke, the technological mediation provided by his pioneering use of the microscope eliminated the imprecision that came with unenhanced observation—or, in effect, rezoned the fieldwork of Penny and Moffett to a different phase of the scientific process as he reaped the benefits that his microscopically enhanced epistemic objects gave him. With the move indoors to the laboratory or the study, Hooke models his bees in vitro as opposed to in vivo—which alters fundamentally the embodied experience of what for Penny and Moffett was not a passive subject but a sovereign polity equipped with their own means of defense.

As Courtney Weiss Smith observes, Hooke "minutely describes" the mechanism of a bee sting, enlarging it to over five inches long in the book and "even keying the particulars to the image."[17] As she elaborates, Hooke's text then deploys successive analogies in order to render or translate the mechanism of the sting itself. Wasting no time on how the sting appears to the "naked eye," Hooke instead curates this sting-object, now detached from the bee, offering that it seems "to consist of two parts, the one a sheath, without a chape or top, shap'd almost like a Holster of a Pistol," which contains "both a Sword or Dart, and the

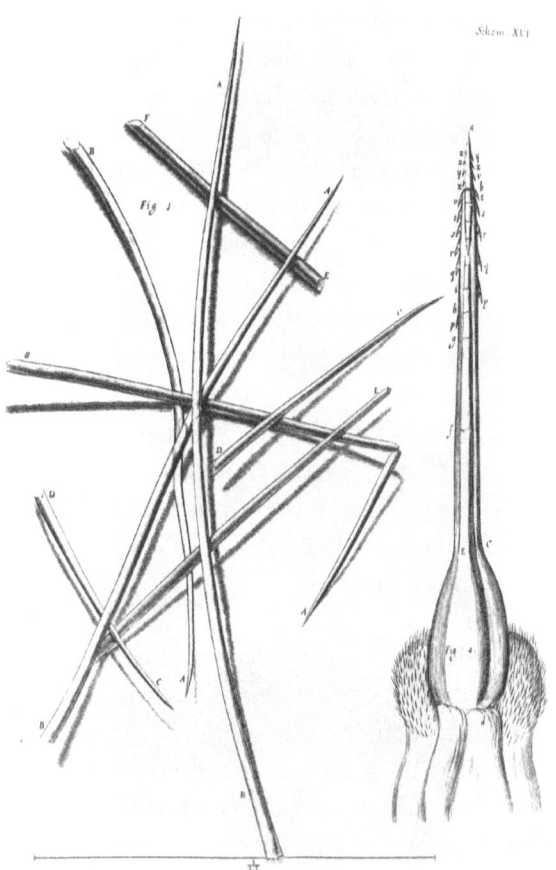

Figure 2.1.1 Robert Hooke, *Micrographia: or, Some Physiological Descriptions of Minute Bodies Made by Magnifying Glasses* (London, 1665). Wellcome Collections, London.

poisonous liquor that causes the pain."[18] The sting has "several crooks or forks" which Hooke analogizes as "Thorns growing on a briar, or rather like so many Cat's claws" (162). "The other part of the Sting," he continues, "is the Sword," which is very sharp and can be retracted or extended as the bee desires. This "very pretty structure," Hooke notes, seems so effective that it is no wonder that the "top of the Sting or Dagger (*a b*) is very easily thrust into an Animal's body" and that by "successive retracting and emitting of the Sting, the little enraged creature . . . can pierce the toughest and thickest hides of his enemies" (163). Armed with such an "Engine" Hooke happily contemplates the way a small band of these "stout and resolute soldiers" can easily fight off "a huge masty Bear." He then offers this conclusion: that the barbed nature of the bee's stinger "shew[s] the world how much more considerable in Warr a few skilfull Engineers and resolute soldiers politickly order'd, that know how to manage such engines, are, then a vast unwieldy rude force, that confides in, and acts onely by, its strength" (164).

By the process of analogy, Hooke renders the bee's sting a sword or dart and so an "engine," a natural-cultural technique of "politick order," that augers and advises for the privilege to be accorded to technology itself as opposed to the "rude force" of brute strength. The bee thereby becomes a biotechnical creature—proof of a particular sense of ordered design written into a divinely inscribed nature that the techniques of science shall render knowable. This observation leads Hooke to generalize further the way in which the "natural contrivance" of the stinger for the bee's venom, much like, say, the "bodkin"-like points on the leaves of the nettle, must have offered the first "hint" of the "Diabolical practice of poisoning of Arrows and Ponyards," which the recently invented "Syringe-Pipe" redeems (144–45).[19]

Hooke's "war-mongering" analogies, as Smith brilliantly names them, speak to the way his powerful means of technical enhancement transforms the life of his objects and the way this analogy underwrites a particular relation of scientific thought to the world. Technology, the world of "engines" and their ingenious applications, finds itself written into the Book of Nature that the microscope deinscribes. Such a powerful epistemology produces an ontological choreography that rezones or rewrites the nature of bees and, in this case, nettles, as they come to serve as natural-historical exempla of a truth about technology to be cultivated in human societies.[20] Such a powerfully altered choreography also sets the human observer spinning, whose "fieldwork" now unfolds in the study or laboratory, being pricked by analogized hybrid plant-animal-technical "bodkins," as opposed to trekking out into the countryside and getting stung by real bees. The mechanism of the sting is described, but its feel migrates to the imaginative realm in which resolute bee-soldiers send the honey-seeking bear packing.

Penny and Moffett would, I am sure, have been captivated by Hooke's discoveries and the quality of the images he provides. But they might also have been a little surprised, perhaps even dismayed, at what their bees and wasps had become. While it is true that the word *sting* derives from a lexicon that includes poles or staffs that could, in times of war, be weaponized into a spear or pike, the root of the word in Old, and Middle, and then in early modern English, zoned *sting* as a farming implement or tool—sometimes referring specifically to a "pointed instrument used in thatching."[21] To Penny and Moffett's ears, then, Hooke's analogizing the bee's stinger to arrows and ponyards and bodkins, while defensible, might also be said to transform the normally peaceable bee, which strives for the common good or commonwealth of the hive, into a warrior of sorts and so to transform the lesser creature of their study from a social or political animal into something else entirely. Where Moffett poses a deep ontological question about the bee's sting— What is it for?—Hooke's techno-scientific elation tends to instrumentalize the sting "Engine" as evidence of a design that inheres to nature and so as a signature to an optimized and optimizing use of technology in his own present. In effect, Hooke transforms the bee from a social or political animal into a schema for a set of abstract technical principles, whose exemplary value can be derived by apprehending the physiology or design that his microscopic mediation now renders knowable.

For Penny and Moffett, however, the unit of analysis was not the individual bee exactly so much as the complex of "Politick, Ethick, and Oeconomick" relations that constitutes the hive itself. As interesting as stings, on occasion, may prove, the hive remains for them the true object of analysis—the real object that makes bees good to think with and through.[22] Thus, where Hooke derives a technical insight to be generalized, Moffett, in *The Theater of Insects*, posits a model of apian government that proceeds on the basis that while their monarch may have a sting and it may be barbed, he refrains from using it—opting for a model of sovereignty in which the king bee uses his sting, so it seems, only in the role of a hygienic cleansing or distributive mode of justice that safeguards the health of the hive or collective. If the king, Moffett observes, "chance to finde amongst his young ones any one that is a fool, unhandsome, hairy, of an angry disposition, ill shapen, or naturally ill conditioned by the unanimous consent of the rest, he gives order to put him to death, lest his souldiery should be disordered, and his subjects being drawn into faction, should be destroyed" (894). The sting embodies not a technique that may be generalized so much as a localization and technical application of violence—not lawmaking violence, but a violence that would, in biopolitical terms, render the king bee a "shepherd" to bees, much as a human shepherd or pastor, in Foucauldian terms, "shepherds" his or her own metaphorical sheep-humans "*omnes et singulatim*" (all together and one by one).[23]

The king bee "sets down a way to the rest, gives order what they shall do, some commands to fetch water, others to make honey-combs within, to build them up, and garnish them." It is he who choreographs and maintains the life of the hive and "as long as the King lives, all the swarm enjoys peace, and all things are in quiet; for the Drones keep themselves willingly in their own cells, the elder Bees are content with their own places, nor do the younger run out of their own into the elders lodgings." In the absence of their monarch, the bees lack order and are prone to an irrational swarm, during which they are likely to sting even if that stinging shall cause their own deaths. For it is then that the bees are "raving mad, or burning with some feaver, anger or hunger," for they are undirected. "Otherwise," Moffett writes, "they do little or no harm at all" (907). What for Hooke serves as a natural-technical mechanism that sports "diabolical" uses in human hands and so must be directed to good ends by science, manifests for Penny and Moffett as an aspect of bee being directed by their monarch's shepherding reticence or technical deployment of the "rude" or unlearned violence deployed en masse by the swarm. All bees have stings, we might say, but their uses are highly differentiated. For Penny and Moffett, then, an inquiry into bee stings yields no biotechnical insight, but instead provides a point of entry into the functioning of the polity of a fellow, if differently political, animal.[24]

Animetaphors

Throughout this chapter, I have been modeling the emerging discourses of entomology in sixteenth-century England as a field science that necessarily functions also as a conceptual trading zone between natural history and political economy. The same observations, the same fieldwork, produce concepts keyed to the human body (remedies for bee stings) and to larger-scale questions about social organization. Questions that arise from preexisting accounts of bees and wasps are tested by direct observation in the field and then revised. By these findings, the object of knowledge, bees and wasps, changes, as do the metaphorical possibilities for understanding humans (and bees) as social animals. In other words, the manner in which Penny, Moffett, Hooke, and we pose questions to and of other creatures will necessarily produce different animetaphors or co-constitutive relations for us all. The different scaling of Penny and Moffett's and Hooke's observations, for example, along with their differently understood epistemic objects, program differently animating relations between the creatures we name "bees" and those we now name "human."[25]

For Hooke, the microscope makes possible a description of the bee and its sting that generalizes a powerful principle of economy in design. Politics, ethics, and economy migrate from the social interactions of the bees as a hive with a king bee to the scheme or blueprint for their bodies. It is a hop, skip, and a jump from the program he installs to the elevation of insectoid design in the modeling of information systems and the production of supposedly ethically and politically neutral technical devices that drone.

For Penny and Moffett, the bee's sting remained a tool, whose name derived from the human world of farming and household maintenance. This sting could, on occasion, be weaponized for the purpose of mutual defense, or it could be used irrationally in distress or despair. But the sting does not define the bee or bees even as its efficacy renders them impressive creatures. Moreover, these bees were not such radically different creatures from the humanist creatures who observed them and who, on occasion, metaphorized their own knowledge-seeking behaviors in apian terms.

To return to where I began, it is to Penny and Moffett's world that Jack Cade's invocation of the bee's sting belongs. Parchment, Jack offers, misuses the skin of an innocent lamb. It parodies the divine efficacy of the Agnus Dei, robs bees of their wax and their stings, and so necessitates that the Commons rally and weaponize the tools that normally they put to everyday use. As the Commons assemble and the likes of Dick the butcher puts his knife to very literal and graphic use, collectively they seek to undo this misuse of resources that produces the world of parchment-backed property rights and contracts. They seek to return the stinger to the bee.

Whether Penny and Moffett or the play supports their actions or might see them, rather, as a misdirected swarm, "burning with some feaver, anger, or hunger" in the absence of their king, is another matter.

Notes

1. On ethos and impersonation as a schoolboy exercise in Tudor England, see Enterline, *Shakespeare's Schoolroom*, 132–33. For a book-length study of wax as a matter-metaphor, see Maxwell, *Wax Impressions*. On sealing letters, see Maxwell, 13, and for a chapter-length treatment of gender and sealing, see Maxwell, 45–66.
2. Shakespeare, *Henry VI, Part 2*, 4.2.94–95. Subsequent references to *Henry VI, Part 2*, appear parenthetically in the text by act, scene, and line number. On the traumatic residues to be found in parchment, see Holsinger's insightful "Of Pigs and Parchment."
3. See Yates, "Skin Merchants," and "Oves et Singulatim." On insurgent writing practices, see Justice, *Writing and Rebellion*.
4. On the figure of the multispecies as a way of representing our ongoing becoming with other entities, see Haraway, *When Species Meet*, and, in anthropology, the work of Philippe Descola. In *Beyond Nature and Culture*, Descola offers a program for reimagining an anthropology that faces "the daunting challenge: either to disappear as an exhausted form of humanism or else to transform itself by rethinking its domain and its tools in such a way as to include in its object far more than the *anthropos*: that is to say, the entire collective of beings that is linked to him but is at present relegated to the position of a merely peripheral role" (xx).
5. On the issue of scale and specifically for a treatment of the way an attention to bees reveals the "interplay of scale and sovereignty" in the early modern imaginary, see Campana, "Bee and the Sovereign?" See also the companion essay, Campana, "Bee and the Sovereign (II)."
6. Harkness, *Jewel House*, 19. My debts to Harkness's pioneering work should be obvious throughout this chapter.
7. See Latour, *Science in Action*, 215–57.
8. Harkness, "Elizabethan London's Naturalists," 46–47.
9. Harkness, *Jewel House*, 37.
10. On "epistemic things," see Rheinberger, *Toward a History*.
11. Harkness, *Jewel House*, 31.
12. Ibid., 38
13. Moffett, *Theater of Insects*, 891. Subsequent references to *Theater of Insects* appear parenthetically by page number.
14. On lawmaking violence, see Benjamin's 1926 "Critique of Violence."
15. On the generally held view that the queen bee was in fact male and a king, along with a survey of the handful of early modern outliers who maintained otherwise, see Woolfson, "Renaissance of Bees."
16. See Gerard, *Herball*. The French physician Ambrose Paré treats bee stings at relative length in his *Anatomie Universelle* (1550); they were included in English in *Workes* (1630), where, in addition to mallows, sucking the wound and drawing out the sting are recommended, followed by washing and treatment with soothing herbs. Other recipes for soothing, if not curing, stings abounded—including rubbing dirt into the wound along with other plant extracts. On the history of treatments for bee stings more generally, see Crane, *World History of Beekeeping*, 329–40.
17. Smith, *Empiricist Devotions*, 57. On Hooke's use of analogy more generally, see ibid., 57–65.
18. Hooke, *Micrographia*, 162. Subsequent references to *Micrographia* appear parenthetically in the text by page number.

19. Also quoted in Smith, *Empiricist Devotions*, 64.
20. On "ontological choreography," see Thompson, *Making Parents*.
21. *Oxford English Dictionary*, s.v., "sting, n.1."
22. This insight is inspired by Botelho's "Thinking with Hives," where he models the hive as a natural-cultural product good to think with.
23. On shepherding and the origins of biopolitics, see Foucault, *Security, Territory, Population*, esp. 128–29.
24. On the rhetorical deployment of the peaceability of the king bee in humanist writing as a figure for a desirable sovereign, see Woolfson, "Renaissance of Bees," 286–87.
25. The phrase "animetaphor" was coined by Akira Mizuta Lippit in *Electric Animal*. The idea that the questions or protocol of animal observation "writes" that animal derives from the work of Vinciane Despret, most recently *What Would Animals Say*.

Bibliography

Benjamin, Walter. "The Critique of Violence." In *Selected Writings*, edited by Marcus Bullock and Michael W. Jennings, 1:236–52. Cambridge, MA: Harvard University Press, 1996.

Botelho, Keith. "Thinking with Hives." In *Object Oriented Environs*, edited by Jeffrey Jerome Cohen and Julian Yates, 17–24. Brooklyn: Punctum, 2016.

Campana, Joseph. "The Bee and the Sovereign? Political Entomology and the Problem of Scale." *Shakespeare Studies* 41 (2013): 93–113.

———. "The Bee and the Sovereign (II): Segments, Swarms, and the Shakespearean Multitude." In *The Return of Theory in Early Modern English Studies 2: From Metaphysics to Biophysics*, edited by Paul Cefalu, Gary Kuchar, and Bryan Reynolds, 59–78. New York: Palgrave Macmillan, 2014.

Crane, Eva. *The World History of Beekeeping and Honey Hunting*. New York: Routledge, 1999.

Descola, Philippe. *Beyond Nature and Culture*. Translated by Janet Lloyd. Chicago: University of Chicago Press, 2013.

Despret, Vinciane. *What Would Animals Say If We Asked the Right Questions*. Translated by Brett Buchanan. Minneapolis: University of Minnesota Press, 2016.

Enterline, Lynn. *Shakespeare's Schoolroom: Rhetoric, Discipline, Emotion*. Philadelphia: University of Pennsylvania Press, 2011.

Foucault, Michel. *Security, Territory, Population: Lectures at the Collège de France, 1977–1978*. Translated by Graham Burchell. New York: Picador, 2007.

Gerard, John. *The Herball or General Histories of Plantes*. London, 1597.

Haraway, Donna. *When Species Meet*. Minneapolis: University of Minnesota Press, 2008.

Harkness, Deborah E. "Elizabethan London's Naturalists and the Work of John White." In "European Visions / American Voices," edited by Kim Sloan. *British Museum Research Publication* 172 (2009): 44–50.

———. *The Jewel House: Elizabethan London and the Scientific Revolution*. New Haven: Yale University Press, 2007.

Holsinger, Bruce. "Of Pigs and Parchment: Medieval Studies and the Coming of the Animal." *PMLA* 124, no. 2 (2009): 616–23.

Hooke, Robert. *Micrographia: or, Some Physiological Descriptions of Minute Bodies Made by Magnifying Glasses*. London, 1665.

Justice, Steven. *Writing and Rebellion: England in 1381*. Berkeley: University of California Press, 1994.

Latour, Bruno. *Science in Action*. Cambridge, MA: Harvard University Press, 1987.

Lippit, Akira Mizuta. *Electric Animal*. Minneapolis: University of Minnesota Press, 2000.

Maxwell, Lynn. *Wax Impressions, Figures, and Forms in Early Modern England: Wax Works*. New York: Palgrave MacMillan, 2019.

Moffett, Thomas. *The Theater of Insects: or, Lesser Living Creatures*. In *The Historie of Four-Footed Beasts and Serpents*, by Edward Topsell. London, 1658.

Paré, Ambrose. *The Workes of That Famous Chirurgion Ambrose Parey*. Translated by Th. Johnson. London, 1630.

Rheinberger, Hans Jörg. *Toward a History of Epistemic Things: Synthesizing Proteins in the Test Tube*. Stanford: Stanford University Press, 1997.

Shakespeare, William. *Henry VI, Part 2*. Edited by Roger Warren. Oxford: Oxford University Press, 2002.

Smith, Courtney Weiss. *Empiricist Devotions*. Charlottesville: University of Virginia Press, 2016.

Thompson, Charis. *Making Parents: The Ontological Choreography of Reproductive Technologies*. Cambridge, MA: MIT Press, 2007.

Woolfson, Jonathan. "The Renaissance of Bees." *Renaissance Studies* 24, no. 2 (2009): 285–88.

Yates, Julian. "*Oves et Singulatim*—A Multispecies Impression." In *Renaissance Post-humanisms*, edited by Joseph Campana and Scott Maisano, 167–94. New York: Fordham University Press, 2016.

———. "Skin Merchants: Jack Cade's Futures and the Figural Politics of Shakespeare's *Henry VI, Part II*." In *Go Figure: Forms, Energy, Matter in Early Modern England*, edited by Judith Anderson and Joan Pong Linton, 149–69. New York: Fordham University Press, 2011.

CHAPTER 2
SCALE
Lesser Living in the Renaissance

Joseph Campana

Lesser Living Creatures appeared, although in predictably smaller letters, blazoned upon the title page of Thomas Moffett's *The Theater of Insects* when it was published in English in 1658, incorporated as the third and final volume of Edward Topsell's *History of Four-Footed Beasts and Serpents*. In 1634, appearing for the first time years after its composition as a stand-alone volume and in the original Latin, it was titled *Insectorum Theatrum: Sive Minimorum Animalium*, although on that title page, the specifying and lowercased subtitle interrupts the title:

INSECTORUM
SIVE
Minimorum Animalium
THEATRUM

The vagaries of print culture might disincline dwelling on the paradoxes of size here, with the largest letters reserved for the smallest things (*Insectorum*) or with *Minimorum Animalium* (the smallest or least of animals) appearing in lowercase yet drawing attention away from both *Theatrum* and indeed from the main title itself. Moffett, as author, seems caught in the eddies of scale recorded in print, as in the

1634 edition his name appears smaller and after three other authors or compilers or sources of this complexly assembled text: Edward Wotton, Conrad Gessner, and Thomas Penny.

The great become small and the small become great in a dizzying interchange of scale, a term that understandably has come to dominate recent thought, though it was no less important for the age of Moffett. In introducing "Writ Large," a recent special issue of *New Literary History*, Krishan Kumar and Herbert Tucker consider the vicissitudes of magnitude. "'Small is Beautiful' was a popular slogan of the 1970s," they argue, but "'Big is Better' might well be the watchword of our times."[1] Hence those essays consider a series of grandiose ideas, practices of generalization, and concepts of grand scope (such as world). It is perhaps a paradox suited to our moment in history that in an age ever more dependent on ever smaller technologies, the desire to scale up is well-nigh irresistible. Of course, it was the Victorian hymnodist Cecil Frances Alexander who codified a more familiar formulation in "All Things Bright and Beautiful," which celebrates "All Creatures Great and Small" in a series of *Hymns for Little Children*. Little children being, themselves, as easily imagined as little not-yet-human creatures as scaled-down instantiations of the human, they would perhaps be particularly attuned to minute particularities and dimensional shifts, which is to say, sweeps of scale. To consider the lesser of lesser living creatures, to consider a theater of insects as opposed to a menagerie of beasts, is to encounter a dynamic we now tend to call "scale" but that also invokes what early moderns might call "measure."[2]

Aristotle's understanding of what came to be known the *scala naturae*, that scheme whereby all the creatures of creation might be arrayed relative to one another in a hierarchy of graduated excellence, has exerted not a little influence on the centuries that followed. As he wrote in *The History of Animals*,

> Nature proceeds little by little from things lifeless to animal life in such a way that it is impossible to determine the exact line of demarcation, nor on which side thereof an intermediate form should lie. Thus, next after lifeless things in the upward scale comes the plant, and of plants one will differ from another as to its amount of apparent vitality; and, in a word, the whole genus of plants, whilst it is devoid of life as compared with an animal,

is endowed with life as compared with other corporeal entities. Indeed, as we just remarked, there is observed in plants a continuous scale of ascent towards the animal.[3]

Scale implies vertical ascent from lifelessness to life, from plant to animal, and, by implication, from animal to human, with creatures divine hovering over humanity. As Paul Emmons puts it in a reflection on scale in architecture from antiquity to computer-assisted design, "Scale is a stair providing means for ascending and descending between the great and the small or in music between the high and the low."[4] The consequences of verticality for the valuation of creatures have been the subject of commentary from a range of scholars, including recently Garrett Sullivan and Tiffany Jo Werth.[5] Although Aristotle here emphasizes the fungible borders between steps and the puzzling nature of intermediary forms, the transformation of a *scala naturae* into a great chain of being offers some index of an evolution toward a series of too, too solid (and also too, too sullied) distinctions between creatures about which so many of late have been so eloquent.

Ecological urgencies make it no surprise that scale would loom so large. In the same year that Dipesh Chakrabarty argued for the need to "think human agency over multiple and incommensurable scales at once," Timothy Clark offered a powerful corrective in insisting that a proper understanding of scale effects emphasizes "the need to accord to the nonhuman a disconcerting agency of its own."[6] Although Clark argues that scale "enables a calibrated and useful extrapolation between dimensions of space or time," the language he uses to describe "scale effects" more often invokes the language of dizziness, contradiction, derangement, and even implosions.[7] "Dominant modes of literary and cultural criticism are blind to scale effect," he argues, for "what is self-evident or rational at one scale may well be destructive or unjust at another."[8] And in an even more damning pronouncement, he continues: "It is as if critics were still writing on a flat and passive earth of indefinite extension, not a round, active one whose furthest distance comes from behind to tap you uncomfortably on the shoulder." Worse still, Clark argues, is the failure to recognize that "non-cartographic concepts of scale are not a smooth zooming in and out but involve jumps and discontinuities."[9] Derek Woods too wonders, "Is the concept of the human scalable?"[10] He then advocates for "scale critique," which emphasizes "disjunctures and incommensurable differences among scales" to counter the all too prevalent "scaled up, abstract notion of the human."[11]

Scale has been taken up most extensively in the humanities in its geographic and cartographic senses, particularly with respect to spatial coordinates such as distance. Nirvana Tanoukhi describes distance as having constituted a "thorny issue" for comparative literature in the wake of conversations about globalization and world literature and yet also suggests that "the concept [of] scale, properly theorized, would enable a more precise formulation of the role of literature, and literary analysis in the production of space."[12] Clark similarly considers quandaries of distance in claims about local, regional, national, and global frames of references, asking, "At what scale or scales should one think and work in environmental politics?"[13] While distance offers one potent vector of analysis, time and, more particularly, considerations of deep time proffer yet another scalar analytic, whether one considers the politics of the literary canon, as Wai Chee Dimock does, or the politics of the Anthropocene, which considers human agency with respect to ecological transformations on the scale of geological time.[14]

With respect to literary studies and reading practices, perhaps few have been so influential as Franco Moretti, whose considerations of scale and reading practices have provoked new and often fractious conversations about distance, proximity, and speed. As he wrote nearly twenty years ago about the "ambition" to conceive of world literature, "that ambition is now directly proportional to the distance from the text: the more ambitious the project, the greater must the distance be."[15] Julie Orlemanski argues in an effort to test out these premises with respect to medieval literature, "While current reflections on the scale of literary study most obviously stem from digitized archives and the increasingly sophisticated means of querying them, I suggest that they take on additional urgency in light of frustrations with historicism. Both 'big data' and 'posthistoricism' worry a sore spot in literary study, which is itself a matter of scale: close reading. . . . Alternative scales of reading, like those in Moretti's experiments, expose the fragile logic of exemplarity by which reading and history have been sutured together."[16]

These spatial coordinates—distance, proximity, and time—constitute only some vectors in the constitution of scale. As Werth argues, "while *scala* in Latin means ladder, in English the word 'scale' encompasses multiple connotations. In addition to its sense as a balance or instrument for weighing, it would also have invoked for its early modern audience things as seeming disparate as a drinking cup, the horny membrane of a fish, reptiles, some mammals, and siege ladders."[17] Justin Sully too describes the etymology of the word as indicating often colliding and sometimes recombinant origins, "etymologically distinct lineages," one referring to "measurement (most commonly of weight)" and the other referring to "a succession of degrees." No wonder, then, as he also holds, "there is no unified field devoted to the study of scale."[18]

Whether early moderns would have made the same associations with scale as recent urgencies have inclined us to make, they were certainly concerned with all too critically neglected questions of scale that concern relative magnitude and that any attention to insect life makes impossible to ignore. As the *scala naturae* makes clear, scalar relations, which are comparative and relative, might be put to a variety of ideological uses, as when all creation may be assessed and ranked relative to a pinnacle of perfection. And yet we might turn back to that evocative moment in Aristotle, whereby "Nature proceeds *little by little*" to glean another, and perhaps equally impactful, sense of scale. "Little by little" is how D'Arcy Wentworth Thompson translates Aristotle's phrase *katà mikrón* (κατὰ μικρόν), which pairs a preposition indicating gradations *(katá)* with a term indicating diminutive proportion *(mikrón,* source of the familiar prefix "micro").[19] In an emergent age of microscopy, insects, as the essays in these volumes indicate, excited reflection on other modalities of scale, modalities not unrelated to and yet also not reducible to the game of comparative creaturely valuation. Thus, although Clark usefully describes scale as "a calibrated and useful extrapolation between dimensions of space or time," other vectors of calibration arise.[20] Insects indicate, with not a little urgency, the complexities of relative magnitudes, making more useful for my purposes here the definition of scale of G. Darrek Jenerette and Jiango Wu, who describe "scale effects" that "result from size differences between a model and the real system."[21] Comparative valuations conjure models, yet as is so often the case when humans understand themselves with respect to diminutive creatures, a question arises: Who or what is a model, and what is the, or even a, "real system"?

"There are no miniatures in nature," Susan Stewart argues; "the miniature is a cultural product."[22] Thus, it would be no surprise that Patricia Fumerton's closely contemporary *Cultural Aesthetics* would pay such exquisite attention to cultural miniatures of the self—the toy-like sonnets and the tiny portraits—that expose an early modern culture of ornament and a dialectic of publicity and privacy. One might be tempted, then, to argue that the fascination with diminutive insects, from Pliny to the present, is a purely "cultural product." But rather than argue for—or against—the nature/culture split enshrined in Stewart's pronouncement, it might be more interesting to consider that scale offers an alternative to static, charismatic miniatures. Scale suggests a constant interplay of comparative assessment, and relative valuation characterizes observation and interaction.

More immediately graspable than increasingly complex comparative relations of scale would be the palpable sense of relative magnitude as comparative heft in scales of measure. The failure of Edmund Spenser's infamous Giant of Equality, for example, is a failure of weighted measure. First, we learn that the Giant's rather substantial ambition—to rebalance all substances in the universe to prevent inequality—is marred by his lack of understanding: "For want whereof he weighed vanity, / And fild his ballaunce full of idle toys."[23] No wonder, then, that he was "admired much of fooles, women, and boys," all avatars of the incomplete, the insubstantial, and the diminutive. After Arthegall's lecture about the justice of divine order, the Giant still fails to properly weigh the things of this world:

First in one ballance set the true aside.
He did so first; and then the false he layd
In th'other scale; but still it downe did slide,
And by no meane could in the weight be stayd.
For by no meanes the false will with the truth be wayd.[24]

Thus, Spenser identifies through heft what we might call a paradox of measure. No matter how prodigious, falsehoods never outweigh even the slenderest truths. For Spenser, insects were associated with a series of insubstantial diminutives, like fools, women, and boys. Indeed, the false measure of the giant has extraordinary appeal as "the vulgar did about him flocke / And cluster thicke vnto his leasings vaine / Like foolish flies about an hony crocke."[25] Spenser may not have expressed, just here, an admiration for the tiny insects that exist a large scalar swing from the magnitude of the giant. But so often in this era, the invocation of the proportions of small creatures, like insects, were wedded to eloquent affirmations of this paradox of measure—what we might call a *diminutive sublime*—that stabilizes discontinuous scale effects when, as Woods puts it, "scale" is "assimilated to measure."[26] Thus, the "lesser" of lesser living creatures constitutes exquisite compactness rather than insubstantial smallness.

This is precisely the opening gambit of Pliny's discussion of insect life as rendered by Philemon Holland in his 1601 *Historie of the World*, which emphasizes the extraordinary craftsmanship required to engineer such tiny treasures:

> In bodies of any bignesse, or at leastwise in those of the greater sort, Nature had no hard peece of worke to procreat, forme, and bring all parts to perfection; by reason that the matter whereof they be wrought, is pliable and will follow as she would have it. But in these so little bodies, (nay prickes and specks rather than bodies indeed) how can one comprehend the reason, the power, and the inexplicable perfection that Nature hath therein shewed? How hath she bestowed all five senses in a Gnat? And yet some there be, lesse creatures than they. But (I say) where have she made the seat of the eies to see before it? Where hath she set and disposts the tast? Where hath shee placed and inserted the instrument and organ of smelling? and above all, where hath she disposed that dreadfull and terrible noise that it maketh, that wonderfull great sound (I say) in proportion of so little a body?[27]

Greatness lies in smallness as paradox stabilizes shifts of scale by creating a smooth zoom from the greatest degree of magnitude, the heavenly creator who brought the universe into being, to the tiny creatures at the diminutive edge of Creation, with the human observer both at the center and in the middle of the scale. Of course, as Clark, Woods, and other theorists of scale indicate, smooth zoom is a fantasy. And, indeed, the more lyrical the articulation of these paradoxes of measure, the more one wonders about these dizzying shifts of scale.

Moffett extends the terms of the diminutive sublime articulated by Pliny, celebrating his realization that "the Greatest God was in the smallest matters."[28] Moreover, Moffett bids "farewel then all those that so much esteem of creatures that are very large. I acknowledge God appears in their magnitude, yet I see more of God in the History of lesser Creatures. For here is more of prudence, sagacity, and ingenuity, and of certain evident divine being." The consequences of this realization turn out to be an error of cultural perception. Moffett insists, "Let us leave off to admire any longer the beast and huge Colosse, and with the chief Master of true wisdom, let us descend from the Cedar to the shrub, that is, from the most highest trees to the most contemptible weeds, or rather the most abject of all vegetables."[29] In this figure, the paradoxical "descent," in which seeking lesser things reveals greater truths, also registers that sense of a *scala naturae* organized around hierarchies of being, as vegetative life becomes as important as animal life and as pulchritude-challenged "weeds" and "the most abject of all vegetables" vie for attention. And yet magnitude constitutes Moffett's primary coordinate when considering scalar divergences.

To fail to appreciate the paradox of measure that insects imply is to mistrust both great and small. "O man," Moffett warns, "thou reliest upon thy own strength, and distrustest God, yet consider that there is so great strength in the smallest creature he hath made, that thou canst not endure it, nor ever be able to do as much. Imitate if thou canst." What humans fail to imitate would be the capacities of these small wonders. "But if I would relate the skill of some of them in building, fighting, playing, working," he avers, "perhaps I might be thought overcurious in these small things, (of which the Law takes no notice) and more negligent in greater matters." And yet in fact, "a man hath need of steel to bore into oaks, which the Wood-worm," we are told, "eats hollow with her teeth."[30] Moffett thus points out another error of perception: that small creatures have minimal capacities relative to humans when in fact humans require extensive apparatus (such as metallurgy and tools) to accomplish what diminutive beings manage on their own. So much for the fabled benefits of technology, which purportedly indicate the elevation of humans above other species.

But this shift of scale is not without resistance. It quickly becomes clear that the diminutive sublime that seems to counter the crass politics of magnitude we might associate with the bigger-is-better logic (or with the Giant of Equality in *The Faerie Queene*) is in fact as easily described as the "microscopic sublime," which is to say as a celebration of the sublimity of small things especially visible in a new age of microscopes but also as a consequence of the logic of dissection in an age already obsessed with the logic of anatomical dissection. Moffett confirms that paradox of measure dictating the greatness of what seems minimal as he derides those, in this case and at first the Italians, "who commonly admire vehemently things notable for magnitude, or new and unusual, but things obvious in al places, and that that are very small they despise, yet if they look exactly to the matter, it will be easie to observe, that the divine force and power shew themselves more effectually in mean things, and they are far more miraculous, than those things the world with open mouth respects so much and admires."[31]

Massive creatures are wonders, to be sure, which is why "if any man bring from far the wonderful Bittour, Elephant, Crocodile, there is no men but runs quickly to see that, because it is a new thing and unusual," and because these creatures are obvious, easy to perceive "under the apprehension of their senses." Greater admiration, however, should be accorded what is difficult to perceive:

> But no man regards Hand-worms, Worms in wine, Earwigs, Fleas, because they are obvious to all men, and very small, as if they were but the pastimes of lascivious and drunken Nature, and that she had been sober only in making those huge and terrible beasts. Nor is this vice peculiar to the Italians only, but it is common to the English and to all mankind, who that they may see those large beasts that carry towers, the African Lion, the huge Whale, the Rhinoceros, the Bear and Bull, take sometimes a long journey to London, and pay money for their places on the scaffold, to behold them brought upon the stage; yet where is Nature more to be seen than in the smallest matters, where she is entirely all for in great bodies the workmanship is easie, the matter being ductile, but in these that are so small and despicable, and almost nothing, what care?[32]

At first these articulations of what I have termed a diminutive sublime arising from a paradox of measure seem to require a redirection of attention. Of the frequently celebrated Samuel Purchas remarks, in the preface to *A Theatre of Politicall Flying-Insects*: "There is some good in all creatures, the meanest hath a beam of Gods Majesty, yet some have more than others, the Bees more than (almost) any. That a little neglected creature should bee so curious in Architecture, and in the fabric of her hexangle Combs should observe as just proportion as the best Geometrician, we should suspect for an untruth, if wee saw it not daily practiced by them."[33] Not only is the bee an exemplary craftsman; it has an innate sense of measure perfectly expressed by the hexagonal structure of combs. But it requires an act of attention, a human perception of a daily event, to realize. Purchas continues this sentiment by citing a familiar anecdote relayed by Claudius Aelianus about the painter Nicostratus, who marvels at the vividness of Zeuxis's depiction of Troy.[34] Purchas leverages this marvel to amplify his celebration of lesser living creatures: "*Nicostratus* in *Aelian*, finding a curious piece of work, and being wondred at by one, and asked what pleasure he could take to stand as he did still gazing on the Picture? answered, Hadst thou mine eyes, my friend, thou wouldst not wonder, but rather bee ravished as I am, at the inimitable art of this rare and admirable peece. I am sure no Picture can express so much wonder and excellency as the smallest Insects: But wee want *Nicostratus* his eyes to behold them."[35] More wonderful than Helen of Troy or any rendering of Helen of Troy is the "wonder and excellency" of these "smallest Insects." For Purchas, as perhaps he imagined for Nicostratus, humans lack "eyes to behold" wonders because they fail to pay sufficient attention. Ordinary human perception, properly trained, allows for appropriate cognition of measure.

But in both Moffett's preface and Thomas Mayerne's epistle dedicatory to Moffett's *Lesser Living Creatures*, the diminutive sublime of the insect ("the miracles of Nature, which are most conspicuous in the smallest things") increasingly relies on both microscopy and anatomy. The genius of the "great Artifice is so great" that "what creature soever you would dissect, you shall find the like art and Wisdome in it."[36] Additive technologies become central to the appreciation of wonders across vast scales of perception. It is merely an extension of this logic of attention that interventions to expose these tiny wonders come to seem both necessary and ordinary. How else could the magnificent workmanship of these tiny creatures be appreciated if not in the extractions, exposure, and analysis of their tiny parts. Mayerne insists:

Thou being an excellent Anatomist, I beseech thee try if you canst, dissect Insects, the great Stagyrite being thy guide, who did not disdain to search into the parts of Animals. Thou shalt finde in the little body of Bees a bottle which is the receptacle of Honey sucked from flowers, and their legs loaded with Bitumen which sticks fast to make wax. Also in the tail there is a horny sting full of revenging poison, that is ready to draw forth as soon as the Bee please. . . . In Gnats you shall observe their sounding trumpet that will suck bloud out of Animals, and will draw out moisture through the joynts of the most solid wood, and wine-vessels. How wilt thou be pleased to see the small proboscis of Butterflies wreathed always into a spiral line, after they have drawn forth nutriment from flowers, their extended large wings painted by natures artificial pencil, with paints cannot be imitated; to which the very Rain-bow is scarce comparable. . . . To behold the pipe of the Grasshoppers that live upon dew, and the organs of the shrill sound they make, that in the heat of the Gog-dairs importunately beats upon the ears of travelers, which are so framed that their concave belly is made vaulted under the Diaphragm, over which is extended a cover of a thin and dry membrane, like to a Drum.[37]

Mayerne offers copious examples of the marvelous greatness of small parts and in the process of cataloging such wonders works himself into a state of near ecstasy when he insists, "What a pleasant spectacle will this be when the artificial hands carefully and curiously guide the most sharp pen-knife, and very fine instrument by direction of the sight!"[38] The wonder of divine creation, which makes such magnificent and diminutive things, suddenly pales before the glorious spectacle of dissection that, however aided by instruments, allows one to almost feel the incision from the point of view of the anatomist. The violence required for this perception is substantial. One might say, of scale, that there is no smooth zoom. Or one might also say that any smoothness of scale, of perceived and comparative magnitude, is a smoothness that comes with the slice of a knife. The sharper and the swifter, the more elegant and marvelous the blade, the easier and more lyrical are the celebrations of the wonders revealed.

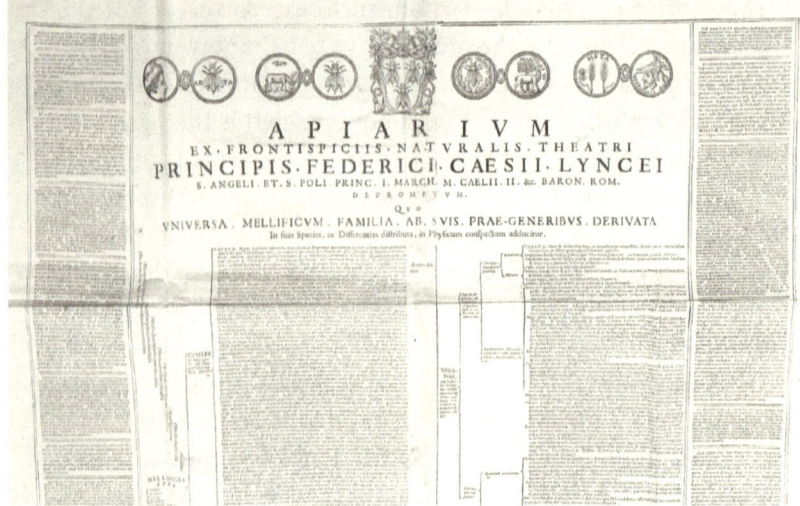

Figure 2.2.1 Francesco Stelluti and Federigo Cesi, *Apiarium* (Rome, 1625). Courtesy of History of Science Collections, University of Oklahoma Libraries.

Of course, neither Moffett nor Mayerne was the first to bring microscopy to bear on the fragile and tiny wonders of the insect world. In 1625, the Accademia dei Lincei (the "Lynx-Eyed Academy")—which was named with the sharp-eyed sight of scientific inquiry in mind, which Federico Cesi founded in 1603 with other inquiring natural historians and which inducted Galileo as a member in 1611—published multiple works celebrating the first of several jubilee years declared by Pope Urban VIII.[39] The Accademia specialized in displays of the power of microscopy. The brief, impressive, and much-noted trio of tributes to the Barberini family—*Melissographia*, *Apes Dianiae*, and *Apiarium*—were no different, one page in the case of the *Melissographia*, a ninety-line elegy in the case of the *Apes*, and four densely packed and complex pages larger than normal broadsheet in the case of the *Apiarium*. The first, as David Freedberg notes, constitutes "the first printed illustration in the history of natural history to have been made with the aid of a microscope."[40] Both the *Apiarium* and the *Melissographia* prominently featured iterations of the family crest of Urban VIII, Matteo Barberini, which was famously composed of a triangle of three bees (figures 2.2.1 and 2.2.2). The Barberini association with bees, along with an older association of the papal tiara with the shape of a hive, would be particularly of interest to John Milton, whose famous epic simile in *Paradise*

Lost features the rebel angels shrinking down and swarming "As bees / In spring time" to enter their newly constructed parliamentary chambers.[41] Cesi's compatriot and collaborator, Francesco Stelluti, created a vision of the bee exquisitely rendered in the engraving by Johann Friedrich Greuter. It might best be described as the infiltration of politics by microscopy and microscopy by politics. These products of the Accademia dei Lincei represent the first published anatomical images produced with the aid of a microscope. Thus, the *Melissographia* features a hybridized heraldic image, with three anatomically detailed images of bees surrounded by a framework of vegetation. In each of the top corners, a cherub holds a papal device: the hive-like tiara on the left and the keys of Saint Peter on the right. The title page to Stelluti's translation of the Roman satirist, *Persio*, similarly includes the Barberini trigon of bees (figure 2.2.3).

Figure 2.2.2 Francesco Stelluti and Federigo Cesi, *Melissographia* (Rome, 1625). Courtesy of National Library of Scotland (MRB.233) by permission of the Scottish Beekeepers' Association.

Figure 2.2.3 Francesco Stelluti, *Persio* (Rome, 1630). Library of Congress, Rare Book and Special Collections Division.

It is perhaps little surprise that a paradox of measure whereby the greatest things may be the smallest would become a tool for managing scalar distributions of power. Elsewhere I have argued, particularly with respect to early modern attention to bees, that sovereignty cannot be thought of without reference to scale.[42] Power, after all, is unstable and ever fleeting; thus, sovereignty, which aspires to perpetuity, relies on paradox for its persistence. And the illusory smoothing out or obscuring of scale discontinuities is part of what sustains sovereignty. What is slightly more surprising is the eruption, in 1630, of the microscopically enhanced illustration of the bee and an accompanying description of this marvelous creature amid Stelluti's translation of the lesser-known Roman poet Persius (figure 2.2.4). Even in a late humanist culture in which intellectuals trafficked in practices so often now

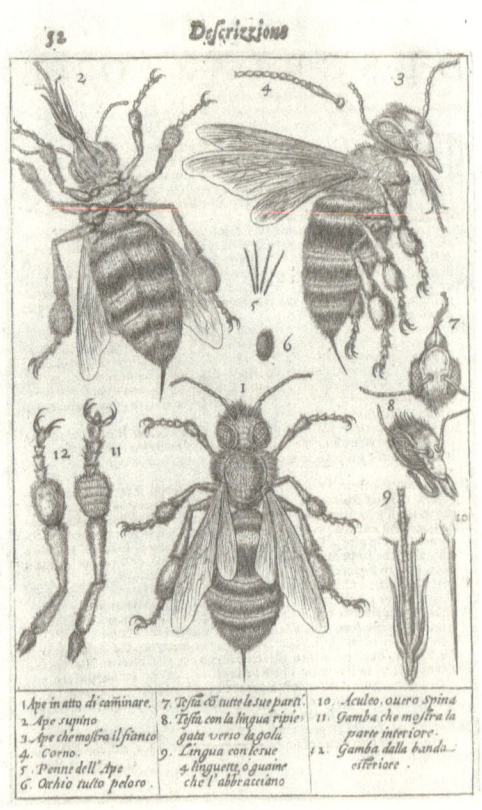

Figure 2.2.4 Francesco Stelluti, *Persio* (Rome, 1630). Library of Congress, Rare Book and Special Collections Division.

Satyra Quarta. 127

Afperfi, ond'è che de fuoi peli priuo
Il Gorgoglion nel anguinaia ftaffi ?
Ma benche cinque forti atleti fuellano

Quella parte della tefta appreffo al collo è tonda, e mobile da ogni parte, e
fi rinchiude dentro al collo, intorno al quale vi è vn cerchietto granellato,
che rapprefenta vn vezzo.
La fpalla è ruuida, tnordinata, e dura come offo.
L'ali fon parimente ruuide, ma dalla parte di fotto lifce, e gialliccie, e per
il lungo hanno alcune linee diritte punteggiate, fra loro equidiftanti.

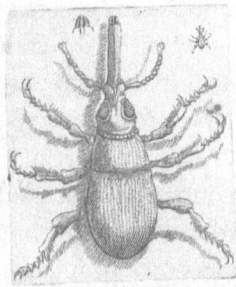

Le gambe fon fei, e ciafcuna ha fette giunture, ouero articoli ; li due primi
doue le dette gambe infieme fi congiungono fon ruuidi, l'altro ch'a quefto
fegue è pilofo dalla parte di dentro, e di fuori lifcio ; gli altri tre feguenti
fon affai piccioli con alcuni peluzzi intorno nella fine di effi.
Nell'vltimo articolo che rapprefenta la palma della mano, e del piede vi fon
due vnghie nere, & acute, e gli vltimi quattro articoli quando cammina gli
appoggia tutti in terra. E quefto è quanto di notabile habbiamo potuto
offeruare in quefto Animale.
2 *Quinque paleftrites. Paleftra* è quel luogo doue fi fa il giuoco della lotta, e
pigliafi ancora per l'iftefla lotta, e *paleftrites* fon quei giouani robufti, che
fogliono effercitarfi nelle paleftre, cioè Lottatori. Virg. al 6. dell'Eneid.
 Pars in gramineis exercent membra paleftris.
ma il Poeta dicendo *quinque paleftrites*, con quefto numero di cinque non
credo voglia altro fignificarci che le cinque dita della mano di qualche
giouane forte per far quell'effetto ch'egli dice, cioè *vt plantaria, vel pilos*
vellant, & exirpent.
Ploto.

Figure 2.2.5 Francesco Stelluti, *Persio* (Rome, 1630). Library of Congress, Rare Book and Special Collections Division.

radically sundered by disciplinary boundaries and mutually exclusive regimes of expertise, this gesture seems surprising, as does, perhaps, the fact that Stelluti retains the triangular composition of the Barberini crest, though without any surrounding heraldic apparatus. Elsewhere in the volume appears, also as a non sequitur to the obscure Roman satirist, the weevil (figure 2.2.5), depicted in a manner equally reliant on microscopy although apparently without the political context of the Barberini bees, a context that always seems to follow bees more generally as they swarm through history and the history of science.

Scale is as much a science as an art of comparative measure that creates relationships through modeling and often therefore also articulates hierarchies of value. And it is a term with an almost exhausting array of uses, as the differences among ladders, weights, and distances might suggest. I have suggested here how much there is to learn from understanding the implications of scale and relative magnitude, especially with respect to life-forms, a subject that can easily get lost in the understandably more primary emphasis on cartographic and spatial analyses of scale. Moreover, and with respect to relative size, I have suggested the importance of considering the diminutive registers of magnitude. Shifts in scale, which are ever more important in the era some call the Anthropocene, are becoming ever more important to observe, as is the fantasy that one might swing seamlessly across massive scalar differences. Thus, compensating devices such as paradoxes of measure work to stabilize scalar instabilities. In the context of early modernity, these paradoxes of measure and sweeps across scale often conceal a founding violence, as we discover in the emergence of microscopy and the reliance on anatomization to secure the accuracy of comparisons that allow for ecstatic articulations of a diminutive sublime.

Yet even as I have made these small labors to keep distinct the various senses of scales, the dangerous conflation of which seems evident in early modern entomological reflections, the scales of nature, cartographic scale, and relative magnitude all come into chilling alignment in Robert Hooke's foundational 1665 *Micrographia: or Some Physiological Descriptions of Minute Bodies Made by Magnifying Glasses with Observations and Inquiries Thereupon*. A complex interplay of scale and power characterizes the preface to this work. Not surprisingly, Hooke deploys various gestures of modesty, including in his dedication to the king. He begins, "I do humbly lay this small present at your Royal majesty's feet."[43] Puns on the smallness of his efforts or his role accumulate, and these gestures are part of a larger set of scalar swings. Of course, with respect to other life-forms, the scale of nature seems secure. "It is the greatest prerogative of Mankind above other Creatures," he writes, "that we are not only able to behold the works of Nature, or barely to sustein our lives by them, but we have also the power of considering, comparing, altering, assisting and improving them to various uses. And as this is the peculiar privilege of humane Nature in general, so is it capable of being so far advanced by the helps of Art, and Experience, as to make some Men excel others in their Observations, and Deductions, almost as much as they Beasts."[44] Comparison, including across scale, emerges as a constitutive capacity of the human. And the failure to make such comparisons accurately makes some humans more like "beasts" in fact. And yet Hooke also describes here not the figure of the triumphant scientist but the depraved human who requires technology to supplement constitutive defects. "By the addition of such artificial Instruments and methods," he argues, "there may be, in some manner, a reparation made for the mischiefs, and imperfection, mankind has drawn upon it self, by negligence, and intemperance, and a willful and superstitious deserting the Prescripts and Rules of Nature, whereby every man, both from a derived corruption, innate and born with him, and from his breeding and converse with men, is very subject to slip into all sorts of errors." As Scott Maisano and I have suggested elsewhere, contrary to critical and historical assertions that this era was characterized by the triumphant assertion of human prerogative, depravity and incapacity were often as commonly associated with the supposed pinnacle of creation.[45] And yet how slyly Hooke swings from minimal to maximal, largely through the aid of technological marvels: "By the means of Telescopes, there is nothing so far distant but may be represented to our view; and by the help of Microscopes, there is nothing so small, as to escape our inquiry."[46]

The triumphant scientist thus does emerge, but only from behind the shadow of human failure and error. And in describing his own method, suddenly his modest inquiries staked out in a small gift to his sovereign reach extraordinary proportions: "I made use of Microscopes, and some other Glasses and Instruments that improve these senses . . . but only to promote the use of Mechanical helps for the Senses, both in the surveying the already visible World, and for the discovery of many others hitherto unknown, and to make with us, with the great Conqueror, to be affected that we have not yet overcome one World when there are so many others to be discovered, every considerable improvement of Telescopes or Microscopes producing new Worlds and Terr-Incognita's to our view."[47] Nothing will be unreachable to the properly and scientifically accessorized human, no terra incognita out of reach. The map and the microscope thus become two of the many rungs on the ladder of the *scala naturae*, which becomes ever more naturalized through the efforts of the era's proponents of scientific inquiry. And if we learn anything from the marvelous and the minute, from the lesser living creatures of the Renaissance and beyond, be they those of Aristotle or Pliny, Thomas Moffett or Robert Hooke, it is this: in scale lies power, especially for those who seem to steady its dizzying swings.

Notes

1. Kumar and Tucker, "Introduction," 609.
2. On larger questions of measure in the works of Shakespeare, see Blank, *Shakespeare and the Mismeasure*. On the broad impact of geometric thinking on Renaissance stages, see Turner, *English Renaissance Stage*.
3. Aristotle, *Complete Works*, 922 (588^b4–12).
4. Emmons, "Size Matters," 227.
5. See particularly Sullivan, *Sleep, Romance, and Human Embodiment*, and Werth, "Introduction."
6. Chakrabarty, "Postcolonial Studies," 1; Clark, "Derangements of Scale," 152.
7. Ibid., 148.
8. Ibid., 150.
9. Ibid., 149.
10. Woods, "Scale Critique," 133.
11. Ibid., 140.
12. Tanoukhi, "Scale of World Literature," 79.
13. Clark, "Questions of Scale," 136.
14. Dimock, "Deep Time."
15. Moretti, "Conjectures on World Literature," 57.
16. Orlemanski, "Scales of Reading," 217.
17. Werth, "Introduction," 3.
18. Sully, "Scale," 503.
19. Many thanks to Nico Aliaga for his thoughts on Aristotle's original.
20. Clark, *Ecocriticism on the Edge*, 71.
21. Jenerette and Wu, "On the Definitions of Scale," 104.
22. Stewart, *On Longing*, 55.
23. Spenser, *Faerie Queene*, 5.2.30.
24. Ibid., 5.2.45.
25. Ibid., 5.2.33.
26. Woods, "Scale Critique," 135.
27. Holland, *Historie of the World*, 310.
28. Moffett, *Theater of Insects*, Ffff6r.
29. Ibid.
30. Ibid.
31. Ibid., Ffff6v.
32. Ibid.
33. Purchas, *Theatre of Politicall Flying-Insects*, A3r.
34. As rendered by Thomas Stanley in a translation nearly contemporaneous with Purchas, "When Zeuxis the Heracleote had drawn Helen, Nicostratus a Painter was astonished at the sight of the Picture. One coming to him, asked what was the reason he so much admired the Workmanship; He answered, 'If you had my eyes you would not ask me'" (*Claudius Aelianus*, 313).
35. Purchas, *Theatre of Politicall Flying-Insects*, A3r.
36. Moffett, *Theater of Insects*, Ffff6r.
37. Ibid., Ffff3r.
38. Ibid.
39. For the best overall account of the Accademia in the context of the development of natural history, see Freedberg, *Eye of the Lynx*. For the *Melissographia* and *Apiarium*, see particularly 160–73.
40. Ibid., 161.
41. Milton, *Paradise Lost*.
42. See Campana, "Bee and the Sovereign" and, "Bee and the Sovereign (II)."
43. Hooke, *Micrographia*, Ar.
44. Ibid.
45. See Campana and Maisano, introduction to *Renaissance Posthumanism*.
46. Hooke, *Micrographia*, Bv.
47. Ibid.

Bibliography

Aristotle. *The Complete Works of Aristotle: Volume 1*. Edited by Jonathan Barnes. Princeton: Princeton University Press, 1984.

Blank, Paula. *Shakespeare and the Mismeasure of Man*. Ithaca, NY: Cornell University Press, 2006.

Campana, Joseph. "The Bee and the Sovereign? Political Entomology and the Problem of Scale." *Shakespeare Studies* 41 (2013): 94–113.

———. "The Bee and the Sovereign (II): Segments, Swarms, and the Shakespearean Multitude." In *The Return of Theory in Early Modern English Studies*, vol. 2, edited by Bryan Reynolds, Paul Cefalu, and Gary Kuchar, 59–80. London: Palgrave Macmillan, 2014.

Campana, Joseph, and Scott Maisano. Introduction to *Renaissance Posthumanism*, edited by Campana and Maisano, 1–36. New York: Fordham University Press, 2016.

Chakrabarty, Dipesh. "Postcolonial Studies and the Challenge of Climate Change." *New Literary History* 43, no. 1 (2012): 1–18.

Clark, Timothy. "Derangements of Scale." In *Telemorphosis: Theory in the Era of Climate Change*, vol. 1, edited by Tom Cohen. Ann Arbor, MI: Open Humanities Press, 2012.

———. *Ecocriticism on the Edge: The Anthropocene as a Threshold Concept*. London: Bloomsbury, 2015.

———. "Questions of Scale." In *The Cambridge Introduction to Literature and the Environment*, 130–40. Cambridge: Cambridge University Press, 2011.

Dimock, Wai Chee. "Deep Time: American Literature and World History." *American Literary History* 13, no. 4 (2001): 755–75.

Emmons, Paul. "Size Matters: Virtual Scale and Bodily Imagination in Architectural Drawing." *Architectural Research Quarterly* 9, no. 3/4 (September 2005): 227–35.

Freedberg, David. *The Eye of the Lynx: Galileo, His Friends, and the Beginning of Modern Natural History*. Chicago: University of Chicago Press, 2003.

Fumerton, Patricia. *Cultural Aesthetics: Renaissance Literature and the Practice of Social Ornament*. Chicago: University of Chicago Press, 1991.

Holland, Philemon. *The Historie of the World*. London, 1601.

Hooke, Robert. *Micrographia: or Some Physiological Descriptions of Minute Bodies Made by Magnifying Glasses with Observations and Inquiries Thereupon*. London, 1665.

Jenerette, Darrel G., and Jianguo Wu. "On the Definitions of Scale." *Bulletin of the Ecological Society of America* 81, no. 1 (2000): 104–5.

Kumar, Krishan, and Herbert F. Tucker. "Introduction: Writ Large." *New Literary History* 48, no. 4 (Autumn 2017): 609–16.

Milton, John. *Paradise Lost*. Edited by Alastair Fowler. New York: Longman, 1984.

Moffett, Thomas. *The Theater of Insects: or, Lesser Living Creatures*. In *The History of Four-Footed Beasts and Serpents*, by Edward Topsell. London, 1658.

Moretti, Franco. "Conjectures on World Literature." *New Left Review* 1 (January–February 2000): 54–68.

Orlemanski, Julie. "Scales of Reading." *Exemplaria* 26, nos. 2–3 (2014): 215–33.

Purchas, Samuel. *A Theatre of Politicall Flying-Insects*. London, 1657.

Spenser, Edmund. *The Faerie Queene*, 2nd ed. Edited by A. C. Hamilton. New York: Longman, 2006.

Stanley, Thomas, trans. *Claudius Aelianus: His Various History*. London, 1666.

Stewart, Susan. *On Longing: Narratives of the Miniature, the Gigantic, the Souvenir, the Collection*. Durham: Duke University Press, 1993.

Sullivan, Garrett. *Sleep, Romance, and Human Embodiment: Vitality from Spenser to Milton*. Cambridge: Cambridge University Press, 2012.

Sully, Justin. "Scale." In *A Companion to Critical and Cultural Theory*, edited by Imre Szeman, Sarah Blacker, and Sully. London: Wiley, 2017.

Tanoukhi, Nirvana. "The Scale of World Literature." In *Immanuel Wallerstein and the Problem of the World: System, Scale, Culture*, edited by David Palumbo-Liu, Tanoukhi, and Bruce Robbins. Durham: Duke University Press, 2011.

Turner, Henry S. *The English Renaissance Stage: Geometry, Poetics, and the Practical Spatial Arts, 1580–1630*. Oxford: Oxford University Press, 2006.

Werth, Tiffany Jo. "Introduction: Shakespeare and the Human." *Shakespeare International Yearbook* 15 (2015): 1–20.

Woods, Derek. "Scale Critique for the Anthropocene." *Minnesota Review* 83 (2014): 133–42.

CHAPTER 3

PEST
Environmental Justice and
the (Early Modern) Rhetoric of Pest Control

Jennifer Munroe and Rebecca Laroche

It is a subgroup of "lesser living creatures"—what early moderns termed "vermin" or "noysome and pestilent things" and what we today deridingly call "pests"—that especially reminds us of our vulnerable bodies, our permeable fleshy coexistence with the nonhuman that confounds notions of human exceptionalism.[1] Controlling "pests" amounts to the attempted regulation of multiple border spaces, sometimes at once—bodily, household, national—but such attempts also underscore our inherent cohabitation. Consideration of these vulnerabilities therefore also necessitates that we trouble multiple dominant systems related to race, class, and gender, the way pest "control" is aligned with multiple forms of inequality and subjection. The presence of pests and our efforts to keep them at bay thus illustrate not only a desire to manage the Other, but also our shared susceptibilities with creeping things and with each other.

This chapter takes up how discourses about pest control demarcate even as they challenge these illusory boundaries and draw on a way of understanding us-versus-them that evokes the tiniest of creatures that multiply in our pantries or on our bodies and build webs in our dark corners, as well as the men and women whose presence within and without our geopolitical territories we aim to regulate or even eradicate out of fear or ignorance. We focus on two insects in particular, ants and lice, and their figuration around the following binaries: them/us, enemy/friend, foreign/domestic, dirty/clean, corrupt/virtuous, and female (and Other) / male. If, however, as Stacy Alaimo posits, the human self and the environment which that self occupies are both jointly the products (and coproducers) of one another, then the notion of discrete boundaries, these binary relationships, is mere illusion.[2] As with our analysis of "domestic transcorporeality,"[3] we draw here on how Natasha Korda proposes the household to be a locus of "multiple exchanges," human and economic, that reveal the permeable boundaries between inside and outside rather than their discrete and manageable borders; here, along with adding the ecological to her materialist feminist approach, we extend this understanding to include national borders as well. These "exchanges" simultaneously serve as coproductive happenings that alter the qualities of the human and nonhuman things in question such that the boundaries between human and nonhuman, as well as the borders between nation-states, are not simply transgressed but prove to be a fundamental human delusion. In the interrogation of these particular boundaries, we thus consider how early modern pest control draws on a rhetoric of war that not only informs these illusory boundaries in early modern England but also pertains to twenty-first-century environmental justice.

We use an environmental justice frame to rethink how, in the way these tiny creatures traverse the porous territories between bodies and environments, to borrow from Mel Y. Chen's work, they "deterritorialize . . . , emphasizing [their] mobility through and against imperialistic spatializations of 'here' and 'there.'"[4] Like Chen's discussion of how the Chinese lead paint scare in the early 2000s constructed "narratives of toxicity," we show how early modern pest control discourses draw on "signifying economies of health, imperialism, and degradation that paint race [and other categories of difference] onto different bodies."[5] For Chen, concerns about the Chinese lead paint on toys express deep-seated anxieties about the traversing of bodily and nationalist boundaries, the mixing of inside/outside, self/Other, yet ultimately prove to be broken "systems of segregation."[6] The very discourses of pest control in early modern England that ostensibly demarcate boundaries between humans and insects may on the one hand serve such "signifying economies," but on the other, they reveal the fundamental interconnectedness of humans and nonhumans, of humans and each other in a way that "deterritorialize[s]" more than it differentiates. Early modern discourses of pest control, that is, perform a fantasy of containment, or purification, that is inherently futile; as such, these discourses of early modern England ultimately reveal not discrete divisions between us and them, but instead punctuated instances whereby "they" are fundamentally "we."

Before we move to Thomas Moffett's treatise, we turn to Gervase Markham, another central figure in discourses of pest control and, more broadly, household management. Markham's chapter from *The Second Book of the English Husbandman*, "How to preserue all manner of Seeds, Hearbs, Flowers, and Fruits, from all manner of noysome and pestilent things, which deuoure and hurt them," includes, along with "Thunder and Lightening," a catalog of small creatures: caterpillars, toads, frogs, field mice, flies, green flies, gnats, pismires (ants), moles, snails, moths, cankers, and garden worms, perpetually locked in conflict with the home's residents. Indeed, to his husbandmen audience, Markham writes of these as if they are an encircled battalion poised to defend garden territory and assault planted seeds if necessary: "It is not enough to bequeath and giue your séedes vnto the ground, and then immediatly to expect (without any further industrie) the fruit of your labours, no goodnesse seldome commeth with such ease: you must therefore know that when you lay your séedes in the ground, they are like so many good men amongst a world of wicked ones, and as it were inuironed and begirt with manie Armies of enemies, from which if your care and diligence doe not defend them the most, if not all, will doubtlesse perish."[7] The garden itself, the first line of defense between "wild" outside and the realm of domesticated habitation, is figured as under siege, where the smallest of creatures threaten to breach its walls. His use of "inuironed" and "begirt" connote not an actual wall, the wood or stone garden perimeter, but instead a vision of fortification in which these tiny foes have the garden surrounded and only the defenses of "care and diligence" will prevail.[8] Creatures are deemed "filthy," "greedy," "pernicious," and "poisonous," "hurting" and "confusing" the seeds. Here, the martial language reinforces the high stakes in the us-versus-them melee and is evocative of nationalist language we find elsewhere in Markham, where "household" stands as synecdoche for the English nation-state.[9] In addition, the offensive-defensive maneuvers throughout pest control here link the military metaphor to gendered language, describing garden snails as "much offensive to Gardens" and feminizing the plants as he does so, speaking of how snails "feed of the tender leaves of the plants" and "of the outmost rinds of the daintiest herbs and flowers."[10] As such, protecting the domesticated space of the garden is a matter of also containing its vulnerable—and feminized—residents, and so the language of pest control becomes enmeshed with other gendered and nationalist discourses related more broadly to "domestication," other binaries of "us/them," constituted by and reifying raced and gendered difference as well as notions of human exceptionalism, while at the same time this language reinforces a fundamental antagonism between humans and nonhuman Others.

In the extended chapter from Markham, the description of "destroying" an anthill with "hot scalding water" particularly calls on the rhetoric of war, as enemies succumb to boiling liquids poured over the ramparts. In this discussion, Markham's material practice may be building on a long classical tradition that martializes the ant. Moffett replicates this tradition even though he wants to invoke it as an example of domestic diligence rather than violent outpourings. Thus, the Myrmidons in Moffett become a people known for their strenuous agricultural labor rather than the army that follows Cephalus in the Ovidian source (*Metamorphoses*, book 7) or Achilles's forces in the *Iliad*.[11] And while Virgil praises "their Black Regiment" that "through narrow wayes passe," Moffett reads only the depiction of labor. Moffett describes "wars" to the death with toads and serpents, compares ant infighting to recent civil wars, and provides an extended passage from Aeneas Silvius about the battle between lesser and greater pismires, but again, all serve as examples of diligence in the face of "intestine necessity."[12] Yet it is these same creatures that "will dig under all walls, will be held by no bands, and they only know neither Lawes nor bounds"; and it is this boundlessness that draws on the anxieties inherent in Markham's imperative for protection.[13]

Not all of Moffett's descriptions of "lesser living creatures," however, are divorced from the us-and-them paradigm (or perhaps for Moffett, the ants are us). When he describes lice, this divide between outside and inside draws on a gendering that resonates with Markham's, but such division takes on additional layers of religious, racial, and national purity as well. Lice are, Moffett writes, "the inevitable scourge of God," brought upon man as punishment from God of original sin: "In the first beginning whilest man was in his innocency, and free from wickednesse, he was subject to no corruption and filth, but when he was seduced by the wickednesse of that great and cunning deceiver, and proudly affected to know as much as God knew, God humbled him with divers diseases, and divers sorts of Worms, with Lice, Hand-Worms, Bellyworms, others call *Termites*, small Nits, and Acares."[14] In fact, lice thrive on corruption, Moffett continues, as they drink of "corrupt blood" and breed out of "corrupt putrefied blood" and "putrefactions."[15] This relationship between lice and forms of decay (both spiritual and physical) extends in Moffett to become associated with a particularly racial and ethnic corruption: "*Vespucius* testifieth of the Isle of *St. Thomas*, that the Blackmoors there are full of Lice, but the white men are free of that trouble. As for dressing the body: all *Ireland* is noted for this, that it swarms almost with Lice. But that this proceeds from the beastiness of the people, and want of cleanly women to wash them is manifest, because the English that are more careful in the way dress themselves, changing and washing their shirts often, have escaped that plague."[16] Here, the "corrupt[ion]" associated with the generation of lice is transferred to those infested with the little creatures—the Blackmoors and, it would seem, all Irish, as well as the women whose own allegedly unsanitary habits propagate (or at least do not prevent) the infestation. And an overabundance of lice is linked to human "beastiness," a blurring of human and nonhuman (by way of such corruption) that gets mapped onto other forms of excess and transgression: "Also what shall I say? Apes, Baboons, will feed on them. And Herodotus and Strabe in Pontus speaks of men that feed on Lice . . . and the Spaniards speake the same of the Inhabitants of the Province of Cuenensis in the West-Indies. And they hunt after them so greedily and desire them, that the Spaniards can hardly keep their slaves from feeding on them. And it is no wonder that they can feed on Lice, that devour Horses, Asses, Cats, Worms (and more than that) men that are raw."[17] Moffett's move from religious impurity—or "wickednesse" resulting from original sin as the origin of lice and other "scourge[ful]" insects and disease—to unclean daily and dietary habits where a "greed[y] desire" for lice becomes a sort of gateway meal that leads to transgressing other dietary prohibitions—from horses, asses, and cats to other dirt-dwelling creatures (worms) and, finally, to cannibalism. The boundaries Moffett constructs throughout these sections align binaries of tame/wild, pure/impure with ones that reinforce gender and racial difference, as well as human exceptionalism.

But such difference proves to be more illusion than reality, as early moderns would have known; lice and spiders (even venomous ones) were part of everyday experience, and infestations were commonplace. Even the martial context in Markham and Moffett serves as a reminder of the give-and-take of daily coexistence more than decisive victory over the insect kingdom. While Moffett associates such infestations with uncleanness and impurity *elsewhere* and in *other* populations, he also describes how they regularly occur not only in prisons but also in army encampments, where men (including English) lived in close proximity with each other and with the little creatures that caused them to itch. "Hence it is that Armies and Prisons are so full of Lice, the sweat being corrupted by wearing always the same cloathes, and from thence ariseth matter for their original by the mediation of heat. So those that keep no diet, but delight in eating and filthines, and feed on *Vipers, Radishes, Basil, Figs, Lignum Aloes, Garden Smallage*, and *Dates* too much, their bodies will from putrefaction of humours breed Lice between their skin."[18] Figuring lice as regular annoyances in army camps on the one hand situates the presence of lice as "over there," in the marginal environments of makeshift (and often mobile) human communities, if not also in foreign territory, and both the exotic origins of the dates and figs and the low-born potables of radishes and smallage associated with a lice-inducing diet evoke fears of repercussions from ingesting the (raced and classed) Others who populate early modern writings about religion, status, and race, including, say, Shakespeare's *Merchant of Venice*. It also serves as a reminder of the mobility of such creatures and the ambiguous boundaries they traverse, of their blurring of "here" as well as "there"—on the bodies of the men who dwelled temporarily in such camps and later returned "home," of the intimacies of the lice-human relationship, whereby lice dwelled on human bodies and nourished themselves with human blood that they brought with them to other human bodies. And the racial and national associations of non-English (and non-Christian) with the corruption and impurity associated with such infestations elsewhere in Moffett yield to the reality of everyday encounters with lice in these army camps, in which it is the English, for instance (and not the enemy Other), who resort to, among other things, using gunpowder on their clothes when they are "lowsie."[19]

Early modern daily life offered countless opportunities for shared coexistence with these tiniest of beings, hardly reserved for exceptional contexts, such as war, prison, or the excesses and "corruption" associated with their presence in Moffett. Samuel Pepys offers numerous accounts of his own battle with the little creatures, including a particularly itchy week, when, he writes, "[My wife] finds that I am lousy, having found in my head and body about twenty lice, little and great, which I wonder at, being more than I have had I believe these 20 years. I did think I might have got them from the little boy [Pepys's footboy, according to the note], but they did presently look him, and found none. So how they come I know not, but presently did shift myself, and so shall be rid of them, and cut my hair close to my head, and so with my content to bed."[20] That he offers numerous examples of such encounters with lice suggests that their eradication was both merely temporary and more difficult than simply getting new clothes and a haircut.

Early modern recipes illustrate the regular presence of lice and the often ordinary ingredients in cures for them, suggesting perhaps the banality, if not also the frequency, of their infestation. While Moffett includes in his book many cures that use quicksilver, he assembles others that are primarily herbal, all of which tend to involve rubbing the materials into the affected area. In Lady Grace Catchmay's manuscript recipe book, we find a pithy recipe "To kill lyce in Childrens heads" that "Take[s] honey and the berreys of Ivy stamped together, and rubb the head therewith it will kill the lice."[21] Nestled between recipes "For the Cramp in the Legs" and "For Chilblanes on the Hands" is "To Cure a Scabbed-Head, and to kill the Lice" in Hannah Woolley's *Supplement to the Queen-Like Closet*: "Take the yolks of six hard Eggs, and bruise them well with a spoon; then put one pound of new-Butter to them that was never salted; boil them together till you find it to be enough, which will be in an hours space, upon a slow fire; let it look blackish when you take it off the fire; then strain it and keep it for your use."[22] Efforts to eradicate insects underscore shared bodies, shared space. Not only do lice clearly traverse the thresholds of the garden, the house, and the blankets used and garments worn by its inhabitants, but lice cures also serve as reminders that the boundaries between nonhuman and human are tenuous indeed. Such recipes, that is, depend on the mixing and comingling of human-nonhuman substances: the combination of honey, ivy, eggs, butter; the concoction generated from such combination (and the addition of fire, which alters its chemistry); the rubbing of these materials into human scalp and hair.

Such recipes as those in the Catchmay and Woolley books capture the intimate relationship between insects and humans within the proximity of private, personal spaces. In Anne Brumwich's mid-seventeenth-century collection can be found the following recipe: "A Medicine to kill any Quick thinge as flye or flea that is crept into *the* eare."[23] While the outer walls may protect the garden from large animals, winged, burrowing, and smaller creatures are undaunted by such barriers. Therefore, given the opportunities presented by chimneys, broken windows, open doors, and rotting wood, these creatures too make their way into houses' interiors. Brumwich's recipe, however, reveals the real anxiety around domestic pest control: that our own bodies are vulnerable, that is, also filled with holes, our skin a ready participant in the transcorporeal interplay between human and nonhuman.

Despite the numerous demarcations present in print and high-profile discussions of pest control, they ultimately show how, as Val Plumwood writes, "the idea that human life takes place in a self-enclosed, completely humanized and cultural space that is somehow independent of an inessential sphere of nature which exists in a remote space 'somewhere else,'" is a delusion.[24] As pest control fails to prevent movement from garden wall to human flesh, from stone to skin (and its success is always only an illusion), it reveals what Alaimo has called the transcorporeality of being: "Imagining human corporeality as trans-corporeality, in which the human is always intermeshed with the more-than-human world, underlines the extent to which the substance of the human is ultimately inseparable from 'the environment.'"[25] In the skin acting as the last barrier to the outside world—the final wall, if you will—its easy penetrability signifies the tenuous line between inside and outside that we struggle so resolutely to maintain.

While the processes of pest control in the early modern period brought the householders into proximity with that which they attempted to eliminate, our own twenty-first-century processes, while arguably more "effective," mean that we attempt to hold pests at arm's length, denying their place in the biodiverse, ecological whole as we do so. As a result of these practices, we have depleted the nutrients of the soil, contaminated the water supply, and contributed to our general ill health. And the detrimental effects of such practices are unevenly distributed across racial, classed, and gendered boundaries.[26] In the previous century, paralleling the boomerang effect of antibacterial soaps and cleansers on the bacterial gene pool, over-the-counter pharmaceutical "solutions" to head lice have fostered a breed of super-lice impervious to these medicaments.[27] We might also recall the history of DDT, a chemical agent developed in the 1940s to "combat malaria, typhus, and other insect-borne human diseases among both military and civilian populations."[28] What began as an insecticide to eradicate fleas, ticks, lice, and mosquitos to fight disease became a widely used pesticide in the American agriculture system with catastrophic effects on our ecosystem (and to human populations) and one of the subjects of Rachel Carson's *Silent Spring*. Indeed, Carson's study references a "propaganda movie" produced by the US Department of Agriculture that showed "horror scenes" around the fire ant, justifying the blanketing of fields in this "war" "between man and the imported fire ant."[29] Paralleling the Red Scare during the Cold War and paranoia about refugee immigration to the United Kingdom, Europe, and the United States today, the "imported" menace that seems to come from other countries may indicate as well a threat from within our own borders. As Carson tells us, for instance, the "fire ant . . . seems to have entered the United States from South America by way of the port of Mobile, Alabama, where it was discovered shortly after the end of the First World War. By 1928 it had spread into the suburbs of Mobile and thereafter continued an invasion that has now carried it into most of the southern states."[30] Carson cites several studies that showed the positive effects of fire ants for agriculture, including their role as a natural predator of the boll weevil and the ways their ant hills loosened the soil. The government's program of eradication, however, killed much beyond the species targeted for eradication, as Carson goes on to demonstrate. The rhetoric surrounding this program should remind us of Markham's boiling liquid, simply ramped up with the parallel technologies of war, as Carson also reminds us that developments in insecticides accompanied the emergence of chemical weapons in 1930s Germany.[31] At the same time, we might recall that for as much as actual threats penetrate our borders—the "Africanized" bees, invasive plants and animals, or a terrorist attack by outsiders—such destruction is as (or more) often homegrown.

As a result of this and other seemingly targeted "pest" eradication, though, we have killed bees, birds, butterflies, dogs, cattle, and children along with the aphids and fire ants, and good bacteria along with the bad.

These obliterating practices depend on strong divisions between human and nonhuman that deny our shared fragility, and in the end they have become increasingly damaging to the biosphere. In so doing, they also inflict damage on some of the most vulnerable, and invisible, members of human populations for the benefit of the most privileged. The illness and injury to migrant workers, the result (among other things) of their repeated exposure to the same pesticides that some American consumers avoid by buying the more expensive organic option or the "safer" conventionally grown vegetables of broccoli and onions rather than pesticide-laced spinach and peaches, underscores the unequal burden of these chemicals on disadvantaged populations. Carson raised this issue around the deadlier pesticides of her day, citing the eleven instances of parathion poisoning among thirty orange pickers in California, but the US Occupational Safety and Health Administration still lists "pesticides and other chemicals" among the hazards to which agricultural laborers are regularly exposed today.[32] The short- and long-term illnesses of farmworkers as a result of exposure, made more extreme for those who actually handle the chemicals, seem to be only partially addressed by accurate labeling and the use of respirators in application.

Moreover, our historical analysis of lice underscores the implications of the increased racialization of labor as it relates to pest control. The xenophobia unleashed in the 2016 election season and by the subsequent Trump administration against a so-called immigrant invasion—a rhetoric at once derisive and aggressive in calling up invasive species and invading armies—has deemphasized the culpability of an industrial agricultural complex dependent on immigrant and migrant labor. Indeed, the invisibility and mobility of this labor force facilitate its exploitation in living conditions and exposure to hazardous chemicals, a precarious existence that may be further compromised by the backroom deals made possible by its invisibility.[33] What is more, this rhetoric ignores the fact that between 3 and 5 percent of US active-duty personnel are immigrants, many of whom put their lives at risk as they seek a path to citizenship.[34] Thus, the rhetoric of invasion, the binaries of self and other, are undermined by actual practice, the intimate interdependence of self and perceived Other and the cultural mobility of certain economic arrangements across borders. The fact that war, a violent expression of the us-versus-them rhetoric, constitutes one of these means of cultural mobility only underscores how the seeming ability to demarcate in fact only further "deterritorializes."

In both contemporary and early modern examples, it is the permeability of our bodies that most disarms us, the porous geopolitical boundaries that provoke fear and defensive postures, even among the most well-meaning, or that incite outright vitriol and calls for mass deportations, special registries for select populations, and rallying cries to "build that wall." Rethinking pest control discourses (both early modern and today) in an environmental justice frame reveals that these domestic encounters may in fact hold the potential for a kind of local activism that engages intersections between environmental destruction and race, gender, and class that environmental justice advocates have long sought to quantify and redress. In the domestic environment, the larger implications are felt deeply, wholly experienced as we make things grow, cook slow food, nurture our human and nonhuman constituents, and live alongside anthills.

Notes

1. Moffett, *Theater of Insects*. See Raber, "Vermin and Parasites."
2. For a more elaborated discussion of transcorporeality, see Alaimo, *Bodily Natures*. Portions of this chapter are extracted from the theoretical frame we established in Munroe and Laroche, *Shakespeare and Ecofeminist Theory*, 19.
3. Munroe and Laroche, *Shakespeare and Ecofeminist Theory*, 20. See Korda, *Shakespeare's Domestic Economies*.
4. Chen, *Animacies*, 167.
5. Ibid., 187–88.
6. Ibid., 167.
7. Markham, *Second Book*, 43. We engage this passage to similar but different ends in Munroe and Laroche, *Shakespeare and Ecofeminist Theory*, 45–46.
8. See, for instance, Morton, "Everything We Need," 79.
9. For a discussion of this aspect of Markham, see Wall, *Staging Domesticity*.
10. Markham, *Second Book*, 46.
11. Moffett, *Theater of Insects*, 1074.
12. Ibid., 1076, 1078, 1079.
13. Ibid., 1079.
14. Ibid., 1090.
15. Ibid., 1092.
16. Ibid.
17. Ibid.
18. Ibid.
19. See Fransen, "Van Helmont," for instance, and the account by scientist Van Helmont and a regiment of soldiers who, ironically, turned their own gunpowder onto their clothes in an attempt to eradicate the lice from their garments.
20. See Pepys, *Diary*, two entries from January 1, 1669, and 1674 (51).
21. Catchmay, "Book of Medicins," f.13r.
22. Woolley, *Supplement*, 52.
23. Brumwich, "Her Book," digital image 36. See Roberts, "Wigging Out," and the discussion of the early modern fear of earwigs entering the ear and consequently the brain. We provide this example of recipe transcorporeality in Munroe and Laroche, *Shakespeare and Ecofeminist Theory*, 58.
24. Plumwood, *Environmental Culture*, 51, quoted in *Ecological Approaches*, 3.
25. Alaimo, *Bodily Natures*, 2.
26. Gross, "Pollution."

27. Ballantyne, "Strange but True" and "What Is Super Lice." See also Michael Pollan, "Some of My Best Friends."
28. US Environmental Protection Agency, "DDT."
29. Carson, *Silent Spring*, 164, a reference that is expanded on in the documentary excerpt quoted here: Godwin, *Rachel Carson's Silent Spring*, min. 27ff.
30. Carson, *Silent Spring*, 161.
31. Ibid., 28.
32. Ibid., 30. US Department of Labor, "Agricultural Operations."
33. Aubrey and Charles, "Big Battles."
34. Zong and Batalova, "Immigrant Veterans"; US Department of Homeland Security, "Citizenship for Family Members."

Bibliography

Alaimo, Stacy. *Bodily Natures: Science, Environment, and the Material Self*. Bloomington: Indiana University Press, 2010.

Aubrey, Allison, and Dan Charles. "Big Battles over Farm and Food Policies May Be Brewing as the Trump Era Begins." *The Salt: What's on Your Plate*. NPR, December 28, 2016. http://www.npr.org/sections/thesalt/2016/12/28/506592753/big-battles-over-farm-and-food-policies-may-be-brewing-as-trump-era-begins.

Ballantyne, Coco. "Strange but True: Antibacterial Products May Do More Harm Than Good." *Scientific American*, June 7, 2007. http://www.scientificamerican.com/article/strange-but-true-antibacterial-products-may-do-more-harm-than-good/.

Brumwich, Anne (and others). "Her Book of Receipts or Medicines." N.d. Wellcome MS 160. http://archives.wellcome.ac.uk/recipebooks/MS160/MS160_0036.pdf.

Carson, Rachel. *Silent Spring*. Boston: Houghton Mifflin, 1962.

Catchmay, Lady Frances. "A Book of Medicins." Wellcome MS 184a.

Chen, Mel Y. *Animacies: Biopolitics, Racial Mattering, and Queer Affect*. Durham: Duke University Press, 2012.

Ecological Approaches to Early Modern Texts: A Field Guide to Reading and Teaching. Edited by Jennifer Munroe, Edward J. Geisweidt, and Lynne Dickson Bruckner. Aldershot, UK: Ashgate Press, 2015.

Environmental Protection Agency. "DDT—A Brief History and Status." Accessed August 11, 2017. https://www.epa.gov/ingredients-used-pesticide-products/ddt-brief-history-and-status.

Fransen, Sietske, with Saskia Klerk. "Van Helmont on the Plague, Again!" *The Recipes Project: Food, Magic, Art, Science, and Medicine*. December 15, 2015. recipes.hypotheses.org/7216.

Godwin, Neil. *Rachel Carson's Silent Spring*. Boston: WGBH Boston Video, 2007.

Gross, Liz. "Pollution, Poverty, and People of Color: Don't Drink the Water." *Scientific American*, June 12, 2012. http://www.scientificamerican.com/article/pollution-poverty-people-color-dont-drink-water/.

Korda, Natasha. *Shakespeare's Domestic Economies: Gender and Property in Early Modern England*. Philadelphia: University of Pennsylvania Press, 2002.

Markham, Gervase. *The Second Book of the English Husbandman*. London, 1614.

Moffett, Thomas. *The Theater of Insects: or, Lesser Living Creatures*. In *The History of Four-Footed Beasts and Serpents*, by Edward Topsell. London, 1658.

Morton, Timothy. "Everything We Need: Scarcity, Scale, Hyperobjects."

Architectural Design 82, no. 4 (2012): 78–81.
Munroe, Jennifer, and Rebecca Laroche. Shakespeare and Ecofeminist Theory. London: Bloomsbury Press, 2017.
Pepys, Samuel. The Diary of Samuel Pepys: Daily Entries from the 17th Century London Diary. Edited by Phil Gyford. Accessed February 19, 2020. https://www.pepysdiary.com.
Pollan, Michael. "Some of My Best Friends Are Germs." New York Times Magazine, May 19, 2013. http://www.nytimes.com/2013/05/19/magazine/say-hello-to-the-100-trillion-bacteria-that-make-up-your-microbiome.html.
Raber, Karen. "Vermin and Parasites: Shakespeare's Animal Architectures." In Ecocritical Shakespeare: Literary and Scientific Cultures of Modernity, edited by Lynne Bruckner and Dan Brayton, 13–32. Farnham, UK: Ashgate Press, 2011.
Roberts, Jennifer Sherman. "Wigging Out: Mrs. Corlyon's Method for Extracting Earwigs from the Ear." The Recipes Project: Food, Magic, Art, Science, and Medicine. December 5, 2015. https://recipes.hypotheses.org/5634.
US Department of Homeland Security. Citizenship and Immigration Services. "Citizenship for Family Members." Accessed 30, 2019. https://www.uscis.gov/military/citizenship-military-personnel-family-members.
US Department of Labor, Occupational Safety and Health Administration. "Agricultural Operations: Hazards & Controls." Accessed February 19, 2020. https://www.osha.gov/agricultural-operations/hazards.
Wall, Wendy. Staging Domesticity. Cambridge: Cambridge University Press, 2002.
"What Is Super Lice and How Can You Treat It?" CNN, March 3, 2016. Video. http://www.cnn.com/videos/health/2016/03/03/super-lice-spreading-pkg.ktxl.
Woolley, Hannah. A Supplement to the Queen-Like Closet; or a Little of Every Thing Presented to All Ingenious Ladies, and Gentlewomen. London, 1674.
Zong, Jie, and Jeanne Batalova. "Immigrant Veterans in the United States." Migration Policy Institute, May 16, 2019. https://www.migrationpolicy.org/article/immigrant-veterans-united-states.

CHAPTER 4

INFESTATION

Out of Africa: Locust Infestation, Universal History, and the Early Modern Theological Imaginary

Lucinda Cole

The problem of infestation—swarms of insects or other vermin overrunning fields and grain bins, decimating agriculture and food reserves—recurs throughout early modern histories, travel writing, and, often in metaphoric form, literature. Drawing on a typology that stretched back to the Old Testament account of the plagues of Egypt, early modern writers and theologians debated whether infestations were scourges sent by God to punish sinful peoples or whether insect swarms were demonic forces, evil in themselves. Although we may think of locust invasions as alien or tangential to early modern European history, they appear in almost every traveler's history of the Near East, and frequently in natural philosophies, such as Thomas Moffett's *Theater of Insects*, intended to describe the nature and habits of creatures. Oliver Goldsmith's *An Historie of the Earth and Animated Nature* (1774), for example, describes locusts in Russia, Poland, and Lithuania in 1690 "in such astonishing multitudes that the air was darkened and the earth covered"; "the trees bent beneath their weight, and the damage which the countrie sustained exceeded computation."[1] While admitting that trying to recount "all the mischiefs these famished insects have at different times occasioned" would be an endless task, Goldsmith emphasizes that in most cases, locusts "come into Europe" out of Africa.

Finding no sustenance in Africa, he writes, they travel to equally barren "sandy deserts," then "proceed forward across the sea, and thus come into Europe, where they alight on the first green pastures that occur" (346). Repeated vermin devastations, like those in 1690, kept the problem of transnational infestation at the forefront of a wide range of discourses about the typological meanings of and remedies for swarming things that threatened the ecological and sociopolitical stability of the state. No geographical area, as Goldsmith suggests, is more important to accounts of infestation than Africa, the breeding grounds from which locusts, in particular, were thought to emerge.

In this chapter, I focus on how Moffett and other English writers imagined and represented the relationships among locusts, Africans, and Europeans in what we might call a politico-theology of infestation. My guiding assumption throughout is that entomology and ethnography developed in tandem and often were mutually constitutive, and that their relationship, in turn, shapes how we interpret the early modern fascination with what Aristotle called "imperfect creatures," those that supposedly bred spontaneously from mud, slime, or putrefying flesh.[2] The first English-language approach to ethnography, by Johann Boemus, appeared under the title *The Fardle of Facions* in 1555, and then, in 1611, as *The Manners, Laws, and Customs of All Nations*.[3] This universal history, an attempt to collect and structure medieval and modern data about the world's cultures, is more or less contemporary with some of the narratives in Richard Hakluyt's better-known *The Principal Navigations, Voiages, Traffiques, and Discoveries of the English Nation* (1589–1600) and those included in Samuel Purchas's 1613 *Purchas His Pilgrimage*.[4] At different points, all three texts describe and try to theorize the nature and meaning of insect infestations in Europe, Asia, and Africa. Insectology as an offshoot of natural history not surprisingly began to develop at the same time and in the same sociopolitical contexts. Ulisse Aldrovandi's *De Animalibus Insectis* (1602) was the first book, according to Brian Ogilvie, "devoted entirely to insects," although Moffett's *Theater of Insects* was probably drafted by the turn of the century; it drew on work by Edward Wotton, Conrad Gessner, and Thomas Penny.[5] Edward Topsell's *Historie of Four-Footed Beastes and Serpents* (1607–1608) borrowed from Moffett's text and was eventually published with it.[6] These early treatises both recast classical and biblical accounts of infestation and incorporate contemporary travelers' narratives. By situating these texts about remote lands and unfamiliar ecologies within changing conceptions of classical authority and biblical typology, these treatises respond, in significant but implicit ways, to the "biological upheaval" that was a by-product of what Alfred Crosby calls the "Columbian exchange."[7]

In the words of Charles C. Mann, after 1492, "the world's ecosystems collided and mixed as European vessels carried thousands of species to new homes over the ocean."[8] Because these new species found no natural enemies in their new homes, their numbers "often exploded," writes Mann, in a "phenomenon known to science as 'ecological release.'"[9] When, for example, Spanish colonists brought African plantains to Hispaniola, they probably also imported some scale insects accompanied by fire ants, which were following their food supply. In Hispaniola, the scale insects destroyed orchards, "as though flames had fallen from the sky and burned them," while the fire ants multiplied into what was described as an "infinite number."[10] According to the missionary Bartolomé de Las Casas, these biting ants "could not be stopped in any way nor by human means."[11] The Spaniards abandoned their new homes until, after a series of religious interventions, "the plague began to diminish."[12] As this description by de Las Casas suggests, European entomology and ethnography in some sense were together born out of global trade and the colonial regimes that were part of its cultural and administrative apparatus.

Within this economic and ecological context, traditional, sometimes apocryphal, stories about plagues of locusts, whose devastating effects had long been recorded by classical and biblical historians, helped model responses to new biological plagues. Both insectology and universal history—disciplines now radically distinguished by subject and scale—confront swarming populations of insects, along with the strategies used to try to mitigate their devastating effects on agriculture and food stores.[13] Before turning to Moffett, however, I explore the lengthy account of locust infestation by Leo Africanus in *A Geographical Historie of Africa*, translated and published in England in 1600.[14] Additions to his original account, in which locusts are represented as a value-neutral staple of a desert diet, demonstrate the extent to which, for early modern Europeans, locusts are always entangled with biblical narratives about God's punishment and mercy. I then situate Moffett's *Theater of Insects* within the interpenetrating contexts of theology, ecology, and universal history, first by examining Moffett's depiction of locust-induced famine, especially in Africa, and then by exploring seventeenth-century debates about whether locusts can or should be regarded as a human food source.[15] Although theological debates about "clean" and "unclean" foods are familiar to scholars working in the early modern period, I argue that these controversies take on new meaning in the light of the global politics of Britain's colonial projects in particular. In James Hart's *Klinike, or The Diet of the Diseased* (1633) and Alexander Ross's *Arcana Microcosmi, or The Hid Secrets of Man's Body* (1652), the practice of locust eating becomes fully pathologized, as are the peoples who include insects in their diet.[16] In these texts, infestation reappears as a form of personal and political infection, in contrast to Judeo-Christian agricultural practices that supposedly offer a real but always precarious protection. For many readers during the period, eating locusts becomes a sign of moral depravity and cultural backwardness, a dietary practice that marks Africans as irrevocably Other.

"A fortunate boading"

The English translation of Africanus's *A Geographical Historie of Africa*, published in 1600, contains three accounts of locus infestations, but only one of these is included in the original text. In Africanus, locusts are the last item on a list of animals not generally found in Europe. "Monstrous swarmes" of locusts "devoure trees, leaves, fruites, and all greene things growing out the earth"; their eggs produce a second generation that continues the feast, thereby "procuring . . . extreme dearth of corne" (349). Although the biblical overtones of the eighth plague of Egypt may hover over this passage, Africanus mitigates the disaster by noting the adaptive measures taken by indigenous peoples: "Howbeit the inhabitants of Arabia deserta, and of Libya, esteeme the comming of these locusts as a fortunate boading: for seething or drying them in the sun, they bruise them to powder, and so eate them" (349). John Pory, the translator, provides two more accounts of locust infestation, the first by Paulus Orosius in *History Against the Pagans* (ca. 417)—"reverend in regard to the authors antiquitie"—and the second by Francis Alvarez in *A True Relation of the Lands of Prester John of the Indies* (1540), which Pory recommends as "credible and to be accepted," given that "the reporter was a most diligent and faithful; eie-witnes of the same" (350). Unlike the descriptions by Africanus, these accounts,

Pory suggests, do a better job of demonstrating how God uses locusts "as a most sharp scourge between times to discipline all the nations of Africa" (958).

History Against the Pagans tells the story of "an horrible and extraordinarie destruction" visited on Africa. In what might be interpreted as punishment for their rejection of Christianity, God sent locusts that devoured corn, bark, and even the wood of the trees. Although a "violent and sudden winde" bore them aloft and out to the African sea, where they drowned, their "lothsome and putrified carcases" were cast back onto shore, where "an incredible stinking & infectious smell" brought about a general pestilence, which first killed birds and beasts, then men by the thousands (350). "Never [before] in the time of Christians," Orosius concludes, did a "scourge of locusts" bring such devastation (351). The idea that the Christian faith offers protection against infestation, disease, and death is reinforced in Alvarez's lengthy description of several locust events in India and Africa. First, he reports on swarms in India, including one that covered twenty-four miles and made the people "halfe dead for sorrow" (352). They implored the Portuguese to help. Alvarez and the ambassador arranged a procession; they marched through fields of wheat with a cross in hand, the Portuguese singing the litany and the indigenes asking, in their language, that God have mercy, until Alvarez performed an excommunication. He

> pronounced over [the locusts] a certaine conjuration, which I had about me in writing, having made it that night, requesting, admonishing, and excommunicating them, enjoining them within the space of three howers to depart towards the sea, or to the land of the Moores, or the desert mountaines, and to let the Christians alone: and they not performing this, I summoned and charged the birdes of heaven, the beasts of the earth, and all sorts of tempests, to scatter, destroy, and eate up their bodies: and to this effect, I took a quantitie of locusts, making this admonition to them present, in the behalfe likewise of them absent, and so giving them liberties, I suffered them to depart. (352)

The conjuration successfully drove the locusts out to sea, where a "great cloud" and thunder "met them full in the teeth" (353). After three hours of rain, thousands of locust bodies lay in "mightie heapes" on the shore;

the next morning, not one locust could be "found alive upon the earth" (353). Stories of this triumph spread so quickly that in a different town three days later, the Portuguese were again enjoined to drive out the locusts; they again formed a procession and again cleared the ground and sky of insect swarms. In this account, Christian conjuration functions as both a rhetoric of prophylactic intervention and a material means of extermination.

Ritual excommunication was not peculiar to African climes. Both Karl Dannenfeldt and E. P. Evans have described European ecclesiastical attempts to control periodic infestation through "sacerdotal conjuring and cursing," proceedings brought against rats, mice, locusts, weevils, and other vermin "in order to prevent them from devouring the crops, and to expel them from orchards, vineyards, and cultivated fields by means of exorcism and excommunication."[17] When Alvarez charges "the birdes of heaven, the beasts of the earth, and all sorts of tempests, to scatter, destroy, and eate up their bodies," he aligns himself with this ritual and tradition. But in South Asia, the "truth" of ritual excommunication operates in a colonizing frame. Pory uses Alvarez's story to present infestation as form of discipline against an errant continent because it was not yet—or not yet completely—Christianized. Far from serving as a "fortunate boading" and as a welcome source of protein, locusts appear as a "scourge," a pestilence, and a source of great sorrow in pagan nations. The sickness and sorrow that result from locust infestations can be relieved only by Christian priests and ambassadors. Pory's version of John Leo therefore transforms geography into naked biopolitics: Africa's and South Asia's creatures (both human and nonhuman) become subject to the power of Christian theology through the logics of infestation and extermination. In this respect, locusts underwrite a new physico-theological order: God instructs Christians to rid Africa and India of the insects that serve as both evidence of these regions' need for colonial intervention and signs of their sins in resisting a divinely sanctioned regime.

Famine and "God's Armies"

Pory's insistence that locusts constitute a "scourge" of pagan Africa indicates how biblical history helped to shape perceptions in sixteenth- and seventeenth-century Europe of the threats posed by swarms of insects to food systems susceptible to periodic crop failures and occasional famine. During the Little Ice Age, cold temperatures, rainfall shortages, and easterly winds from the Baltic regions often brought with them crop shortages, higher grain prices, and dearth of food.[18] In fledgling agricultural economies, the presence or absence of hungry animal populations could constitute the difference in villages and cities between sufficiency and hardship, even between life and death. In 1533, Parliament passed an act requiring citizens to make and maintain nets and snares for trapping crows, rooks, and choughs, birds that fed on seeds before they could sprout and take root. In 1566, under Elizabeth, the earlier act was "revived," but this time it was expanded to include a larger range of vermin, including foxes, weasels, otters, rats, mice, and moles.[19] In his 1616 treatise *The Fall of Man, or The Corruption of Nature*, Godfrey Goodman exhorts his readers, "Let not the plagues of Aegypt seem so incredible," when, within living memory (1580), swarming mice infested Essex and made it "almost [un]inhabitable."[20] The England of James I, like the Egypt of Exodus, is plagued, its nature corrupt. "Wee stand not onely in feare of fierce Lions, cruell Tigers, rauening Wolues, deuouring Beares," writes Goodman, "but Gats, Flies, and the least wormes doe serue to molest vs."[21] As the title of his jeremiad suggests, the "Fall of Man" is bound inextricably to the corruption of a natural world, figured not only by traditional images of wild beasts (all but extinct in seventeenth-century Britain) but by small, noxious creatures, ubiquitous and familiar vermin.

As I have argued elsewhere, Europe had its share of animal plagues, even occasional plagues of grasshoppers or locusts.[22] Moffett reports on insect-induced famine events in France in 455, 874, 1337, 1353, and 1374, in which a third of the inhabitants died. In 1476, locusts "wasted almost all *Polonia*"; in 1536, they invaded first eastern Europe, then Germany and Italy, returning in 1543, their bodies "forming heaps above a cubit high" (987). At times during the early modern period, locust-like insects devastated crops as far north as Wales and Ireland.[23] Moffett reports that while he was drafting his chapter on locusts—"whilest ... writing this"—he "received news that the Spaniards were sorely afflicted with swarms of Locusts brought thither out of Africa": "For they flew like Armies through the skies and darkned the air. And the people when they saw them, rang all their bels, shot off ordinance, sounded with trumpets, tinkled with brazen vessels, cast up sand, did all they could to drive them away; but they could not obtain what they desired, wherefore sparing their labour in vain, they died everywhere of hunger and contagion: as the Mariners and steer-men reported to us, who escaped very hardly from that danger themselves" (987). As the military imagery in this passage suggests, locust infestation was more than a historical curiosity or a faraway threat. The Spaniards responded with the weapons and signals of war in trying to repel these "Armies . . . that darkned the air." A locust swarm can extend from 150 to 400 square miles; 50 million locusts, according to one expert, can eat 100 tons of food every night.[24] Even if England for the most part offered a less habitable climate to these hungry insects than more southerly nations, the English were vicarious witnesses to the damage they could do and deeply aware of the close, if mysterious, relationship among infestation, famine, and infection.

In this context, Moffett's *The Theater of Insects* should be regarded as more than a scholarly compendium of early modern knowledge about insects in the known world. As its title suggests, the text stages a world—a theater—in which insects are actors and agents. In addition to serving as experimental subjects whose anatomies threw into chaos early modern ideas about the possibilities of spontaneous generation, insects led natural philosophers to expand their definitions of life. The anthropomorphizing of locusts in particular as "Armies" reveals the widespread recognition that insect swarms could affect human populations in ways sometimes more immediate and powerful than the dictates of monarchs and their emissaries.

Within the Christian tradition, the Four Horsemen of the Apocalypse—War, Famine, Disease, and Death—often were heralded by, if not directly attributed to, vermin, "given power," according to Revelations 6:7–8, to "kill with sword, and with hunger, and with death." George Wither's *Britain's Remembrancer* (1628) begins with a description of how Famine, personified as a general, commands a host of "Troups" that include caterpillars, locusts, birds, and worms:

The crawling *Caterpillars*, wastfull *Flyes*,
The skipping *Locust* (that in winter dies)
*Floods, Frosts, & Mildewes, Blastings, Windes, & Stormes,
Drounth, ravnous Fowles, & Vermine, Weedes, & Wormes*:
Sloth, Evill husbandry, and such as those,
Which make a scarcenesse where most plenty grows.[25]

Although Wither puts locusts under the command of Famine, in the Bible they usually are represented as part of God's militia, as "war horses" (Joel 2:4–5) or as a "great army, which I sent among you" (Joel 2:25), says God, often by way of an east wind. In Exodus, an east wind brings with it locusts that have "invaded" Egypt, covering "all the ground until it was black" and devouring all that was left after an already devastating plague of hail. "Nothing green remained on tree and plant through all the land of Egypt." In early modern texts devoted to natural history—as we have seen in Moffett's description of the contemporary infestation in Spain—swarms of locusts were described as flying "armies," often sent by God to scourge sinful populations. Those "creatures," writes Moffett, "are not the smallest amongst the Armies of the Lord of hosts, when he pleaseth to punish the sins of men, and to revenge himself on the despisers of his Lawes" (987). Samuel Purchas uses almost identical language: we "must conclude that these small creatures have a chief place among Gods Troops and Armies."[26] In such cases, the logic of the scourge structures biblical and natural history alike.

Pronouncements about God's vengeance, however, fit somewhat uneasily beside more naturalistic accounts of the effects of famine and the sympathetic descriptions of the efforts throughout recorded history to combat infestations. Moffett includes verses from "the author of *Naumachia*" about the devastation caused by locusts that "came flying out of Africa":

> The nurse childe of death,
> Famine was present with her empty veins,
> The poor with hunger starved, their breath
> Was spent; for neither broth nor bread remains:
> Upon their mouthes and guts hunger laid hold,
> They move their chaps, and bite their teeth, not meat,
> Through wrinkled skin their bowels might be told:
> Nothing but skin and bone, they'd nought to eat,
> In stead of belly stood an empty place. (986)

This passage reinforces what is at stake in the "battle" against what Moffett calls "so cruel an Army," vividly emphasizing the capacity of locusts to beggar or wipe out entire populations. His chapter on locusts concludes with a summary of strategies to fight them, to reassure readers that a "great abundance" of locusts may be "driven away by the providence and wisdom of man" (988). Like many other writers, he mentions Pliny's account of Cyrene (present-day Libya) and its "war" against locusts. By decree, people were compelled to break locust eggs, destroy the hatchings, and kill the grown insects (988). Greeks, he reports, "march out in military orders against them": in "the Island Lemnos, all Soldiers are bound to bring a certain measure of Locusts to the Magistrates every day" (988). Syria similarly fights "against them in a souldierly posture" (988). The methods used against locusts vary: ploughing eggs under, ringing bells, driving locusts into ditches, and hanging bats from the trees to encourage natural predation.

In the end, though, Moffett rejects most of these solutions, at least those practiced in the spirit of paganism. That ancient history offers so many examples of locust-driven famine, he says, "should admonish us Christians that are entred into the rites of the true God, and are instructed by the perfect light, that the sure way to drive from us hurtful Locusts is to call upon God by prayer joyned with true repentance and unfeigned piety, without which all our force and inventions will come to nought, nor will all our devices avail at all" (989). With this theological affirmation, Moffett underscores his commitment to providentialist history, in which God, acting through Moses or other divinely inspired agents, is alone capable of controlling "God's Armies" and alone capable of determining the success or failure of verminous battle: "For I highly approve of that saying," he concludes, "*For all remedies without Gods assistance are idle enterprises of men, but when God is pleased, and blesseth the means, then are they remedies indeed*" (989). Prayer, repentance, piety: in Moffett's view, these are the essential strategies to banish insect swarms; without faith, the "providence and wisdom of man" are little more help than chasing after the wind.

God's Mercy, Locust Meat, and the Body Politic

Built into Moffett's account of locust infestation is a paradox that characterizes Judeo-Christian redemptive histories: locust infestation can serve as both a scourge for sin and a sign of God's benevolence. Africanus's description of locust swarms as a "fortunate boading" or welcome food source easily could be allied with the third chapter of

Matthew, in which John the Baptist, wandering the deserts, lived on locusts and "wilde honey." Moffett acknowledges both the threat and beneficence of infestation. Even though these "Armies of the Lord" can be used to "revenge himself on the despisers of his Lawes," Moffett writes, even in his "greatest severity Mercy is not wanting" (987). Invoking a host of ancient and contemporary writers, including Africanus, he turns to the thorny theological and biopolitical question of eating locusts:

> For being that Locusts have brought sundry Nations to want and hunger, and they have had no thing to eat, these Locusts have died suddenly, and became meat for the people they afflicted before: the people of hot Countreys, (whom especially they spoil of their increase of fruits) as the *Aethiopians, Tagetenses, Parthians, Arabians, Lybians, Mellenses, Zemenses, Darienenses, Africans*, and those that live about *Lepris*, the *Azanaghi, Senegenses*, people of *Mauritania*, and others, live chiefly upon Locusts, and account their eggs to be dainties; others prepare them thus: First in a low large place they make a great smoak, by which the Locusts in flying are hindred and forced to fall; than when they have taken them they dry them with salt, the Sun and smoke, and cutting them in pieces, they keep them for their yearly provision, as we do fish, not only those which have large legs, but the *Attelabi*, the *Aselli, Asiraci*, and almost all kindes of Locusts. (987)

In such passages, Moffett recognizes that locusts may serve as more than famine food, and his catalog of insect-devouring people across Africa and the Near East reveals the extent to which dietary practice became implicated in both biblical history and his incipient ethnography. Although locusts may be eaten out of necessity, they are regarded in many non-Western regions as a staple food source, even a delicacy, because peoples of several countries "account their eggs to be dainties." Because the countries that are included in this catalog include both ancient lands and contemporary regions that marked the reaches of European imperial desires, questions about insects as instruments of God's will become entangled with questions of food consumption and dietary practices. Tellingly, Moffett compares the drying and eating of locusts in "hot Countreys" to the English ways of salting and drying fish. Mosaic history becomes bound up with both his incipient ethnography of peoples in Africa and the Middle East and the familiar English practices of food preservation.

Moffett's comments reveal how complicated the issue of eating insects becomes when locusts and other vermin are considered, at different times and in different circumstances, as agents of divine retribution and as diabolical or "imperfect" creatures born from putrefaction. John the Baptist's diet had long been debated by biblical scholars and theologians, who attempted to reconcile the story in Matthew with other, seemingly contradictory passages. Proscriptions against eating "winged things" in Deuteronomy 14:19, in particular, run counter to the allowance in Leviticus 11:22, which states, "These of them you may eat: the locust in its kinds, and the devastating locust in its kinds, and the cricket in its kinds, and the grasshopper in its kinds." James A. Kellhoffer argues persuasively that locust eating was part of a chosen diet, including among the wealthy, in the ancient Near East.[27] Far from serving merely as famine food, locusts on a stick are depicted as parts of royal banquet scenes for an ancient Assyrian king. Judeo-Christian dietary practices, in contrast, are characterized by contradictory attitudes toward eating insects in general and locusts in particular. The Mishnah "reflects a rather lively discussion" under what conditions locusts are permitted as food, but even it reinforces the ubiquity of the practice. Such commentary stokes further debate about the types of locusts that can be considered "clean."[28] The anxiety and confusion accompanying these debates gave rise to interpretations that John the Baptist was not eating insects at all but a fruit or the tender tops of trees.

Perhaps somewhat surprising in a text devoted to insects' taxonomy, Moffett sidesteps the theologically driven questions about which locusts might have been considered kosher. Clearly he was aware of such debates: "S. *Matthew* in the 3. chapter," he writes, "saith that *John the Baptist* lived upon them and wilde honey; and God appointed four sorts of em to be clean, and suffered the people of *Israel* to feed upon them" (987). Rather than join the theological fray, he simply points his reader to Bede: "Whosoever desireth more concerning Locusts for food, let them read the most learned Annotations of Venerable *Bede* upon St. *Matthew*" (987).[29] Although Moffett freely admits that locusts are edible and can serve as a sign of God's mercy, he nonetheless insists that they are detrimental to individual and national health: even though the locusts "have no venome," people who "feed on them are not long lived, and seldome live to 40 years, and frequently die young" (987). Moffett bases this assumption on Greek historians Diodorus Siculus and Strabo, who, as we shall see, were cited as sources to caution readers against incorporating swarming insects into normative understandings of agricultural and food systems. For this reason, Moffett takes some pain to distinguish the appetites of people in "hot Countreys" who eat not only legless weevils but "almost all kinds of Locusts" from those of diasporic Jews, presumably bound by the proscriptions in the Old Testament.

In the first century BCE, Diodorus of Sicily describes a North African tribe of locust eaters he calls the Acridophagi as "lesser" than other Africans, "of lean and meager bodies and exceedingly black."[30] In the spring, he writes, southerly winds blow locusts out of the desert and into their valley; the inhabitants set grasses and other combustible matter on fire, thereby smoking the locusts from the skies so that they "lye in great Heaps." These locusts are then salted and "preserved for a long time sweet without the least Putrefaction, so that they have Food ever ready at hand from these Insects during all the rest of the Year."[31] The Acridophagi, however, live truncated lives and suffer horrifying deaths, which Diodorus recounts in clinical detail:

> They are a little sort of People, very swift of Foot, but exceeding short liv'd, for they that live the longest never exceed forty: And as the Manner of their Death is strange and wonderful, so it's sad and most miserable: For when they grow old, wing'd Lice breed in their Flesh, not only of divers Sorts but of horrid and ugly Shapes. This Plague begins first at the Belly and Breast, and in a little time eats and consumes the whole Body. He that is seiz'd with this Distemper, first begins to itch a little, as if he had the Scab, Pleasure and Trouble being mixt together. But afterwards when the Lice begin to break out at the Skin, abundance of putrid Matter . . . issues out with them. Hereupon the sick Person so tears himself in Pieces with his own Nails, that he sighs and groans most lamentably, and while he is thus scratching of himself, the Lice come pouring out in such

Abundance one after another as out of a Vessel full of Holes, and thus they miserably close and end their Days. Whether this proceeds from the Nature of their Food or the Temper of the Air is uncertain.[32]

Although Diodorus is unwilling to assert that locust eating is the cause of internal infestation, Moffett maintains that there is a causal relationship between locust eating and the short life spans of these North Africans. In this respect, he reinforces a discourse about peoples and diet that dominated the early modern period. As travelers brought back stories about alien food systems and diets that often differed radically from European eating habits, such cultural differences had to be ordered into more generalized and theologically driven notions of what constituted acceptable, "civilized" practices of food preparation and consumption. In this respect, Diodorus helps anchor a nationalist, or at least Eurocentric, rhetoric about the nature and value of English diets.

Such Eurocentric assumptions and values inform the work of the Puritan Hart, who takes on the question of locust eating in his 1633 text *Klinike*. One justification for attending to "strange and uncoth Diet[s]," which includes eating dogs, cats, horses, mules, rats, snails, and locusts, he argues, is that the reader will be better positioned to "laud and magnifie the great and extraordnarie bountie of our great and gracious God, in affording us such plentie and varietie of good and wholesome food for susteining these fraile bodies"; a second and more practical reason is that "travellers," forced to be at such places, will have to become acquainted with "uncoth" food.[33] Although "uncoth," as a synonym for "foreign" or "strange," does not necessarily imply a harsh moral judgment, Hart uses it in the more derogatory sense of "unpleasant" or "distasteful." Because he frames the "Diet of the Diseased" as a fundamental difference between (blessed) Europeans, with their livestock and cornfields, and the rest of the world, Hart makes it clear very quickly that the "diseased" are those outside this agricultural economy, including diasporic Jews. Locusts, he claims—"which we commonly call Caterpillars"—are a creature God often used to "scourge the inhabitants of hot countries" along with "the rebellious and stif-necked people of the *Jewes*." But in the seventeenth century, locusts constitute "ordinary food among many Nations," especially Africans.[34] Because this text turns on the distinction between "coth" and "uncoth," civilized and uncivilized, healthy and "diseased," Hart's *Klinike* casts locus eating and locust eaters, Jews and Africans, as the primitives against whom the English define their culinary and national identities.

The Scottish Aristotelian Ross returns to the diseased diet and lives of the Acridophagi in his less anti-Semitic but equally polemical *Arcana Microcosmi*. He paraphrases Diodorus's account, including the etiology of diseases supposedly caused by eating insects, but offers a more confident diagnosis: "This disease doubtlesse proceeds partly from the corruption of the aire, and partly from the unwholesomnesse of their diet, which turns to putrid humours in their bodies, whence the disease is Epidemical."[35] Ross, however, explicitly associates the disease with *phthiriasis*, or the "lousy disease," first described by Aristotle as *morbus pedicularis*, about which there were many marvelous stories.[36] The assumption that the "lousy disease" implied what Jan Bondeson calls "divine punishment to tyrants, desecrators, and enemies to religion" is common to both classical and Christian history.[37] This network of associations among insect eating, moral corruption, and grisly death fascinates Ross, who includes the example of the tyrant "Sylla" (Sulla), whose sensationalistic demise was described by Plutarch. According to Bondeson, Plutarch ignored the more historically and medically accurate versions for a horrific account marking Sulla's death as divine retribution: "The tyrant's corrupted flesh became one mass of lice," reports Bondeson, "and although many men were employed to remove and wipe away the vermin, they still multiplied."[38] In this vein, Ross invokes the death of Herod, who, according to Acts 12:23, was smitten by "an angel of the Lord" and "was eaten by worms, and gave up the ghost." Ross attributes the suffering brought about by this disease to "the immediate hand of God as a punishment of sinne and tyranny."[39]

Drawing on Aristotelian theories of infection, Ross fully pathologizes the practice of insect eating and entire peoples as a source and symptom of moral and spiritual disease. Both Aristotle and later Galen imagined that the lousy disease arose from warm moisture in the body, an attitude reflected in Ross's assumption that such "vermin breed most in those who are given to sweat" and "whose constitutions are hot and moist."[40] But more than Diodorus, Ross emphasizes the element of "nastinesse" or lack of hygiene in the lousy disease. "And it is certain," he writes, "that wild and savage people are most given to them, because of their carelesse uncleanlinesse," a behavioral category that includes not only Ethiopians but "some wilde *Irish*" who wear a shirt "six months together without shifting."⁴¹ By virtue of such statements, Ross tethers a disease that, according to Bondeson, had been associated historically with "highly placed men" to populations that lie outside the bounds of Eurocentric civilizations.⁴²

Finally, having associated northern Africans with "wild and savage people" whose diets and bodies reflect their physical and moral corruption, Ross uses his diagnosis of phthiriasis to argue from a medical rather than theological perspective that locusts were never "used in Judea"; those who believe that John ate them or that Leviticus allowed them to be "clean food" likely were misinterpreting the biblical text. Neither "Hebrician[s]" nor "*Rabbins*," he continues, "doe know the true meaning or signification of the proper tearms there used. Therefore the Hebrew word *Harbe*, which we translate *Locust*, the Septuagints call *Bruchus*, which is another kind of Insect. And the *French* in their Bibles have left the Hebrew word untranslated. And so did *Luther* before, as not knowing what that word meant, nor the other three Hebrew words."⁴³ In this passage, entomology and etymology become entangled in an argument that may appear to be about locusts but ultimately is more about the place of Jews in Christian history. Where Hart willingly assigned Africans and Jews to the same category of pagan or near-pagan people, Ross wants to reclaim the latter as proto-Christians whose moral fiber must be distinguished from those corrupt nations and people capable of being infested by such an "unwholesome food," God's scourge of insects.

Conclusion: What Does Othello Eat?

I have argued that insect infestation was both a real danger and a collective fear in the early modern period as England reimagined itself in relation to a larger world, vulnerable to biopolitical forces and the new and threatening disease vectors that accompanied transoceanic trade. In this early modern context, locusts are never simply locusts, but instead are creatures deeply entangled in theologically inflected arguments about punishment and mercy, diet and disease, self and other.⁴⁴ Africa becomes marked as the global source of infestation and Africans as the insect-eating others of civilized Europeans, even as Europeans failed to agree on what exactly it was that sustained John the Baptist during his time in the wilderness. Because "locust" has no stable definition, the entire discourse is open to assumptions, projections, and, as Ross acknowledges, inevitable controversies. Thomas Blount's *Glossographia* (1656) describes the locust as "a kind of flying insect, or Fly ... of which we have none in England," noting that some species "were commodious for meat." He refers to Matthew 3:4—"His meat was locusts"—and to Thomas Browne's argument in *Vulgar Errors* that John the Baptist was indeed consuming insects.[45] Without entirely undermining his interpretation, Blount then acknowledges that "some conceive" these locusts "to be the tops of herbs and plants."[46] In a seventeenth-century account of West Barbary, Lancelot Addison connects this controversy to Moors. He describes a tree whose fruit is "eat by the *Moors* of an inferior Condition" but "chiefly preserved for their Horses, to whom it both physic and repast."[47] "Some have called the fruit *Locusta*," he continues, and assume this is what John the Baptist ate in the wilderness, even though other commentators "interpret the Baptist's Locusts to be a kind of Fly or Grashopper, wch in warmer Climates are very large and many, and were formerly dried and eaten by the Inhabitants."[48] The locust remains embedded in a series of self-replicating and proliferating controversies that mark the limits of historical interpretation.

Our own century, however, seems to have reached some consensus, at least in interpreting Shakespeare. Although Shakespeare's plays are filled with references to moths, flies, glowworms, caterpillars, and other insects, "locust" appears only once—in a play whose hero is a native of Africa. In act 1 of *Othello*, Iago tries to persuade Roderigo to resurrect his suit to Desdemona, claiming that she "cannot ... long continue her love to the Moor ... nor he to her" (1.3.342-44). "These Moors," he continues, "are changeable in their wills.... The food that to him now is as luscious as locusts shall be to him shortly as bitter as coloquintida" (1.3.347-50). Noting that Britain had no locusts, Robert Patterson's 1842 *Natural History of the Insects Mentioned in Shakspeare's Plays* claims flatly that in *Othello*, the word *locust*, associated with "luscious," is "introduced in such a manner as to show it is the vegetable production that is meant."[49] Although noting a French infestation of insects in 1553 and Alvarez's Ethiopian excommunication seven years later, Emma Phipson posits that Shakespeare "in all probability" refers to the "bean" and not to the "insect."[50] Henry C. Hart's 1905 edition provides a lengthy note, informed by natural history and philosophy, about the "varied interpretations of locust" but concurs that Shakespeare refers here to vegetable matter.[51] A venerable twenty-first-century edition of Shakespeare's works annotates "coloquintida" as "bitter fruit" and "locusts," simply and significantly, as the "fruit of the carob tree."[52] This assumption is replicated in the Bedford and Norton editions; the former refers to Matthew 3:4, and the latter describes locusts as "sweet, exotic fruit, perhaps carob or honeysuckle."[53] In effect, these modern editors make silent decisions about what John the Baptist ate without actually exploring the early modern contexts or controversies.[54] This collective unwillingness to entertain the idea that Othello might have found insects "luscious" probably says more about Anglo American dietary and literary habits than it does about Shakespeare's play.

In their depictions of infestation, Moffett and his contemporaries give voice, implicitly and explicitly, to early modern anxieties about newly global ecologies, changing biopolitical systems, and the contested interpretive structures of literary and theologically inflected narratives. If we have not yet come to terms with the role of infestation in colonial regimes, it is partly because insects have until recently been erased from European cultural-historical records. And literary animal studies have more or less followed in those footsteps. But as Martha Few argues in her powerful analysis of locust extermination in colonial Latin America, "colonialism was decisively shaped by locusts and by campaigns against the locust economically, politically, and socially."[55] To her list, I would add, "semiotically." As we have seen, imperialism was accompanied and reinforced by a deeply textured superstructure of universal history through which natures and values were being defined and contested. This history, in all its complications, affects how we read early modern texts, how willing we are to explore the implications of Othello's locust eating, and how we figure the sources of real and imaginary infestation.

Notes

1. Goldsmith, *Historie of the Earth*, 344. Subsequent references to *Historie of the Earth* appear parenthetically by page number.
2. I take Brian Ogilvie's point that to speak of "entomology" before 1745 is anachronistic. Moffett and other insectologists nevertheless helped create the conditions for entomology, just as Boemus helped create the conditions for anthropology. See Ogilvie, "Nature's Bible," 6. The discourses

that were codified in the eighteenth century into entomology and anthropology were deeply indebted to classical texts and to Aristotelian notions of development, which they borrowed and contested. See Cole, *Imperfect Creatures*.
3. Boemus, *Fardle of Facions*. See Hodgen, "Johann Boemus."
4. Hakluyt, *Principal Navigations*; Purchas, *Purchas His Pilgrimage*.
5. Aldrovandi, *Animalibus Insectis*. Ogilvie outlines this history in "Attending to Insects," 358.
6. Ogilvie, "Attending to Insects," 358.
7. See Crosby, *Columbian Exchange*.
8. Mann, *1493*, 7.
9. Ibid., 13.
10. Ibid.
11. Las Casas, *Historia*, quoted in ibid.
12. Mann, *1493*, 13.
13. On insects, interpretation, and problems of scale, see Campana, "Bee and the Sovereign?"
14. Africanus, *Geographical Historie*. Subsequent references to *Geographical Historie* appear parenthetically by page number.
15. Moffett, *Theater of Insects*. Subsequent references to *Theater of Insects* appear parenthetically by page number.
16. Hart, *Klinike*; Ross, *Arcana Microcosmi*.
17. Evans, *Criminal Prosecution*, 3. See also Dannenfeldt, "Control of Vertebrate Pests."
18. On the Little Ice Age, see Fagan, *Little Ice Age*, esp. 101–12. In relation to the early modern period, see Markley, "Summer's Lease." In relation to insects and the Columbian exchange, see Crosby, *The Columbian Exchange*; and Mann, *1493*, 38–43..
19. Dannenfeldt, "Control of Vertebrate Pests," 553–54.
20. Goodman, *Fall of Man*, 219.
21. Ibid.
22. See Cole, *Imperfect Creatures*, esp. 49–80.
23. "Locust-like" is a term used to acknowledge ongoing debates about the differences between locusts and grasshoppers. On insect infestation in Ireland and Wales, see Thornton, "Locusts in Ireland"; and Cole, "Swift Among the Locusts."
24. Schmetzer, "Worst Locust Plague in History."
25. Wither, *Britain's Remembrancer*, 41.
26. Purchas, *Theatre of Politicall Flying-Insects*, 201.
27. Kellhoffer, "Did John the Baptist."
28. Ibid., 308–9.
29. Here is Bede's analysis: "The smallest species of locusts, the kind that John the Baptist ate, appears even today. Having slender and short bodies, about the size of a finger, they are easily caught in the grass and, when cooked in oil, supply meagre nourishment. In that same desert are trees having broad round leaves of milky colour and a honey taste. Naturally fragile, the leaves are rubbed in the hand and eaten. This is said to be the wild honey" (*Biblical Miscellany*, 21).
30. Diodorus, *Historical Library*, 97.
31. Ibid.
32. Ibid.
33. Hart, *Klinike*, 83.
34. Ibid., 84.
35. Ross, *Arcana Microcosmi*, 94.
36. On the lousy disease, see Bondeson, "Phthiriasis."
37. Ibid., 428.
38. Ibid., 329.
39. Ross, 94–95.
40. Ibid., 94.
41. Ibid.
42. Bondeson, "Phthiriasis," 329.
43. Ross, *Arcana Microcosmi*, 94.
44. For a similar argument about bedbugs, see Sarason, "nauseous venomous insect."
45. Blount, *Glossographia*, n.p. See Browne, *Pseudodoxia Epidemica*, 354–55.
46. Blount, *Glossographia*, n.p.

47. Addison, *West Barbary*, 78.
48. Ibid.
49. Patterson, *Natural History*, 107.
50. Phipson, *Animal-Lore*, 395.
51. Shakespeare, *Tragedy of Othello*, ed. Hart, 56–57n354, 355.
52. Shakespeare, *Othello*, ed. Neilson and Hill, 1104n354, 355.
53. See Shakespeare, *Othello*, ed. Hall; and Shakespeare, *Norton Shakespeare*.
54. The Folger edition, in contrast, at least acknowledges that the Geneva Bible glosses "locusts" as "grasshoppers" (Shakespeare, *Othello*, ed. Mowat and Werstine, 52n391).
55. Few, "Killing Locusts," 65.

Bibliography

Addison, Lancelot. *West Barbary, or, A Short Narrative of the Revolutions of the Kingdoms of Fez and Morocco with an Account of the Present Customs, Sacred, Civil, and Domestick*. Oxford, 1671.

Africanus, Leo. *A Geographical Historie of Africa*. Translated by John Pory. London: George Bishop, 1600.

Aldrovandi, Ulisse. *De Animalibus Insectis Libri Septem*. Bologna: Bellagambam, 1602.

Bede. *A Biblical Miscellany*. Translated by W. Trent Foley and Arthur G. Holder. Liverpool: Liverpool University Press, 1999.

Blount, Thomas. *Glossographia, or A Dictionary Interpreting All Such Hard Words . . . Now Used in Our Refined English Tongue*. London: Tho. Newcombe, 1661.

Boemus, Johann. *The Fardle of Facions, Conteining the Auciente Maners, Customes, and Lawes, of the Peoples Enhabiting the Two Partes of the Earth, Called Affrike and Asie*. Translated by Henry Waterman. London: John Kingstone and Henry Dutton, 1555.

Bondeson, Jan. "Phthiriasis: The Riddle of the Lousy Disease." *Journal of the Royal Society of Medicine* 91 (1998): 328–34.

Browne, Thomas. *Pseudodoxia Epidemica*. London: T.H., 1646.

Campana, Joseph. "The Bee and the Sovereign? Political Entomology and the Problems of Scale." *Shakespeare Studies* 41 (2013): 94–113.

Cole, Lucinda. *Imperfect Creatures: Vermin, Literature, and the Sciences of Life, 1600–1740*. Ann Arbor: University of Michigan Press, 2016.

———. "Swift Among the Locusts: Vermin, Infestation, and Natural Philosophy in the Eighteenth Century." In *Animals and Animality in the Literary Field*, edited by Bruce Boehrer, Molly Hand, and Brian Massumi, 136–55. Cambridge: Cambridge University Press, 2018.

Crosby, Alfred W. *The Columbian Exchange: Biological and Cultural Consequences of 1492*. Westport, CT: Greenwood, 1972.

Dannenfeldt, Karl H. "The Control of Vertebrate Pests in Renaissance Agriculture." *Agricultural History* 56 (1982): 542–59.

Diodorus. *The Historical Library of Diodorus the Sicilian in Fifteen Books: Book Three*. Bibliotheca de Fulvio Orsini, 1529–1600.

Evans, E. P. *The Criminal Prosecution and Capital Punishment of Animals*. London: William Heinemann, 1906.

Fagan, Brian. *The Little Ice Age: How Climate Made History*. New York: Basic Books, 2000.

Few, Martha. "Killing Locusts in Colonial Guatemala." In *Centering Animals in Latin American History*, edited by Few and Zeb Tortorici, 62–92. Durham: Duke University Press, 2013.

Goldsmith, Oliver. *An Historie of the Earth and Animated Nature: Volume 7*. London: J. Nourse, 1774.

Goodman, Godfrey. *The Fall of Man, or The Corruption of Nature*. London: Felix Kingston, 1616.

Hakluyt, Richard. *The Principal Navigations, Voiages, Traffiques, and Discoveries of the English Nation*. London: George Bishop and Ralph Newberie, 1589.

Hart, James. *Klinike, or The Diet of the Diseased*. London: John Beale, 1633.

Hodgen, Margaret T. "Johann Boemus (Fl. 1500): An Early Anthropologist." *American Anthropologist* 55 (1953): 284–94.

Kellhoffer, James A. "Did John the Baptist Eat like a Former Essene? Locust-Eating in the Ancient Near East and at Qumran." *Dead Sea Discoveries* 11 (2004): 293–314.

Las Casas, Bartolemé de. *Historia de las Indias*. 3 vols. Mexico City: Fondo de Cultura Economica, 1951.

Mann, Charles C. *1493: Uncovering the New World Columbus Created*. New York: Vintage Books, 2012.

Markley, Robert. "Summer's Lease: Shakespeare in the Little Ice Age." In *Early Modern Ecostudies: From Shakespeare to the Florentine Codex*, edited by Karen Raber, Tom Hallock, and Ivo Kamps, 131–42. New York: Palgrave, 2008.

Moffett, Thomas. *The Theater of Insects: or, Lesser Living Creatures*. In *The History of Four-Footed Beasts and Serpents*, by Edward Topsell. London, 1658.

Ogilvie, Brian. "Attending to Insects: Francis Willughby and John Ray." *Notes and Records of the Royal Society* 66 (2012): 357–72.

———. "Nature's Bible: Insects in Seventeenth-Century European Art and Science." *Tidsskrift for Kulturforskning* 7 (2008): 5–21.

Patterson, Robert. *Natural History of the Insects Mentioned in Shakspeare's Plays*. London: A. K. Newman, 1842.

Phipson, Emma. *The Animal-Lore of Shakespeare's Time*. London: Kegan Paul, Trench, 1883.

Purchas, Samuel. *Purchas His Pilgrimage*. London: William Stansby, 1613.

———. *A Theatre of Politicall Flying-Insects*. London: R.I., 1657.

Ross, Alexander. *Arcana Microcosmi, or The Hid Secrets of Man's Body*. London: Tho. Newcombe, 1652.

Sarason, Lisa T. "'That nauseous venomous insect': Bedbugs in Early Modern England." *Eighteenth-Century Studies* 46 (2013): 513–30.

Schmetzer, Uli. "'Worst Locust Plague in History' Threatens Europe." *Chicago Tribune*, May 2, 1988. http://articles.chicagotribune.com/1988-05-02/news/8803130590_1_swarms-desert-locust-locust-larvae.

Shakespeare, William. *The Norton Shakespeare*. 2nd ed. Edited by Stephen Greenblatt, Walter Cohen, Jean E. Howard, and Katherine Eisaman Maus. New York: Norton, 2008.

———. *Othello*. Edited by Kim F. Hall. New York: Bedford / St. Martin's Press, 2006.

———. *Othello*. Edited by Barbara A. Mowat and Paul Werstine. New York: Simon and Schuster, 2004.

———. *Othello*. Edited by William Allan Neilson and Charles Jarvis Hill. In *The Complete Plays and Poems of William Shakespeare*. Cambridge, MA: Houghton Mifflin, 1942.

———. *The Tragedy of Othello*. Edited by Henry C. Hart. In *The Works of Shakespeare*. London: Methuen, 1903.

Thornton, David E. "Locusts in Ireland? A Problem in the Welsh and Frankish Annals." *Cambrian Medieval Celtic Studies* 31 (1996): 37–53.

Wither, George. *Britain's Remembrancer*. Manchester, UK: Charles Simms, 1880.

CHAPTER 5

HABITAT AND POLITICS
"*Regardles of his gouernaunce*":
*Exploring Human Sovereignty and
Political Formation in Early Modern Insect Habitats*

Andrew Fleck

Edward Topsell, to whose massive bestiary the English translation of Thomas Moffett's own weighty *The Theater of Insects: or, Lesser Living Creatures* is appended in 1658, served primarily as a Protestant minister. Even in his printed sermons, he takes to heart the lesson that the book of nature might provide insight into divine providence, though his interpretation of the behavior of some creatures points to the equivocal meaning to be derived from them. In a popular series of sermons focused on the book of Ruth, for instance, Topsell explores the possibility of efficacious prayer for others. At Ruth's wedding to Boaz, the witnesses "celebrated with prayer." Ruth's exemplary marriage offers a contrast with those Topsell sees around him in Elizabethan England, where typically the witnesses "are none but godless ruffians" who come to the ceremony vainly to display their fine silks and gluttonously to gorge themselves on the "delicate diuersities of meates" at the marriage feast. What "prayers can these powre forth, for their newe marryed frendes," Topsell asks, any more than "the Cockatrice [can] breath forth any thing but poyson, or the spider spinne any sounder cloth then her webbe?"[1] The prayers of the wicked, if not pouring a curse on the couple, certainly appear insubstantial and fleeting. The preacher here emphasizes one aspect of the spider's web, its deceptive fragility, but other early modern readers find reasons to praise the spider and its web. Looking back to classical and biblical precedent, for instance, Moffett would recall that Aristotle spoke in praise of spiders as "the wisest of all Insects" and that in the book of Proverbs, a touchstone for humans reading God's providence in the cosmos, Solomon marveled at the webs found even in the palaces of kings, woven by spiders "that man cannot do the like."[2] In fact, as Plutarch had asserted and some English writers agreed, human beings had originally looked to "the spider" when learning the arts of "spinning, weaving, derning, and drawing up a rent."[3] In a number of interesting and equivocal ways, the remarkable material of the spider's habitat—a web that is alternately weak and strong, silky and tacky, fragile and durable—engaged the imagination of early modern readers, particularly as they considered the functions of law and sovereignty in just societies.

Spiders, like bees, ants, and butterflies, lived in habitats that many early modern writers treated politically. Peering into the dwellings of insects to find examples of the supposedly natural order of society, early modern thinkers imported their own prejudices into their imaginings of these habitats, confirming their own sense of what makes it possible for individuals to live in harmonious, efficient community.[4] In his encyclopedic *Foreste*, for instance, the Spanish humanist Pedro Mexía compiles many examples of lessons humans can learn from nonhumans, suggesting that a person who "diligently and attentiuely, will consider as well the nature, as the properties also of beastes, he thence shall not onelie take good instructions of life ... but lessons also to frame, and perfect his maners."[5] Mexía begins immediately with insect societies and the political lessons humans should draw from them. The subjects of a kingdom could learn "true seruice and honour to their Prince, consideryng the true loue, and obedience, of the litle Bee towardes her soueraigne," while they can learn to cooperate with each other "with out grudge, or mutinie, of the foresaide litle antes, whiche dwell together in greate multitudes, with good order, doyng iustice, eche one, to the other."[6] The lessons apply to the sovereign as well, who can learn "with what lenitie, and curtesie, they ought still to vse their subiectes especially when thei behold the Kyng of the Bees, for no cause to greue or offende any of the others."[7] Mexía, like Topsell, Moffett, and many other early modern writers, participates in the "zoographic" process of using the nonhuman, including insects and their habitats, "to think with."[8] Jean Bodin, for instance, in his treatment of the ideal princely commonwealth, frequently imagines the operations of social insects to justify actions in human community. Suggesting that the ideal commonwealth would employ censors to monitor the number and employment of citizens as the Roman Empire had done, Bodin argues that one benefit would be "the discouery of euery mans estate and faculty, and whereby he gets his liuing, therby to expell all drones out of a commonweale, which sucke the hony from the Bees."[9] This early modern treatment of the hierarchical operation of monarchical beehives may be familiar from a set speech like the Archbishop of Canterbury's in the second scene of Shakespeare's *Henry V*; the communal, republican nature of ant colonies in the early modern imagination may be familiar as well.[10] The early modern politicization of the spider web and the butterfly's field, however, may be less so. In John Heywood's lengthy allegory of *The Spider and the Flie* and in Edmund Spenser's *Muiopotmos*, the web of the arachnid tyrant and the liberty of flies, especially butterflies, point to Tudor writers' ability to project imagined political formations onto the habitats of insects.

Heywood's poem recounts the tribulations of a housefly caught in the web a spider has recently woven across the center of a window. In the ensuing allegorical parable—in which the spider accuses the fly of a crime, necessitating an ant's and a butterfly's participation in the trial, which breaks down and ignites a war between the victorious spiders and defeated flies, reversed at the last moment when the maid, a figure for Mary Tudor, intervenes and destroys the spider—Heywood comments ambiguously on early Tudor conflicts between the aristocracy enclosing territory and the resentful commoners rebelling against that encroachment.[11] As the wool trade assumed greater importance in early modern England, landowners enclosed more and more land that tenant farmers had once cultivated for agriculture, replacing small, tilled tracts and the adjacent commons with larger areas devoted to raising sheep.[12] The conflict between the plebeian fly, enjoying his customary access to the open spaces in the lattice of a window, and the encroaching spider that has unjustly taken possession, via his web, of some of the holes, quickly reveals the poem's use of an apparently natural and eternal conflict between spiders and flies to explore contemporary human debates about the private enclosure of public commons.

Although the narrative includes a mock-heroic centerpiece, a battle between spiders and flies that seems to represent popular midcentury uprisings like Kett's Rebellion, the fly's criminal trial dominates most of the poem. When the spider chastises the entangled fly, claiming that if it has not attempted a burglary, "at the least, thou has trespassed me," the debate between them turns to a question of jurisdiction and the nature of the fly's and the spider's property.[13] The lordly spider tries to trick the fly into granting that he must adjudicate the conflict, since the fly agrees that in the abstract "thoffender being taken in place, / Where he hid the dede, to stande to the grace, / Of lawful lawe, in that precinkte presente" (24.3). Because the fly has been caught in the sticky habitat of the spider, the spider declares himself the judge: "Thy dede done here: hath by lawe here, death sure, / Alonely to be tride at wyll of me" (24.6). The fly, however, denies the spider's jurisdiction, since the strands of his web stretch across a window that does not belong to him. If "this window [were] your maner in freholde / And flies here your copie holders knowne clere," the fly concedes, with reference to the early modern terms that govern rural habitats, perhaps the spider would have jurisdiction, but "you are not my lorde, nor I your tenant," and thus a landlord's authority over a tenant does not apply in this case (24.10–11).[14] Although he does not specifically allude to Proverbs 30:28, "The spider taketh holde with *her* hands, and is in Kings palaces," the reminder that the spider builds his habitat only in the window frame at all through custom established by the benign neglect of the house's owner and his careless maid plays an important part in the call for reformation in the dramatic reversal of the poem's conclusion.[15] In fact, the fly asserts, the open spaces of the window lattices, by powerful legal custom, "be flies freholde" and therefore "flies at libertee, in and out might chop" (25.1). The flies have made a habit or custom of passing through these holes from time out of mind, and the spider's sudden encroachment introduces disorder.

Throughout the trial, the fly treats the spider with the deference due to a superior, but the case eventually reaches an impasse, and a second "quarreling" spider and a second "cocking" fly receive permission to argue the conflict more frankly. In this later episode, the railing fly makes clear his fellow plebeians' view of the dislocating effects of landlords' enclosures of the commons. The cocking fly recalls that historically the holes in window lattices were "ours in comon right" and were

"Late comonly ours," though they are "now seuerally yours" through the spiders' recent construction of webs across them "where ye set in foote, by right or by might" and lay claim to formerly open spaces (44.7).[16] Looking at it now, covered in new webs, "this window showth your vsurped pours," this fly complains. Flies had been content to concede the sturdy "tops: and top sides: of all windows" to the spiders, provided spiders would "graunt likewise all holes," the vacant spaces of the windows, to the flies for their use, creating a shared "comon welth" for spiders and flies as "the worlde before went" (44.11). Spiders and flies cooperated and "stood with our degre" in this social hierarchy (44.12). The flies may only claim the traditionally unused spaces by custom, but the spiders' own claims to the edges of a window they do not own rely on custom as well. Recently, however, usurping spiders have claimed more and more of the formerly open holes in windows so that now "you: we: and our windowes to: all go to wracke. / By your couetous cutthrotes" (44.13). The greedy spiders, spurning custom in order to satisfy their avarice, have upset the social cohesion of the common habitat of the window. Their disorderly aggression contrasts with the natural orderliness sometimes ascribed to spiders. Mexía, for instance, had argued that humanity learned to love geometry from contemplating that "better proportion . . . whiche vseth the litle poore Spider."[17] Heywood employs these allegorical spiders' encroachment to criticize the unchecked acquisitiveness of the social elites and their desire to enclose territory, threatening the English commonwealth through their disregard of mutual obligation enshrined in custom.

The conflict between the aristocratic spider and the plebeian fly turns on an English understanding of the nation's eccentric access to common law and the power of feudal custom. On one hand, customary privileges govern both insects' habitats: the window in the dwelling of an absent human owner. On the other hand, custom is not enshrined in legal codes, and reliance on it runs the risk of foolishly trusting an unstable legal foundation. As Bodin would argue in his treatise on sovereignty in the ideal princely commonwealth, "Custome hath no force but by suffereaunce, and so long as it pleaseth the soueraigne prince."[18] Law, Bodin claims, serves the tyrant, while custom suits a king. The spider may have violated the custom by which he limited his habitat to the frame of the window and infringed on flies' customary access to the lattice holes in the window's center, but the flies seem to have no recourse to prevent this sweeping away of custom. However, the window is in an English house, and English common law limits the tyrannical power of the spider. Sir John Fortescue defended the unique quality of English law. Unlike the civil law of Europe that Bodin describes, English laws "are made not onlye by the Princes pleasure, but also by the assent of the whole royalme: so that of necessitie they must procure the wealth of the people, and in noe wise tende to their hynderaunce."[19] The dramatic reversal at the end of Heywood's poem, in which the maid destroys the spider and sweeps away its encroaching webs, points to the poem's embrace of traditional possession of habitats and the virtue of custom. The conflict of bloodsucking spiders with their annoying insect prey allows the poet to explore the risk to the fragile tissue of the commonwealth without simply taking the side of one party over the other.

And yet this ambiguous allegory involving a contest between the perspectives of two insects implicates the human beings who are endangering the social fabric. Just as the poet uses the conflict of insects over the encroachment of one webbed dwelling onto another signified by vacancy and absence, all within the larger habitat of the shared window, so the insects make use of human behavior to argue about their conflict over the holes in the lattice. When he counters the charge that he has trespassed onto the spider's web, the fly's theory of the law relies on and is most intelligible to Heywood's readers through reference to human experience. The fly argues that if a carter turned out of a muddy road and onto higher ground and accidentally bumped the support post of a person's house on private property, "law and lauful reason, showth it right, / That recompense punishe [the] ouersight"; but if that house were constructed "within this high way," the carter has no liability for "houses in high wayes encroaching so," meaning he would be "bounde by reason nor by law, / To recompence, the value of a straw" (19.5–6). Heywood not only uses an artfully constructed narrative about natural habitats to explore the limits of human society, but also acknowledges the artifice of that construct by representing the insects appealing to human behavior to explain the limits of insect habitats in regard to other insects.

In order to explore the tension between the landed nobility and the landless peasants, Heywood might have chosen any number of other creatures for his allegory. They could have been wolves or sheep, a common figure for the enclosures that prompted the rebellions in the first place. Heywood could have figured them as bees and ants, both of which are industrious social insects but only one of which produces something of value, if he wanted to make insects the central figure in his allegory. Spiders striving with bees might have been more appropriate, since early modern writers might see these lesser creatures as inversions of each other, both of them able to transform natural materials and excrete them. In Ben Jonson's *Volpone*, for instance, the English rumormonger Sir Politic Would-Be distinguishes his supposedly serious pursuits from his wife's frivolous ones by remarking that "the spider and the bee oft-times / Suck from one flower."[20] Although bees and spiders both take in the same raw material, only bees—often a figure of productive humanist readers—create something appealing and useful—honey—while spiders transform the same material to create webs and "venims . . . gathered out of old philosophers and heathen authors."[21] Perhaps Heywood thought to connect the proud nobility with the vanity of spiders. As Jeremy Corderoy would note in a dialogue critical of those amassing wealth in this world, the estates of those who devote themselves to ephemeral trifles rather than to godly virtue could be "very well compared to ye house of a Spider, who," as Job remarks, "by wasting his own bowels, spinneth his web, and passing curiouslie composeth it, yet a little puffe of wind calleth it and him downe."[22] Spenser would himself employ this trope at the outset of "Virgils Gnat," published in the *Complaints* along with *Muiopotmos*, when he self-deprecatingly dismisses his ephemera as "like a cobweb weauing slenderly" with which he has "onley playde."[23] In characterizing his work in this way, he echoes his patron, Sir Philip Sidney, whose self-effacing dedication of the *Arcadia* dismisses this "idle work of mine, which I fear (like the spider's web) will be thought fitter to be swept away than worn to any purpose."[24] A more intriguing possibility is that Heywood associated the constricting webs woven by spiders over the formerly unfettered vacancies of the lattice holes as reflecting the power of despotic laws to restrict the liberty of the commoner. This is certainly the fly's complaint as the spider threatens him with a crime. He demands that "you spiders, show your selues among, / By any kynd of law, what wey ye may / Lawfully bylde, within this my high way," assigning the transgression to the spider, which has violated the customary access through the center of the window (19.10).

The representation of laws as the strands of a spider's entangling web appears in many early modern contexts. Sometimes the figure suggests the literal feebleness of the law in the face of determined transgressors. In a sermon on the proper limits to a godly sovereign's power, for instance, Richard Eedes considers the nature of tyrants, who rashly "thinke to breake through [God's] lawes, as it were through the web of a spider" only to learn of the mighty, immutable chains of divine law.[25] The connection of the flimsy bands of the spider's habitat with failures in justice occurs in many early modern writers. For example, in Antonio de Guevara's popular *Epístolas Familiares*, translated into English by Geoffrey Fenton as the *Golden Epistles*, the historian advises "that great theeues should not so hang up the little ones, nor the lawes be made like to Spyder webbes, who suffer the great ones to pearce and passe thorow without punishment, and strangle the little flie, in whom is least offence."[26] The injustice of a web that punishes the weak but permits the powerful to escape punishment—expressed as a paradox, since the larger flying creatures pass through the web while its strands capture the smaller flies—appears in a variety of literary and humanistic texts of the early modern period. In their poetic response to the plague, for instance, Thomas Dekker and Thomas Middleton lament that the poor suffer the most in the epidemic, just as "The lesser fly / Now in the spider's web doth lie."[27] The sense that unjust laws more often entangle the poor receives its most complete treatment and explication in a digest of commonplaces attributed to Conrad Lycosthenes and his early sixteenth-century predecessor Lucio Domizio Brusoni. Brusoni cited the authority of an ancient Scythian observer of classical Athens, Anacharsis, who supposedly made a number of acerbic comments about the flaws in Athenian justice. Brusoni notes that Anacharsis "called lawes spiderwebs, bicause they take the silly flees, but let the great birds through them. Meaning ye the poore only are punished for their offences, but the riche and mighty by bribing, and other shiftes, escape unpunished."[28] Whether they ascribe specifically to Anacharsis the idea of the spider's habitat as a mesh of laws that unjustly entangles only the lowly or not, the figure persists in early modern writing on politics.

Jean Bodin, the French humanist whose influential *Six Livres de la République* serves as an important touchstone for Derrida's thinking about sovereignty, makes reference to nonhuman habitats in his arguments with about as great a frequency as other early modern writers on the nature of human societies. Near the beginning of his treatment of the commonwealth as a collection of families under a sovereign power, for instance, Bodin makes allowance for even a very small collection of families to be its own commonwealth, "for it is neither the wals, neither the persons, that maketh the citie, but the vnion of the people vnder the same soueraigntie of gouernment, albeit there be in all but three families."[29] Size does not matter, Bodin argues, since "an Emot [or ant] is as well to be called a liuing creature, as an Elephant."[30] Analogies to other nonhuman creatures abound in Bodin, including an unacknowledged appropriation of the saying others attributed to Anacharsis. As Bodin makes the argument that every proper commonwealth must appoint censors to account for the property of the members of society, he comments as well on their duty to observe citizens' morals. The law, he notes, may address murders and thefts, but "lawes punish those offences onely, which trouble the quiet of a commonweale: and yet the greatest offendors doe easily escape the punishment of the law, euen as great beasts do easily breake through the spiders web."[31] Laws, like the webs of spiders, ought to apply to individuals equally, but the lowly invariably suffer more. Heywood's allegorical treatment of the covetous nobility who threaten the commonwealth's harmony as arachnids spinning their webs over open spaces to entangle more of the plebeian flies might be seen as an extended treatment of the injustice of these sticky laws.

Heywood's lengthy insect fable did not inspire many printed responses. As the French humanist Jean Talpin might have warned, in Fenton's translation of *Christian Pollicie*, the risk of secretly weaving an obscure political and moral allegory over the course of several decades and three changed regimes might amount to "The glorious webbe of the Spider . . . stretched out to none other ende but to take the foolishe flye."[32] And challenging arguments about the proper order of a commonwealth, as Bodin would show in the ease with which he dismisses arguments in favor of the popular state, may "haue a goodly shew, but in effect they are like vnto spiders webs, the which are very subtill and fine, but haue no great force."[33] After a quarter of a century, Heywood's poem does eventually leave a ripple in an Elizabethan text, however. William Harrison, in describing his English habitat, includes a chapter on the relative dearth of venomous creatures in his beloved homeland. After remarking on the decadence of Rome's caesars, who enjoyed watching the combat of stout flies and crafty spiders, Harrison mentions that closer to home, a poet "hath made a booke of the spider and the flie, wherein he dealeth so profoundlie, and beyond all measure of skill, that neither he himselfe that made it, neither anie one that readeth it, can reach vnto the meaning therof."[34] Heywood might have been disappointed that his allegory remained so obscure. He would have company, if not solace, in a similarly obscure allegory of Spenser, however. In *Muiopotmos*, Spenser uses the etiological impulse of Ovidian epyllion to explore not only the mythographic origins of the butterfly's wings and the spider's enmity toward the beautiful butterfly, but also the idea of liberty and tyranny under the cover of a beast fable.

Spenser's *Muiopotmos* uses the mock-heroic entomological conflict of a carefree butterfly and a treacherous spider to explore a variety of Ovidian etiologies. Alluding ironically to Virgilian epic, Spenser's narrator "sing[s] of deadly dolorous debate, / Stir'd vp through wrathfull Nemesis despight, / Betwixt two mightie ones of great estate."[35] The two mightily insignificant rivals are Clarion, prince of the butterflies, and Aragnoll, a tyrannical spider. As the narrative begins, Clarion surveys the realm of his father. Emulating the heroes of epic, Clarion dons a breastplate as magnificent as "that, which Vulcane made to sheild / Achilles life from fate of Troyan field" (63–64).[36] Clarion then explores the garden, pausing to luxuriate in an epic catalog of flowers during his progress through his father's empire.[37] Surveying the open spaces of this unencumbered habitat, the princely butterfly fleetingly experiences contentment as "Lord of all the workes of Nature . . . rain[ing] in th'aire from earth to highest skie" (211–12). This delight lasts only for a moment. In keeping with the themes of the other items in the *Complaints*, the poet must change his notes to tragic—for "what on earth can long abide in state?"—and Clarion's happiness must soon come to an end (217). The speaker introduces Aragnoll at this point. This "wicked wight" perversely detests the free pleasure Clarion has found "in this faire plot dispacing too and fro" in the garden without a care, and his "heart did earne" to bring about the hero's demise (243, 250, 254). Aragnoll spins a subtle web and waits for Clarion to stumble into his trap. Then, "Like a grimme Lyon rushing with fierce might / Out of his den, he seized greedelie / On the resistles pray" and slips a "weapon slie" into a gap in Clarion's armor (434–36).[38] The poem concludes with gestures to the *Aeneid* as Clarion's "deepe groning spright / In bloodie streames foorth fled into the aire, / His bodie left the spectacle of care" (438–40).[39] Studded with Virgilian and Ovidian gestures, Spenser's *Muiopotmos* combines the classical outlines of Elizabethan epyllia with the period's interest in allegorical beast fable.

Spenser knew the power of the beast fable as a means of exploring human nature. This form has ancient roots, going back to Job 12:7–9 and the recognition that in cases where the divine does not speak explicitly on some matter of human behavior, humans should "Aske now the beastes, and they shal teache thee, and the foules of the heauen, and they shal tel thee.... Who is ignorant of all these, but that the hand of the Lord hathe made these?" Complementing the biblical advice to read divine intentions in the book of nature, Aesop had given to the classical tradition the power of the beast fable to carry advice on the nature of human political formations, particularly on the invaluable nature of liberty and the dangers of tyrannical kings. In one fable, frogs demand that Jupiter place a king over them and end up with a stork who proceeds to devour them. The moral Aesop offers his reader is that "he that hath lyberty ought to kepe it wel, for nothing is better than libertie, for libertie should not be well sold for all the gold and siluer in the world."[40] In addition to encountering these traditions in the classroom, Spenser knew them from the "Ister Bank" song of the *Old Arcadia*.[41] Like Aesop's frogs, Philisides's free beasts demand a king, creating a man who then becomes a tyrant, teaching Sidney's human readers not to permit "gloire to swell in tyranny" and a reminder to the oppressed that if they "know your strengths, and then you shall do well" (225).[42] Spenser himself made use of beast fables elsewhere, as in the problematic and imprudent *Mother Hubberds Tale*, printed at the same time as *Muiopotmos*, and in *The Shepheardes Calendar*, whose fourth edition appeared in the same year.[43]

Spenser's poem, like most other Elizabethan epyllia, constructs several Ovidian etiologies.[44] Like his peers, Spenser not only transforms his Ovidian model but invents mythological origin stories of his own. In the episode of arming the heroic Clarion, the poet turns finally to the hallmark of the butterfly's anatomy, its beautiful gossamer wings. These are "Painted with a thousand colours, passing farre / All Painters skill" (90–91).[45] Pausing to dilate on the beauty of Clarion's wings, which inspire the "secret enuie [envy]" of the ladies at his father's court, the poet creates a myth of the butterfly's origins (106). These wings derive from an episode when Astery, one of the nymphs of Venus, responded to her mistress's request that damsels "gather flowers, her forhead to array"

(117). Outperforming her peers through her nimbleness and industry, Astery "gathered more store / Of the fields honour" than the rest (122–23). Her friends, now "enuying sore" the success of Astery, spread a rumor that the amorous Cupid helped the object of his desire to this plenty, inspiring Venus, from "iealous feare" to prevent the union of her son and one of her maids. The goddess punishes Astery by turning her "into a winged Butterflie" and, "for memorie / Of her pretended crime, though crime none were," she decorated "her wings" with "all those flowres, with which so plenteouslie / Her lap she filled had" (138, 140–43).[46] Astery's power to inspire envy among her peers and jealousy in her mistress persists in her descendant Clarion's ability to generate envy in the ladies of the court.

Spenser's figuration of Clarion as a prince resonates with the popular estimation of the gaudy butterfly. Moffett, perhaps unsurprisingly, filters his treatment of butterflies through human institutions, as he had with spiders and lesser creatures. As he describes the colors and markings on the abdomen, legs, and wings of one kind of butterfly, the Phalena, he likens them to human rulers. Nature intended one sort of Phalena as "King of Butterflies" and decorated them accordingly, "that is to say, strong, valiant, blackish, freckled," while Nature "spent her whole painters shop" on a second sort, which Nature meant to be "the Queen, delicate, tender, fine, all beset with pearls and precious stones, and priding it self in embroidery and needle-work: her body downy like Geese," her ineffable wings "having eyes of divers colours" that are ultimately "of so elegant and notable figure, that it is easier to wonder at and admire, than with expressions to describe."[47] The beauty of butterflies and their wings is certainly a very old notion, and in Shakespeare's Lear's fevered "laugh[ter] / At gilded butterflies," that trope easily traverses into critique of gaudy aristocrats and courtiers, but Moffett's figuration of these remarkably beautiful butterflies as the king and queen of their species takes the notion of political metaphors applied to the habitats of the animal "kingdom" in a new direction.[48] For Moffett casually to imagine these insects as kings and queens, their beautiful wings as the extravagant luxuries possessed and displayed by a human monarch, is to cross the human/nonhuman divide in an unexpected way.[49]

In a subsequent and more obviously Ovidian origin story, Spenser takes up and transforms the genesis of Aragnoll's and all spiders' hatred of Clarion and all butterflies. This spider, "The foe of faire things, th'author of confusion, / The shame of Nature, the bondslaue of spight" detests Clarion (244–45). The poet dilates on material from Ovid to explain the "cause why he this Flie so maliced" and says that "in stories written it is found" (257–58). The story he has in mind is that of Arachne and her contest with Minerva, recounted in the sixth book of the *Metamorphoses*.[50] In the Ovidian original, Arachne, "famous for the place / In which she dwelt, not for hir stocke, but for hir Art," excelled in weaving, a skill associated with Minerva.[51]

> ... But Arachne nathelesse
> Denyeth and disdaining such a Mistresse to confesse,
> "Let hir contend with me" she saide: "and if she me amend
> I will refuse no punishment the which she shall extend."[52]

Arachne's hubris entices the deity to observe the weaver in disguise and then confront her about the boast. They engage in a contest in which Arachne produces a "goodly worke, full fit for Kingly bowres"—probably an allusion to Proverbs 30:28—inspiring "Enuie pale" in Minerva's heavenly breast (300–301). Minerva finds herself nearly outmatched by her mortal rival, and the envy she experiences, like that Venus and her companions directed at Astery the future butterfly, contributes to the metamorphosis this goddess directs at the future spider. When the suicidal Arachne hangs herself, Minerva condemns Arachne to live on "in shape of Spider still" practicing "The Spinners and the Websters crafts of which she erst had skill."[53] Spenser transforms key elements of Ovid's etiology of this bug. In Spenser's myth, Minerva follows Arachne in the contest and outdoes the mortal, who "stood astonied long" and jealously "did she inly fret" so that "She grew to hideous shape of dryrihed" (339, 343, 347). Most important for this etiological digression in Spenser's poem, the mark of Minerva's triumph in the second tapestry is "a Butterflie, / With excellent deuice and wondrous slight, / Fluttering among the Oliues" (329–31). For Spenser, this addition explains the animosity of spiders toward butterflies, the beautiful mark of their ugly, dreary existence.

This second, inventive transformation of an Ovidian etiology points to another form of origin that Spenser explores in *Muiopotmos*. In the ekphrastic Ovidian tapestry that Minerva creates on her loom, she depicts "the storie of the olde debate" between Neptune and herself for the privilege of sponsoring a prosperous new urban habitat (305). Before a gathering of Olympian deities who will determine the outcome and award sovereign authority over the exemplary city of Athens, the "God of Seas" initiates the debate (313). Because he has maritime dominion, Neptune "Claym[s] that sea-coast Citie as his right" (314). In the image Minerva weaves, Neptune "strikes the rockes," out of which "issues a warlike steed," a sign of the deity's martial power and one that impresses the other gods, which "surely deeme the victorie his due" (315–16, 319). Minerva, however, counters Neptune's miracle. The tapestry, depicting Minerva's warlike self, displays the basis of her victory, when "A fruitfull Olyue tree, with berries spredd" emerges when she "smote the ground" (325–26). Not only does her miracle impress the immortal assembly—"all the Gods admir'd" the tree—but it also produces the joint symbol of peace and Athenian prosperity, the fruit of the olive tree (327). The deities will award the sovereignty of Athens to Minerva, and the city will take the name of its Greek patron, Athena. Not content simply to retell Ovid's version of this contest, Spenser himself weaves an innovative detail into his poem to explain the enmity of spiders and butterflies. The Elizabethan poet's Minerva weaves a deceptively lifelike butterfly "That seem'd to liue, so like it was in sight," alighting on the olive tree (332).[54] This lively addition seals her victory over Aragnoll's foremother. Sovereignty and spiders emerge from the web of Minerva's loom, gesturing obliquely to the figure at work in Anacharsis's insight into the flaws of Athenian law. The poem's abundant story of origins—the origins of Athenian prosperity, the origin of Minerva's sovereignty, the origins of the spider, and the origins of its animosity toward the butterfly—connects to other political questions attached to the habitats in Spenser's epyllion.

Muiopotmos figures the habitat of the butterflies that Clarion surveys as a kingdom open to the skies. Butterflies "doo possesse the Empire of the aire, / Betwixt the centred earth, and azure skies" in the poet's estimation (18–19). This realm, coincidentally, is one usually granted to Neptune in his sibling contest with Jupiter and Pluto. Clarion undertakes a quest at the start of the mini-epic to

> . . . range abroad in fresh attire,
> Through the wide compas of the ayrie coast,
> And with vnwearied winges each part t'inquire
> Of the wide rule of his renowmed sire. (37–40)

His and his kind's habitat is the open, unconstrained champaign. Once he has clad himself in his beautiful accoutrements, Clarion flies out "Over the fields in his franke lustinesse, / And all the champion he soared light, / And all the countrey wide he did possesse" (148–50). In the center of his domain he finds a magnificent garden and, after the catalog of flowers he samples there, he "rests in riotous suffisaunce / Of all his gladfulnes, and kingly ioyaunce" in a fleeting moment of perfect contentment, soon to be interrupted by the malice of the tyrannical Aragnoll (207–8).

The garden, a paradoxical habitat that joins the green world of nature with the cultivated world of art, offers a figure for the proper ordering of early modern sovereignty. Some laws and some boundaries are surely necessary, as the fly in Heywood's allegory had conceded. In Fenton's translation of Talpin's treatise on a godly commonwealth, a magistrate's moral laws share equal footing with strong walls and iron gates as "the verye Soules of common weales."[55] However, when there "is a negligent or partiall countenunce geuen to the lawes and authority . . . they be but as spiderwebbes, wherein the small flies are taken and sucke the blood and great waspes do pearse and passe thorow at pleasure," the commonwealth descends into injustice, followed by "an uniuersall reuersement of all pollecye."[56] Unjust laws create a situation not unlike when a "garden being strongly fensed with hedge or ditche, there is great seueritye, that neyther the night theefe, nor the hungry beast, can haue power to enter and commit it to praye, where, if there bee neyther wall nor closure, the negligence of the owner offereth occasion to the theefe or Beast, to inuade his ground, to the spoile of his commoditye and fruictes."[57] The apparent openness of the garden Clarion explores also invites the depredations of his rival, Aragnoll, who resides in this garden. His destruction of the carefree butterfly results in part from his envy, not of the beautiful wings of his enemy, but from jealousy of his careless freedom. In the garden where Clarion reposes in unfettered kingly joy, Aragnoll "Had lately built his hatefull mansion," encroaching on the butterfly's open habitat with an entangling web like those of the spiders of Heywood's allegory (246). When the spider observes the detested butterfly taking his ease, he retreats into "the caue, in which he lurking dwelt" and spins his "subtil gin" (358, 369). The strands of this wondrous net will entangle the poem's protagonist and immobilize him when his enemy attacks.

The poem thus pits the sovereign liberty of Clarion, abroad under the open air, against the mesh of restrictions and claustrophobic confines of the despotic Aragnoll. In the transition between Clarion's free movement across his habitat and the moment of pathetic change to captivity, the poet asks, apparently rhetorically, "What more felicitie can fall to creature, / Than to enioy delight with libertie?" (209–10). The poet describes the butterfly's final moments of freedom as he "wandred too and fro / In the pride of his freedome" and "regardless of his gouernaunce" falls into the web Aragnoll has woven (379–80, 384). Captured at last by the wily spider's weaving, he finds himself struggling against the web "in vaine. / For striuing more, the more in laces strong / Himselfe he tide" (427–28). He discovers that he cannot escape the web of "treasons" laid out by Aragnoll and then must observe in horror as, "his youthly forces idly spent," he lies powerless beneath Aragnoll's "weapon slie" (395, 431). Figuring the spider's web explicitly as treason, the poet links the conflict of lesser creatures to the political life of human beings and their conflicting forms of governing their habitats. In this final moment, the poet represents the bound young hero as at the mercy of a "greisly tyrant," cementing the political contest latent in the poem between freedom and tyranny, movement and restraint, joy and dreariness (433).

Early modern entomologists, and early modern culture more broadly, thought that humans could peer into insect habitats and take lessons for themselves from the nonverbal ways of the divine. Moffett, as he concludes his chapter on butterflies, addresses his readers, warning them to "Learn therefore, O mortal Man, who ever thou art, that God that is best and greatest of all, made the butterfly to pull down thy pride" (974).[58] Human beings could learn humility if they observed the butterfly properly. Its complex beauty reflected God's handiwork, beyond any human's ability to replicate it. But the butterfly might also put human beings to shame in other ways. They enjoyed a natural liberty, free to roam through a habitat of meadows and gardens and the open air. No human beings still enjoyed such liberty. For Laurie Shannon, *King Lear* figures prominently as a canvas on which to explore the "zoomorphic" mentality of the early modern, pre-Cartesian exploration of human and nonhuman relations. Near the end of the second act of Shakespeare's tragedy, Lear finds himself reacting against the domestic tyranny of his daughters, who strip him of his marks of sovereignty and ultimately attempt to restrict his movements. In one last gesture of strength and autonomy, as madness begins to take hold, Lear rejects his daughters and declares that he would rather

. . . abjure all roofs, and choose
To wage against the enmity o' th' air,
To be comrade with the wolf and owl,
Necessity's sharp pinch. (2.4.207–10)

Fleeing the claustrophobic web of his manipulative daughters' despotism, Lear seeks out the liberty of the heath. Although he briefly disentangles himself from their machinations, the punishing storm he encounters there may point in its own way to the limitations of the idealized habitat of the carefree butterfly.

Notes

1. Topsell, *Revvard of Religion*, 255.
2. Moffett, *Theater of Insects*, 1065.
3. Plutarch, *Philosophie*, 967. As Erica Fudge has forcefully demonstrated, a tradition of Plutarchianism cropped up in early modern England, using human ideas about animals to shape the outline of the human (*Brutal Reasoning*, 97).
4. Jacques Derrida notes that "real" predatory beasts like wolves (and for my purposes, spiders) exist, but that their meaning is a function of the stories we tell in specific "cultures, nations, languages, myths, fables, fantasies, histories" (*Beast and the Sovereign*, 5). Gail Kern Paster, writing about animal emotions and human passions, recognizes the anthropocentric tendency of early modern writers, including Topsell (*Humoring the Body*, 154).
5. Mexía, *Foreste*, fol. 145v.
6. Ibid.
7. Ibid.
8. I borrow this term from Shannon, *Accommodated Animal*, 8.
9. Bodin, *Six Bookes*, 641. Bodin's treatment of sovereignty and his recourse to tropes of the nonhuman figures importantly, as we shall see, for Derrida, who (perhaps unintentionally) discusses early modern political philosophers as entangled in "the political web of their time" (*Beast and the Sovereign*, 51).
10. On the monarchical beehive as an image of natural hierarchy, see most recently Lake, *How Shakespeare*, 350. On the republic of ants, see Fleck, "Dutch Ants."
11. James Holstun persuasively argues that the poem dramatizes "the great battleground of sixteenth-century agrarian struggle," between greedy landlords and powerless tenants, with Heywood attempting to counsel an increasingly erratic Queen Mary to align with the interests of the traditional commonwealth against the forces of "aristocapitalism" ("Spider," 62, 56).
12. Roze Hentschell surveys the transformation of early modern England's rural landscape under the pressure of enclosure and discusses the variety of historiographical treatments of the phenomenon (*Culture of Cloth*, 32).

13. Heywood, *Spider and the Flie*, 19.1. Subsequent references to *The Spider and the Flie* appear parenthetically by chapter and stanza. Alice Hunt argues that questions of authority—political, juridical, and authorial—emerge as central to the allegory ("Marian Political Allegory," 343).
14. Judith Rice Henderson unpacks the impact of the different leases on the jurisdiction of different courts in this episode ("John Heywood's," 252).
15. Geneva Bible.
16. Articulated in these terms, the flies' objections to the spiders' infringement of their free passage through the window could be read in terms of Pierre Bourdieu's theory of habitus, the social conditioning that comes to govern "mythically structured space," as well as "between man and the natural world" (*Outline of a Theory*, 91).
17. Mexía, *Foreste*, fol. 146v.
18. Bodin, *Six Bookes*, 162.
19. Fortescue, *Learned Commendation*, 40r.
20. Jonson, *Volpone*, 2.1.30–31.
21. Harvey, *Theologicall Discourse*, 98.
22. Corderoy, *Warning for Worldlings*, 141.
23. Spenser, "Virgils Gnat," lines 3–4.
24. Sidney, *New Arcadia*, 506.
25. Eedes, *Six Learned and Godly Sermons*, fol. 17r.
26. Guevara, *Golden Epistles*, 16v.
27. Middleton and Dekker, "News from Gravesend," lines 974–75.
28. Brusoni, *Extracte of Examples*, 154–55.
29. Bodin, *Six Bookes*, 10.
30. Ibid.
31. Ibid., 644.
32. [Talpin], *Forme of Christian Pollicie*, 119.
33. Bodin, *Six Bookes*, 701.
34. Harrison, *Firste Volume*, fol. 112r.
35. Spenser, *Muiopotmos*, lines 1–3. Subsequent references to *Muiopotmos* appear parenthetically by line number.
36. As Andrew Hadfield remarks, the humor of this scene derives from a fragile and airy butterfly encumbered with such heavy armor (*Edmund Spenser*, 283). Curiously, the butterfly plays a role in some unlikely martial contexts. John Boswell, in discussing the figures to be found on coats of arms, mentions that the butterfly "is borne of diuers" in their family crests (*Workes of Armorie*, 21r). The butterfly on the family crest of James Tuchet, seventh Baron Audley, is recalled in the 1563 edition of *Mirror for Magistrates*.
37. Heather James sees the passage as a tour de force of "the humanist activity of gathering rhetorical flowers and maxims for storage in commonplace books" ("Flower Power," para. 8).
38. Mark David Rasmussen reads their conflict and this conclusion as pitting aristocratic carelessness embodied in Clarion against the brute strength and cankered perversity of the stronger Aragnoll ("*Complaints* and *Daphnaïda*," 229).
39. Namratha Rao explains the epyllion's final, puzzling Virgilian gesture, in which the protagonist's death resembles that of Turnus, as an acknowledgment of divine injustice creating a "powerful dissonance" between its "totalising symmetries and its underlying ethical expectations" ("Fearful Symmetry," 153).
40. Aesop, *Fables*, sig. F3v.
41. Shannon argues that this poem does much more than the traditional "beast fable" in its treatment of its nonhuman figures, pointing in fact to the shared constitution of human and nonhuman in the fallen cosmos (*Accommodated Animal*, 73).
42. Sidney, *Old Arcadia*, 223. For Sidney's use of Aesop, see Patterson, *Fables of Power*, 67.

43. Patterson shows how imprudent Spenser's *Mother Hubberds Tale* was and traces Spenser's engagement with beast fable in other texts, though she passes over *Muiopotmos* (*Fables*, 67). Hadfield treats the scandal of this beast fable at greater length (*Edmund Spenser*, 268).
44. On this Ovidian impulse in Shakespeare and others, see Weaver, *Untutored Lines*, 71. Lynn Enterline traces the vogue for Elizabethan Ovidian verse to humanist pedagogy (*Shakespeare's Schoolroom*, 79).
45. For Eric Brown, the deluxe accoutrements of Clarion's wings signal the hero's proud ambition and highlight his "insufficient inward preparation" for the allegorical trials the soul will soon face ("Allegory of Small Things," 261).
46. Robert A. Brinkley notes the lack of remorse to be found in this episode, given that the poet transmutes Astery's suffering for a crime she did not commit into a mark of great beauty ("Spenser's *Muiopotmos*," 673). For Ayesha Ramachandran, the poem does more than simply meditate on the "recurrent trope of Nature and Art contending" ("Clarion in the Bower," 86).
47. See Moffett, *Theater of Insects*, 958–59.
48. Shakespeare, *King Lear*, 5.3.12–13.
49. As Joseph Campana argues, attention to the "negative sublime" of the perfectly minute forms of insect society inspired early modern thinkers to reflect on human society as well ("Bee and the Sovereign?," 98–99). Brown sees in Shakespeare's engagement with the life cycle of the butterfly in *Coriolanus* a meditation on dramatic synecdoche, as well as the fragile bonds of political society ("Performing Insects," 30).
50. As Rao observes, Spenser balances the invented story of the butterfly's beautiful wings with this transformed version of Ovid's version of the Arachne myth ("Fearful Symmetry," 142). She builds on the careful attention of Richard Danson Brown to the balanced symmetry of *Muiopotmos* in "*The New Poet*," 219.
51. Ovid, *Metamorphosis*, 75.
52. Ibid.
53. Ibid., 77.
54. On the contest of art and nature embodied in this deceptive butterfly, see Fleck, "'Arte,'" 112.
55. Talpin, *Forme of Christian Pollicie*, 13.
56. Ibid., 13–14.
57. Ibid., 14.
58. Fudge adeptly shows how early modern writers like Topsell, in which Moffett's treatment of butterflies and other lesser living creatures eventually appeared, write about nonhuman creatures "through a filter of human vision and for a particular (human) purpose" (*Brutal Reasoning*, 109).

Bibliography

Aesop. *The Fables of Esope in English*. Translated by William Caxton. London, [1570].

Bodin, Jean. *The Six Bookes of a Commonweale*. Translated by Richard Knolles. London, 1606.

Boswell, John. *Workes of Armorie, Deuyded into Three Bookes*. London, 1572.

Bourdieu, Pierre. *Outline of a Theory of Practice*. Translated by Richard Nice. Cambridge: Cambridge University Press, 1977.

Brinkley, Robert A. "Spenser's *Muiopotmos* and the Politics of Metamorphosis." *ELH* 48, no. 4 (1981): 668–76.

Brown, Eric C. "The Allegory of Small Things: Insect Eschatology in

Spenser's *Muiopotmos*." *Studies in Philology* 99, no. 3 (2002): 247–67.

———. "Performing Insects in Shakespeare's *Coriolanus*." In *Insect Poetics*, edited by Brown. Minneapolis: University of Minnesota Press, 2006.

Brown, Richard Danson. *"The New Poet": Novelty and Tradition in Spenser's "Complaints."* Liverpool: Liverpool University Press, 1999.

Brusoni, Lucio Domizio. *An Extracte of Examples, Apothegmes, and Histories. Collected out of Lycosthenes, Brusonius and others.* Translated by John Parinchef. London [1572].

Campana, Joseph. "The Bee and the Sovereign? Political Entomology and the Problem of Scale." *Shakespeare Studies* 41 (2013): 94–113.

Corderoy, Jeremy. *A Warning for Worldlings, or A Comfort to the Godly and a Terror to the Wicked*. London, 1608.

Derrida, Jacques. *The Beast and the Sovereign*. Vol. 1. Translated by Geoffrey Bennington. Chicago: University of Chicago Press, 2009.

Eedes, Richard. *Six Learned and Godly Sermons*. London, 1604.

Enterline, Lynn. *Shakepseare's Schoolroom: Rhetoric, Discipline, Emotion*. Philadelphia: University of Pennsylvania Press, 2012.

Fleck, Andrew. "'Arte with her contending, doth aspire T'excell the naturall': Contending for Representation in the Elizabethan Epyllion." In *Elizabethan Narrative Poems: The State of Play*, edited by Lynn Enterline, 95–118. London: Arden, 2019.

———. "Dutch Ants and Dutch Uncles: Sorting out Englishness Among the Exile Community in the Low Countries." *Studies in Medieval and Renaissance History* 3 (2006): 211–39.

Fortescue, John. *A Learned Commendation of the Politique Lawes of Englande*. London, 1567.

Fudge, Erica. *Brutal Reasoning: Animals, Rationality, and Humanity in Early Modern England*. Ithaca, NY: Cornell University Press, 2006.

The Geneva Bible: A Facsimile of the 1560 Edition. Edited by Lloyd E. Berry. Madison: University of Wisconsin Press, 1969.

Guevara, Antonio de. *Golden Epistles, Contayning Varietie of Discourse*. Translated by Geoffrey Fenton. London, 1575.

Hadfield, Andrew. *Edmund Spenser: A Life*. Oxford: Oxford University Press, 2012.

Harrison, William. *Firste Volume of the Chronicles of England, Scotlande, and Irelande*. London, 1577.

Harvey, Richard. *A Theologicall Discourse of the Lamb of God and His Enemies*. London, 1590.

Henderson, Judith Rice. "John Heywood's *The Spider and the Flie*: Educating Queen and Country." *Studies in Philology* 96, no. 3 (1999): 241–74.

Hentschell, Roze. *The Culture of Cloth in Early Modern England: Textual Constructions of a National Identity*. Farnham, UK: Ashgate, 2008.

Heywood, John. *The Spider and the Flie*. Edited by A. W. Ward. London: Spenser Society; New York: Burt Franklin, 1967. First published 1894.

Holstun, James. "The Spider, the Fly, and the Commonwealth: Merrie John Heywood and Agrarian Class Struggle." *ELH* 71, no. 1 (2004): 53–88.

Hunt, Alice. "Marian Political Allegory: John Heywood's *The Spider and the Fly*." In *Oxford Handbook of Tudor Literature, 1485–1603*, edited by Mike Pincombe and Cathy Shrank. Oxford: Oxford University Press, 2009.

James, Heather. "Flower Power." *Spenser Review* 44, no. 2 (2014).

Jonson, Ben. "Volpone, or The Fox." In *The Cambridge Edition of the Works of Ben Jonson*, edited by David Bevington,

Martin Butler, and Ian Donaldson. Cambridge: Cambridge University Press, 2012.

Lake, Peter. *How Shakespeare Put Politics on the Stage: Power and Succession in the History Plays.* New Haven: Yale University Press, 2016.

Mexía, Pedro. *The Foreste or Collection of Histories.* Translated by Thomas Fortescue. London, 1571.

Middleton, Thomas, and Thomas Dekker. "News from Gravesend: Sent to Nobody." In *Collected Works of Thomas Middleton,* edited by Gary Taylor and John Lavagnino, 128–48. Oxford: Clarendon Press, 2010.

Moffett, Thomas. *The Theater of Insects: or, Lesser Living Creatures.* In *The History of Four-Footed Beasts and Serpents,* by Edward Topsell. London, 1658.

Ovid. *Metamorphosis.* Translated by Arthur Golding. London, 1575.

Paster, Gail Kern. *Humoring the Body: Emotions and the Shakespearean Stage.* Chicago: University of Chicago Press, 2004.

Patterson, Annabel. *Fables of Power: Aesopian Writing and Political History.* Durham: Duke University Press, 1991.

Plutarch. *The Philosophie, Commonlie Called, The Morals.* Translated by Philemon Holland. London, 1603.

Ramachandran, Ayesha. "Clarion in the Bower of Bliss: Poetry and Politics in Spenser's 'Muiopotmos.'" *Spenser Studies* 20 (2005): 77–106.

Rao, Namratha. "Fearful Symmetry in Spenser's *Muiopotmos.*" *Essays in Criticism* 69, no. 2 (2019): 136–56.

Rasmussen, Mark David. "*Complaints* and *Daphnaïda.*" In *The Oxford Handbook of Edmund Spenser,* edited by Richard McCabe. Oxford: Oxford University Press, 2010.

Shakespeare, William. *King Lear.* Edited by Stephen Orgel. New York: Pelican, 1999.

Shannon, Laurie. *The Accommodated Animal: Cosmopolity in Shakespearean Locales.* Chicago: University of Chicago Press, 2013.

Sidney, Philip. *The Countess of Pembroke's Arcadia (The New Arcadia).* Edited by Victor Skretkowicz. Oxford: Clarendon Press, 1987.

———. *The Countess of Pembroke's Arcadia (The Old Arcadia).* Edited by Katherine Duncan-Jones. Oxford: Oxford University Press, 1985.

Spenser, Edmund. "Muiopotmos: or The Fate of the Butterfly." In *The Shorter Poems,* edited by Richard McCabe. New York: Penguin, 1999.

———. "Virgils Gnat." In *The Shorter Poems,* edited by Richard McCabe. New York: Penguin, 1999.

[Talpin, Jean]. *A Forme of Christian Pollicie,* translated by Geoffrey Fenton. London, 1574.

Topsell, Edward. *The Revvard of Religion, Deliuered in Sundrie Lectures vpon the Booke of Ruth.* London, 1596.

Weaver, William. *Untutored Lines: The Making of the English Epyllion.* Edinburgh: Edinburgh University Press, 2012.

CHAPTER 6
CONSUME
Consuming Insects

Amy L. Tigner

People in most Western countries view entomophagy with feelings of disgust.
—ROZIN AND FALLON

Take a hand full of Bees new out of the hive and beat them in a wooden morter and as you beat them pore in a litell beare to them and so beat them againe and thus must you doe two or three times tell your Bees be well beaten then strane them and then let the patient drinke this a good draft once or twise but you must have a great care that the bees be kept awhile tell you beat them.
—ANONYMOUS RECEIPT BOOK MANUSCRIPT (Egerton 2608)

For most people in North America and Europe, the thought of consuming insects is revolting, yet a new trend on the horizon advocates the agricultural production and consumption of insects. In 2008, the UN Food and Agriculture Organization and Wageningen University together sponsored researchers in compiling a comprehensive study about the importance of edible insects for the world's food supply for the coming population explosion, projected to reach 9 billion by 2050.[1] Speaking as one of the researchers from this project, Professor Marcel Dicke walked onto the TED Talks stage in 2010 and argued for the benefit of eating insects, citing their high conversion factor (1 kilogram of feed will produce 9 kilograms of locust, as opposed to producing 1 kilogram of beef, for example); their relatively low rate of the waste that creates greenhouse gases; and their comparable nutrition rate, which is equal to that of beef, pork, or chicken.[2] This call for insects as food has inspired many new businesses to fill the niche. Writing for the *New York Times Style Magazine*, Ligaya Mishan notes that "start-ups dedicated to entomophagy . . . have raised millions of dollars in venture capital. And the American market for edible insects exceeded $55 million in 2017 and is projected to increase more than 43 percent by 2024, according to the research firm Global Market Insights."[3] As outlandish as these foods seem to be, on average American and European eaters already consume 2 pounds (900 grams) of insects per year in industrialized foods, such as tomato soup, peanut butter, and chocolate. But what seems either invisible or absolutely strange to us was common in the preindustrial, early modern world, as the recipe from Egerton 2608 at the start of this chapter—which calls for live bees as the key ingredient—attests.

In the sixteenth and seventeenth centuries, English eaters were no strangers to consuming insects and other lesser creatures. Undoubtedly their foods—from fruits and vegetables to flours and dried legumes—also contained bits and pieces of insects, but we also know from early modern recipe books (receipt books, as they are called) that bees, flies, worms, and beetles occur regularly as ingredients in household recipes. Although this chapter is primarily concerned with insects, I also include other "lesser creatures," such as snails and lizards, in my study, for despite the fact that these other faunas are not categorically the same as insects, they would occupy a similar place in the early modern kitchen and often in the same recipes. Studying lesser living creatures can tell us much about the early modern period, as this book argues, and thinking about how early moderns used insects and other small faunas in their recipes helps us to understand how humans interacted with the minute nonhumans of the world. Rebecca Laroche notes that "recipe books reveal a pragmatic rather than idealized, intimacy between early moderns and their nonhuman counterparts."[4] Though we generally associate intimacy with sexuality, eating constitutes an equal, or perhaps even greater, intimacy, for all creatures interact with the outside world most intimately by ingestion: what goes into the body becomes the body. Humans and nonhumans understand the world by what we taste and what we eat. By considering the pragmatic intimacy of consumption chronicled in recipes, this chapter investigates the entanglement of human and small-creature bodies and the shared environment in which humans and nonhumans live. Though certainly these small beasts would in many circumstances have been considered undesirable pests, I argue that within early modern household kitchens, these minute nonhumans were often highly esteemed for their particular culinary, medicinal, and even aesthetic value.

These days, a recipe book is synonymous with a cookbook, but in the early modern period, a recipe book, or more properly a receipt book, often contained both culinary and medicinal recipes—sometimes categorized separately but often interspersed, whereby a recipe "To make a sumer custard" might face "To make a salue for a bourne or a scalde," as it does in Margaret Baker's seventeenth-century receipt book.[5] Early moderns recognized the difference between the culinary and the medicinal, but the divide between what was food and what was medicine was not wide, as the prevailing culture followed the Galenic humoral system in which food and medicine worked in tandem to affect health. Food functioned medicinally to restore the body's natural state of health. As Ken Albala explains, "Rather than thinking of food as fuel, most [Renaissance] theorists were inclined to describe it as a restorative, something that replaces the dissipated flesh, blood, and spirits."[6] Early modern health was dependent primarily on the ability of the housewife, working together with family and household staff, to procure, process, and store both foods and medicines—the two sides of the same coin—or, literally, the same receipt book.

We see how an early modern aristocratic woman worked in tandem with her "Maides" planting and harvesting in the garden and later processing in the kitchen foods and medicines in the seventeenth century in the Yorkshire diary of Lady Margaret Hoby.[7] In her entry from April 4, 1601, Hoby "was all the after none in the Garden Sowing seed"; on April 8, she "went with my Maides in to the Garden"; and on Sunday, April 11, she "was busie in the Kitchin and garden tell diner time." On July 22, 1600, Hoby discloses specifically, "I was busie with Roses," which we can assume meant harvesting them for their distillation. On several other occasions, she mentions that she is "busie presaruinge," and in August 1600, she says she was "busie about presaruinge sweetmeat" and "I went about my stilling." Her cabinet of distilled and preserved medicines functioned as a kind of local pharmacy, particularly for her own workmen and servants but also for the community surrounding her estate; Hoby served this population as physician and surgeon, and her practice relied on both plants and animals collected from her own garden. Although no receipt book from Hoby is extant, many recipe collections have survived the ravages of time, and increasingly they are being digitized and transcribed.[8] Elaine Leong has argued, "Study and analysis of these [receipt] collections suggests that interest in maintaining one's health was a fairly universal concern, and that making medicine at home was a common pastime—or, for many early modern housewives, even a duty."[9] Though only a few of the recipes that feature insects and other lesser creatures are strictly culinary, they were regularly ingredients in the medicinal. In both cases, however, the bodies of insects and small faunas were acting on the bodies of humans as sustenance or as health correctives, or both, when they were consumed.

Significantly, human bodies were also acting on insect bodies—flies and bees, for example—as these small nonhumans might be said to "taste" or "consume" human flesh during the act of stinging or biting. In this way, insects differ from other animal bodies that are regularly consumed by humans, as there seems to be at least some parity when insects bite back. In the case of worms, these creatures customarily feed on humans, either as parasites in the living body or along with beetles and flies as consumers of dead flesh. To the insect world, the human body is animal and part of the range of their edible possibilities. Post-Cartesian thought divides the human from the animal; however, the sixteenth- and seventeenth-century practical women (and sometimes men) who cared for the bodies of the household understood the bound relationship between animals and humans, or what Stacy Alaimo calls "transcorporeality," which proposes the interconnectivity of humans, nonhumans, substance, and place.[10] The notion of transcorporeality is particularly manifest when we think of the relationship between the human body and insects (such as worms, flies, and beetles) that eat the body until it decomposes into soil, from which new life can originate.[11] "The human body," as Moira Gatens explains in regard to Spinoza's worldview, "is radically open to its surroundings and can be composed, recomposed, and decomposed by other bodies."[12] And the most direct way that bodies interact with each other is through the act of eating. As Hamlet astutely quips, "We fat all creatures else to fat us, and we fat ourselves for maggots" (4.3.22–23).

Bodies and the Recipe Practice, or "These violent delights come to violent ends" (*Romeo and Juliet* 2.5.9)

Insects indeed are creatures with which humans share a particularly close kind of transcorporeality, especially apparent in the early modern period: worms eat humans and humans eat worms. Julian Yates has read Donna Haraway's notion of the "messmate" as a way to consider multispecies relationships in Shakespeare's various "kitchens." Yates interprets the term *messmate* to include "those with whom we eat at table; to those we eat, and to those who, in the event of our demise or by dint of our continued breathing, eat us."[13] In his discussion of Hamlet's "convocation of political worms" that consumes Polonius's flesh, Yates argues that Hamlet "extends the fact of cooking to beings other than humans and so convokes worm and worms as cook and kitchen."[14] If we look to early modern receipt book manuscripts, most frequently written and compiled by women, we can understand how the early modern kitchen evidences the "interconnectivity" between human body and insect body, manifesting as a kind of circular table—each acting in turn as eater and eaten.

Unlike what Hamlet imagines for Polonius, whose dead body is food for worms, the receipt books decidedly deal with worms that feast on live human bodies, and in turn these receipts use worms and small creatures as consumable ingredients to cure various diseases of the human body. For a worm or other parasite to feed on a living human, the human first has to eat the worm through contaminated water or food, such as undercooked meat or unclean fruits or vegetables. Intestinal worms were indeed quite common: nearly all receipt books that contain medicinal recipes include at least one for worms, an affliction that most often affected children but was not unusual in adults. In her receipt book, dated from 1666, Rebeckah Winche provides "A Pouder for Wormes," and Mary Granville's family receipt book (ca. 1640–1750) has "For Worms in Man Woman or Child."[15] Both recipes have similar ingredients, calling for rhubarb, burned hartshorn (literally the burned shavings of deer antler, a source of ammonia), and wormseed (wormwood, or *Chenopodium ambrosioides*), so named for its known effectiveness against worms. The effectiveness of wormwood against worms has been recently proved in a study conducted in Peru that found that *C. ambrosioides* given to seventy-two patients had antiparasitic efficacy in 56 percent of the cases. However, when they looked at the specific parasites, they found that the efficacy was 100 percent for hookworm (Ancylostoma) and whipworm (Trichuris) and 50 percent for small roundworm (Ascaris), three very common parasitical worms.[16] Early modern women also regularly undertook trials and tests of drugs (albeit perhaps on a lesser scale) and then often left efficacy notations on the recipes. The Granville receipt "For worms" ends with the note "*Probatum est*" (It is proved), which marks the receipt as proven effective against the affliction. Proving a receipt was essential in maintaining the health and welfare of the household and was standard practice in receipt book writing. "In the 'proving' and experimenting with recipes," Catherine Field argues, "women were acting as scientists within the kitchen."[17]

Much of the scientific experimentation in the kitchen would have been conducted with ingredients that were close at hand—even just outside in the garden, where worms and snails would have been plentiful in the damp English climate. These small creatures were essential to the well-stocked closet where medicines and foodstuffs were stored.[18] Most often earthworms and snails were distilled into waters or processed into oils that would be taken orally or given topically for a variety of ailments. Recipes for snail water, which nearly always included earthworms as an ingredient, appear with great frequency in both manuscript and print receipt books. Lady Grace Castleton's snail water recipe, attributed to Lady Frankland, is a cure for "jandis for opening the liver & for obstrouctions for the colic & wind in the stomock," and calls for the snails to be cleaned, boiled in beer, and then beaten (shells and all), to which is added slit and cleaned earthworms, also boiled in beer and beaten. To this mixture some twelve herbs and hartshorn are added; then the whole lot is placed in an alembic (still) and distilled.[19] The distilling process preserved the medicinal essence of these plants and animals so that it could be stored (sometimes for years) in the closet, ready for use when the need arose. As the recipe specifies at the end, the patient was to drink the water in the morning while fasting and then again at four o'clock in the afternoon. The thought of drinking this concoction made of snails and earthworms likely has a significant "yuck factor" for modern readers, but in fact, both the cosmetic and the medical industries have recently found snails to be beneficial to cell restoration; in essence, the bodies of snails rebuild the bodies of humans. Though not taken orally, snail slime as a topical application has become a high-end facial treatment (an EscarGlow facial, a microneedling snail treatment, runs $300) and is starting to gain traction for medicinal uses in wound recovery. According to a recent study conducted by the all-female research team of Agnes Sri Harti, Dwi Sulisetyawati, Atiek Murharyati, and Meri Oktariani, "Snail slime gives a positive reaction to test for protein contents, comprising amino acids and proteins which play a role in cell regeneration and growth. The animal protein content of snail slime has a high biological value in wound healing and in the inhibition of inflammatory process."[20] Another study from the 1990s found earthworms to be effective in healing wounds, especially surgical wounds.[21] These findings confirm what early modern women knew about the properties of these lesser creatures. In "A Booke of Medicens" (1625), Lady Francis Catchmay includes a snail oil recipe that is clearly meant to help with wounds, as she instructs, "Take the oyle of them and anoynte the soare place," and also a recipe for an "oyle of the greate red wormes" that "is good for bruses, aches, or shrinkinge of sinowes."[22] The receipt books written by Castleton, Catchmay, and their contemporaries demonstrate both a shared communal knowledge base and a culture of individual experimentation through the practice of proving recipes.

When we look to how the recipe writers and compilers dealt with the nonhumans that made up the many ingredients, we see the almost casual brutality inherent in the recipes. Common in the period, the snails and earthworms of both Castleton's and Catchmay's concoctions are processed live, just as are the bees in the Egerton 2608 recipe at the start of the chapter, which are taken "new out of the hive, and beaten in a morter," or the "4 lizards aliue" for "The Queens Oil" in Lady Ann Fanshawe's mid-seventeenth-century receipt book.[23] One might surmise that the efficacy of the recipe is dependent on the freshness of the ingredients, and there is nothing fresher than a newly killed live animal. And for kitchens that regularly butchered and sometimes tortured animals that were larger and closer in form to the human body, the recipe maker would hardly consider cooking or eviscerating these lesser creatures as anything out of the ordinary.[24] However, the Egerton 2608 recipe does caution "that the bees be kept awhile tell you beat them," presumably so that they do not fly up and sting back. The early modern kitchen was far from sentimental; rather, it was pragmatically violent or a "theater of cruelty," as both Wendy Wall and David Goldstein have observed.[25] Even the very language of early modern recipes possesses unequivocal violent verbs: "bruising," "breaking," "beating," and "whipping" regularly occur in the directions. Most of these terms are so normal for modern cooks that we might hardly notice them, but a less common term like "bruise" can conjure another kind of domestic violence or violence induced by patriarchal practice, such as criminal punishment or slavery. These violent kitchen actions "bruise," "beat," or "break" nonhuman bodies into usable or digestible essence for human consumption.

As much as humans were breaking and consuming animal bodies, human bodies and bodily fluids did not escape the violence of the kitchen. Recipes regularly called for human excretions. Rebeckah Winche's remedy for what was called the king's evil (scrofula) lists "3 spoonfulls of the urin of a man child he being not aboue 3 years old."[26] And, perhaps stranger, recipes also called for human bodies, mummy or mummia, as an ingredient. Louise Noble explains, "The medical circulation and consumption of the human body is a part of a long and complex history.... The early modern English distributed and consumed as medicine the flesh and excretions of the human corpse."[27] Lady Grace Mildmay lists "mummia" as an ingredient for her recipe for the opiate "laudanum."[28] Given the early modern notion that sleep is the imitation of death, perhaps it is not surprising that a formula for an opiate might include the most direct form of a memento mori—remains from the corpse itself. Such usage of the human body was an accepted, if morbid, practice in the period. In *The Merry Wives of Windsor*, for example, Falstaff, commenting on his near-death experience in the river with the dirty laundry, jokes that he "should have been a mountain of mummy" (3.5.15).

The acquisition of human bodies, just as with newly killed bees, earthworms, snails, or lizards, required significant violence: "The most highly prized mummy was that from a fresh corpse, preferably a youth who had died a sudden and violent death, because of the widespread belief that a swift death captured the body's healing life force, while a slow death depleted it."[29] Although the majority of medicinal uses for human corpses are for humans, Margaret Baker's receipt book lists mummy in a recipe for a dog: "To make a pupy to growe noe more," includes "muma" along with "draggons blood" (which originates not from a dragon but from the sap of the *Dracaena draco*, or dragon tree) and instructions to whip the puppy and feed it only once a day.[30] This rather brutal treatment of a dog seems both awful and somewhat incomprehensible to this dog lover, but as Lisa Smith suggested to me, perhaps the recipe's purpose is to make a small and complacent lapdog. In this case, then, the "muma" would work to diminish rather than enhance the vitality of the puppy. And the vicious process functioned as a way to tame the animal into a pet, potentially one that would be cared for (at least I like to think so). Nevertheless, when we look at these various recipes, we can clearly see that the kitchen was indeed a theater of cruelty, but it was also a theater of trans-corporeality, in which all bodies, nonhuman and human, were deconstructed into base substance—in Hamlet's words, "the quintessence of dust" (2.2.298)—that transfers from one body to another.

Transcorporeal Exchange, or "so work the honeybees" (*Henry V*, 1.2.187)

Having gone down the transcorporeal path to mutual nonhuman and human death, I now step back and consider a more symbiotic transcorporeal relationship between humans and nonhumans—in particular, humans and bees. Though some recipes do call for bee bodies, as we have seen above, a much greater number of recipes list the bee's by-product, honey. The bee and its production of honey inspired great admiration in Thomas Moffett, who writes in his treatise, "Of all insects, Bees are the principal and are chiefly to be admired, being the only creature of that kinde, framed for nourishment of Man. But the rest are procreated to be useful in physick, or for delight of the eyes, the pleasure of the ears, or the compleating and ornament of the body: the Bee doth exceed them all in every one of these."[31] Certainly early modern humans benefited greatly from the bees and their production, but bees also benefited from the human-cultivated gardens and orchards in which they often lived. And the symbiosis between the garden and orchard and the bees goes much deeper, as bees both feed on and pollinate flowers; this fact, however, was not clearly known until the mid-eighteenth century.[32]

Nonetheless, bees and their hives constituted a living part of the early modern household infrastructure, its management and production, or what Lynnete Hunter and Sarah Hutton define as "oeconomics," which referred to the primary economic unit of the household and its contribution to the community.[33] Many early modern manuals specifically mention that beekeeping was linked to the household garden, an important productive location of any estate. In William Lawson's "The Husbandry of Bees," a section in his *A New Orchard and Garden* (1618), any housewife worth her salt must keep bees: "I will not account her any of my good Housewives, that wanteth eyther Bees or skilfulnesse about them." The placement of the bee skeps enables the bees to have easy access to their food source, but as most gardens were adjacent to the house, bees were also close to the human dwelling: "The first thing that a Gardiner about Bees must be carefull for, is a house. . . . Therefore you must have an house made a long time sure, dry wall in your Garden, neare, or in your Orchard, for Bees love flowers, and wood in their hearts."[34] Their nearness to the house is significant in that the bees and their hives are literally part of the domestic architecture, as their hives or woven skeps were often placed within recesses, or what are technically called "boles," in the garden walls. The advantage of such proximity is that the honey could be easily brought to the kitchen, where it would be kept for use by itself or processed in other concoctions, and the bees had ready access to carefully managed flower gardens and orchard trees. The by-product of honey, the combs or beeswax, would also be used in the household for candles or for sealants on bottles or jars. Both the honey and the wax, then, were employed as preservative agents in keeping the household goods that maintained the health of the family and its dependents. Bees thus were a significant part of the larger context of the domestic female sphere that produced food, medicine, and many household products, such as cosmetics and cleaning supplies. Further, more than any other insect, bees had a particularly close gendered symbiotic relationship with human females, as women often were the bee caretakers, the makers of bee products, and the principal consumers.

In speaking of gender, however, we should also consider the gender in the beehive, for it is in the seventeenth century that the gender of the central or monarchal bee was contested. Before Charles Butler wrote his 1609 treatise, the bee monarch was thought to be male and was thus referred to as the king; Butler nevertheless advanced the argument that the hive was governed by a "Feminine Monarchie."[35] Moffett, however, publishing his Latin treatise in 1634, still considered the monarch of the beehive to be male and therefore a king.[36] So whether seventeenth-century women were aware of it or not, the female-dominated kitchen space was interacting with and exchanging in direct transcorporeality with the female-dominated hive.

Of course, women were not the only humans who interacted with bees, but they did supervise what was needed for the household and therefore often directed the management of both kitchen and garden. The soil, the plants, the bees, and the women and their households worked together in mutual benefit: the soil and the plants fed each other through seasonal cycles; the bees fed on but also pollinated the fruit trees and flowers; the household consumed the bee honey, honey by-products, and the fruit, but they also enriched the soil, cultivated plants, and provided the bole homes for the bees. However, bees could and did exist outside the confines of the garden and therefore were not reliant completely on humans. The reverse was not, and is not, true. Humans need these lesser creatures to pollinate edible plants that flower, but the bees, like most other insects, could live quite happily and perhaps better without human intervention, especially given our current use of pesticides and herbicides that threatens the world's bee population.

Insect Trade or "By her high forehead and her scarlet lip" (*Romeo and Juliet* 2.1.18)

Bees, snails, flies, lizards, and worms were all easily obtainable domestic creatures that populated the recipes and the concoctions of the household closet, but the other most common insects were scale insects, imported from abroad. Insects therefore became part of the growing market that relied on colonial trade and the growing number of foreign commodities that made up the seventeenth-century shopping list. The recipes demonstrate how these insects comprise part of the larger project of imperial practices in the home.

The alkermes, kermes, or sometimes kermis berries (some thought them to be flora, not fauna) and the cochineal are scale insects, members of the superfamily Coccoidea, and were used for medicine and red dye. Native of the Mediterranean and the Far East, kermes or *vermiculus* (meaning small worm, from which is derived the word *vermilion*) was the most important animal dye of the Old World and had been used in English households throughout the Middle Ages.[37] Although used medicinally, kermes was primarily valued as vermilion or scarlet color dye, so desired by kings, cardinals, and the aristocracy. In the mid-sixteenth century, however, a more brilliant scarlet dye from the cochineal insects came onto the European market from the New World. First encountered in the 1520s by the Spanish in Mexico, the cochineal are parasites found on several related species of cacti in the New World. Franciscan friar Bernardino de Sahagún recorded Aztec use of the insect in *Historia General de las Cosas de Nueva España* (also known as the *Florentine Codex*), written between 1540 and 1585. By the 1550s, the Spanish were actively importing tons of dried cochineal in their flotillas that sailed from Mexico and Peru to Spain; from Spain, cochineal was primarily distributed to the rest of Europe by way of Amsterdam, the major trading hub for Spanish dye.[38] John Donne, writing in the early 1590s, makes references to English piracy of Spanish ships full of cochineal in his Satire 4: "As pirates which did know / That there came weak ships fraught with cochineal (188–89).[39] Donne's poem attests to the value that this small insect commanded in a world demanding the color red. Generally, we tend to think about Spanish colonial exploitative "trade" primarily in terms of gold and silver, and even plants, but the trade in insects was extensive. Spanish naturalist José de Acosta recorded that 5,677 *arrobas* (approximately 144,000 pounds or 72 tons) of cochineal, worth 283,750 pesos, was shipped from Lima to Spain in 1587.[40] By 1585, the English were already importing cochineal from Spain, mostly via Amsterdam; a trading directory from 1575 to 1585 mentions *quchinilla* "from southern Spain."[41] We can see by seventeenth-century receipt books the growing popularity of cochineal for household use.

Although cloth dye was the driving force behind the scale insect trade from the Mediterranean and the New World, both kermes and cochineal show up as valuable medicinal ingredients and coloring agents in household receipt books. The 1659 *Pharamacopoea Belgica* considers the insect's medicinal properties: Kermes "hot and dry, a good Cordiall, [and good at stopping] the Terms [menses]." This tome also supplies a recipe for "Confectio Kermis," which appears as an ingredient in household recipes.[42] The Granville manuscript also uses kermes in a recipe, "The Milk Cordial Water," a distillation of red cow's milk, snails, an assortment of herbs, and "alkarmes." The recipe does not specify what ailment it cures, though cordial waters (taking their name from the Latin for heart, *cor, cordis*) were generally used for issues having to do with the heart.[43] One might suppose in a Galenic worldview that the red from the kermis might be particularly invigorating to the heart. Rebeckah Winche includes kermes in a cosmetic recipe that appears to be a kind of rouge for cheeks or perhaps "scarlet lips," "The Lady Kents pouder," which also calls for crab eyes and claws (a known purplish dye), red coral, bezoar (*Lapis bezoar orientale*, an organic "stone" found in the intestines of Persian goats), pearl, and amber (fossilized tree resin).[44] These exotic ingredients are all organic, derived from non-human bodies or excretions, but the early modern recipe writer (and recipe maker), whether an aristocrat like Lady Kent or not, would be unlikely to forget that the ingredients come from plant or animal bodies (although it was not always clear whether the kermes and cochineal were berries or bugs). Because the rouge did not simply come from a store—already made up, packaged, and therefore divorced from its origins—the early modern housewife understood the value of these ingredients as nonhuman bodies, not separate in kind from the human body. Further, as topical cosmetic or ingestible medicine, insects along with other nonhuman bodies are absorbed into the human body, demonstrating the material connections that contemporary industrialized humans tend to deny or forget. As these insects and other lesser creatures were used specifically for cosmetics, they were chiefly acting on female bodies; thus the process of transcorporeality was often one that was gendered, not only because women were making the recipes but also because they were the prime consumers of them.

The American insect cochineal seems most often to be used as a colorant due to its superior brilliance and less well understood New World pharmacological properties. But color and health may not be completely separate aspects of this insect, as some medicinal recipes that include cochineal seem to have been used medicinally but also work aesthetically, making the concoction an appealing reddish color. For example, the anonymous receipt book W.b. 653 and the Granville manuscript include cochineal in recipes for bitters that includes bitter Seville oranges and gentian roots; the addition of cochineal would turn this orangish water a more vibrant and pleasing red. Most certainly Hannah Woolley's *Queen-Like Closet* (published in 1670) recipe, "To Candy Almonds to look as though they had their Shells on," makes clear that cochineal is to be used as a food dye: "Take Iordan Almonds and blanch them, then take fine Sugar, wet it with water, and boil it to a Candy height, colour it with Cochineal."[45] These Jordan almonds are not so very different from those that are produced today, as cochineal is still used as a colorant not only in these candies but also in a number of other red or pink foods that are labeled with "natural dyes," from frozen meats to jams.[46] Similarly, some cosmetic companies currently use cochineal—a much less toxic alternative to red dye 40, a known carcinogen, for example—in their makeup.[47]

The multiple ways in which humans have interacted with the cochineal as well as other insects and lesser creatures—wearing their color on garments, coloring skin with their pigment, and consuming their bodies as dye, medicine, food, or drink—demonstrate the permeability of the human body—in essence, our embedded transcorporeality that is shared with nonhumans. Of course, this viewpoint may seem anthropocentric—as humans predominantly "use" these nonhumans for their own benefit—and this is true in our disconnected industrialized society. But the early moderns who dealt directly with nonhumans, such as the recipe writers and makers, had a greater understanding of transcorporeal exchange. The use of insects and lesser creatures works only as a kind of borrowing that will be paid back in full post mortem: in the end, humans are food for worms. The modern practice of embalming bodies is one of the greatest robberies we perpetrate on these miniature faunas, as we refuse to allow our bodies to return to primal matter and instead poison the ground with lethal chemicals. In the next few decades, with the looming population explosion, we may have no choice but to eat insects, but we should also remember to pay back the favor by returning our (unembalmed) bodies to the insects and the earth. This gesture may seem insignificant in the face of large-scale industrial pollution, but perhaps this one small act may change the way we see ourselves in correlation with nonhumans: as transcorporeal beings whose mutual welfare is inextricably bound.

Notes

1. Huis et al., *Edible Insects*, ix.
2. Dicke, "Why Not Eat Insects?"
3. Mishan, "Why Aren't We."
4. Laroche, "Roses in Winter," 52.
5. Baker, "Receipt Book," 42, 43.
6. Albala, *Eating Right*, 65. For a good explanation of the Galenic humors as they relate to food and medicine, see chapter 2.
7. Hoby, *Private Life*.
8. The Wellcome Library and the Folger Shakespeare Library have a great number of receipt books, now available digitally. The Early Modern Recipe Online Collective (EMROC) runs a digital humanities project whose aim is to transcribe one hundred receipt books in the next five years. To learn more about EMROC, visit the website: https://emroc.hypotheses.org. Most of the receipt books I have cited in this chapter are part of the EMROC project.
9. Leong, "Making Medicines," 146.
10. Alaimo, *Exposed*, 77.
11. Rebecca Laroche and Jennifer Munroe also discuss Alaimo's term *transcorporeality* in relation to early modern ideas about pests, especially in chapter 2 of *Shakespeare and Ecofeminist Theory*.
12. Gatens, *Imaginary Bodies*, 110, quoted in Alaimo, *Exposed*, 28.
13. Yates, "Shakespeare's Messmates," 131; Haraway, *When Species Meet*.
14. Yates, "Shakespeare's Messmates," 183.
15. Winche, "Receipt Book," 80; Granville, "Granville Family Receipt Book," 203.
16. Nakazawa, "Traditional Medicine."
17. Field, "Many hands hands," 85. For more about "Probatum est," see chapter 5 of Wall, *Recipes for Thought*.
18. For an explanation of the complexities of the closet in the early modern period, see Herbert, *Female Alliances*, 83–85.
19. Castleton, "Receit Booke," 6–7.
20. Harti et al., "Effectiveness," 76. I mention that this study is done by an all-female team of researchers from Indonesia because I think it is significant that women are doing this work with traditional medicines.
21. Cooper and Roch, "Capacities of Earthworms."
22. Catchmay, "Booke of Medicens," 184.
23. Fanshawe, "Mrs. Fanshawe's," 74. This recipe also calls for four ounces of flies, but I would imagine that these would be dead, since it would be rather difficult to collect the live variety and put them in the recipe. Sometimes practicality seems to overrule the preference for live nonhumans in the recipes.
24. For example, Fumerton and Hunt discuss in their introduction the gleeful torture of plucking and then slowly roasting a goose alive to garner the greatest flavor, which is described in John Wecker's *Secrets of Nature* (published in Latin 1582; translated into English 1660); see *Renaissance Culture*, 2.
25. The term "theater of cruelty" in the context of the kitchen comes from Goldstein. Wall, *Staging Domesticity*, 3; Goldstein, "Woolley's Mouse," 106.
26. Winche, "Receipt Book," 63.
27. Noble, *Medicinal Cannibalism*, 1.
28. I thank Elaine Leong and Lisa Smith for drawing my attention to Richard Sugg's important work, *Mummies, Cannibals, and Vampires*. The information about Mildmay is on p. 82.

29. Noble, *Medicinal Cannibalism*, 2.
30. Baker, "Receipt Book," 43.
31. Moffett, *Theater of Insects*, 889.
32. Grant, "Arthur Dobbs."
33. Hunter and Hutton, *Women, Science, and Medicine*, 2.
34. Lawson, *New Orchard*, 19–20.
35. Butler, *Feminine Monarchie*.
36. Moffett, *Insectorum*, 4; Moffett, *Theater of Insects*, 892.
37. Donkin, "Spanish Red," 9–10. This is the most extensive study of cochineal.
38. Phipps, *Cochineal Red*, 14, 27–28.
39. Donne, *Complete Poems*, 411.
40. Acosta, *Historia*, 183.
41. Donkin, "Spanish Red," 39; Tawney and Power, *Tudor Economic Documents*, 3:202.
42. *Pharmacopoea Belgica*, 26, 92.
43. Granville, "Granville Family Receipt Book," 184.
44. Winche, "Receipt Book," 31.
45. Wolley, *Queen-Like Closet*, 97.
46. http://www.nicoletta.co.za/shop/nicoletta-speciality-coated-nuts-and-treats/pastel-mix-candy-coated-almonds/. For a list of other foods that use cochineal as a colorant, see Flinn, "Natural Colors."
47. Curran, "Food Dyes."

Bibliography

Acosta, José de. *Historia Natural y Moral de las Indias*. Mexico City: Fondo de Cultura Económica, 1962.

Alaimo, Stacy. *Exposed: Environmental Politics and Pleasures in Posthuman Times*. Minneapolis: University of Minnesota Press, 2016.

Albala, Ken. *Eating Right in the Renaissance*. Berkeley: University of California Press, 2002.

Baker, Margaret. "Receipt Book of Margaret Baker, V.A.619." Folger Shakespeare Library, c.1675.

Butler, Charles. *The Feminine Monarchie or A Treatise Concerning Bees, and the Due Ordering of Them Wherein the Truth, Found Out by Experience and Diligent Observation, Discovereth the Idle and Fondd Conceipts, Which Many Haue Written Anent This Subiect*. Oxford: Ioseph Barnes, 1609.

Castleton, Lady Grace. "Receit Booke, V.A. 600." Folger Shakespeare Library, 17th century.

Catchmay, Lady Frances. "A Booke of Medicens Ms 184a." Wellcome Library, ca. 1625.

Cooper, Edwin L., and Philippe Roch. "The Capacities of Earthworms to Heal Wounds and to Destroy Allografts Are Modified by Polychlorinated Biphenyls (Pcb)." *Journal of Invertebrate Pathology* 60, no. 1 (1992): 59–63.

Curran, Laurel. "Food Dyes Linked to Cancer, ADHD, Allergies." *Food Safety News*, July 8, 2010. http://www.foodsafetynews.com/2010/07/popular-food-dyes-linked-to-cancer-adhd-and-allergies/#.WEIGKHeZOCQ.

Dicke, Marcel. "Why Not Eat Insects?" TEDGlobal, July 2010. Video. http://www.ted.com/talks/marcel_dicke_why_not_eat_insects?language=en#t-97579.

Donkin, R. A. "Spanish Red: An Ethnogeographical Study of Cochineal and the Opuntia Cactus." *Transactions of the American Philosophical Society* 67, no. 5 (1977): 1–84.

Donne, John. *The Complete Poems of John Donne*. Edited by Robin Robbins. New York: Routledge, 2013.

Fanshawe, Lady Ann. "Mrs. Fanshawe's Book of Receipts." Wellcome Library, 1651–1680.

Field, Catherine. "'Many hands hands': Early Modern Englishwomen's Recipe Books and the Writing of Food, Politics, and the Self." PhD diss., University of Maryland, 2006.

Flinn, Angel. "Natural Colors—Carmine & Cochineal." Gentle World: For the

Vegan in Everyone, December 14, 2010. http://gentleworld.org/natural-colors-carmine-cochineal/.

Fumerton, Patricia, and Simon Hunt, eds. *Renaissance Culture and the Everyday*. Philadelphia: University of Pennsylvania Press, 1999.

Gatens, Moira. *Imaginary Bodies: Ethics, Power, and Corporeality*. New York: Routledge, 1996.

Goldstein, David B. "Woolley's Mouse: Early Modern Recipe Books and the Uses of Nature." In *Ecofeminist Approaches to Early Modernity*, edited by Jennifer Munroe and Rebecca Laroche, 105–27. New York: Palgrave Macmillan, 2011.

Grant, Verne. "Arthur Dobbs (1750) and the Discovery of the Pollination of Flowers by Insects." *Bulletin of the Torrey Botanical Society* 76, no. 3 (1949): 217–19.

Granville, Mary. "Granville Family Receipt Book." Folger Shakespeare Library, 1640–1750.

Haraway, Donna J. *When Species Meet*. Minneapolis: University of Minnesota Press, 2008.

Harti, Agnes Sri, Dwi Sulisetyawati, Atiek Murharyati, and Meri Oktariani. "The Effectiveness of Snail Slime and Chitosan in Wound Healing." *International Journal of Pharma Medicine and Biological Sciences* 5, no. 1 (2016): 76–80.

Herbert, Amanda. *Female Alliances: Gender, Identity and Friendship in Early Modern Britain*. New Haven: Yale University Press, 2014.

Hoby, Margaret. *The Private Life of an Elizabethan Lady: The Diary of Lady Margaret Hoby, 1599–1605*. Thrupp, UK: Sutton, 1998.

Huis, Arnold van, Joost Van Itterbeeck, Harmke Clunder, Esther Mertens, Afton Halloran, Guilia Muir, and Paul Vantomme. *Edible Insects: Future Prospects for Food and Feed Security*. FAO Forestry Paper 171. Rome: Food and Agriculture Organization of the United Nations, 2013.

Hunter, Lynette, and Sarah Hutton, eds. *Women, Science and Medicine: 1500–1700*. Thrupp, UK: Sutton, 1997.

Laroche, Rebecca. "Roses in Winter: Recipe Ecologies and Shakespeare's Sonnets." In *Ecological Approaches to Early Modern English Texts: A Field Guide to Reading and Teaching*, edited by Jennifer Munroe, Edward J. Geisweidt, and Lynne Bruckner. Farnham, UK: Ashgate 2015.

Laroche, Rebecca, and Jennifer Munroe. *Shakespeare and Ecofeminist Theory*. London: Bloomsbury, 2017.

Lawson, William. *A New Orchard and Garden . . . With the Country Housewives Garden*. London, 1618.

Leong, Elaine. "Making Medicines in the Early Modern Household." *Bulletin of the History of Medicine* 82, no. 1 (2008): 145–68.

Mishan, Ligaya. "Why Aren't We Eating More Insects?" *New York Times Style Magazine*, September 9, 2018.

Moffett, Thomas. *Insectorum sive Minimorum Animalium*. London: T. Cotes, 1634.

———. *The Theater of Insects: or, Lesser Living Creatures*. In *The History of Four-Footed Beasts and Serpents*, by Edward Topsell. London, 1658.

Nakazawa, Giove. "Traditional Medicine in the Treatment of Enteroparasitosis." *Revista Gastroenterología Peru* 16, no. 3 (1996): 197–202.

Noble, Louise. *Medicinal Cannibalism in Early Modern English Literature and Culture*. New York: Palgrave Macmillan, 2011.

Pharmacopoea Belgica; or, The Dutch Dispensatory. London: E.C., 1659.

Phipps, Elena. *Cochineal Red: The Art History of a Color*. New York: Metropolitan Museum of Art, 2010.

"Receipt Book, Egerton 2608." British Library, 17th century.

Rozin, P., and A. E. Fallon. "A Perspective on Disgust." *Psychological Review* 94, no. 1 (1985): 23–41.

Shakespeare, William. *The Norton Shakespeare*, edited by Stephen Greenblatt, Walter Cohen, Jean E. Howard, and Katharine Eisaman Maus. New York: Norton, 1997.

Sugg, Richard. *Mummies, Cannibals and Vampires: The History of Corpse Medicine from the Renaissance to the Victorians*. London: Routledge, 2011.

Tawney, R. H., and Eileen Power. *Tudor Economic Documents*. London: Longman, Green, 1924.

Wall, Wendy. *Recipes for Thought: Knowledge and Taste in the Early Modern English Kitchen*. Philadelphia: University of Pennsylvania Press, 2016.

———. *Staging Domesticity: Household Work and English Identity in Early Modern Drama*. Cambridge: Cambridge University Press, 2002.

Winche, Rebeckah. "Receipt Book." Folger Shakespeare Library, 1666.

Wolley, Hannah. *The Queen-Like Closet; or, Rich Cabinet*. London: R. Lowndes, 1670.

Yates, Julian. "Shakespeare's Messmates." In *Culinary Shakespeare: Staging Food and Drink in Early Modern England*, edited by David B. Goldstein and Amy L. Tigner, 179–98. Pittsburgh: Duquesne University Press, 2016.

CHAPTER 7
DECOMPOSE
Worm Work

Frances E. Dolan

This is a tale of two worms, one maligned as a consumer and destroyer and the other idealized as a paragon of both industry and artistry. One was associated with the lowly element it grubbed around in and, it was thought, ate up, and undermined. The other was associated with the gossamer luxury fabric it spun. Our protagonists are the earthworm and the silkworm. Theirs is an early modern story; the meanings assigned to these opposites, and the hopes and fears pinned to them, are specific to that period. They are also central players in two distinctly early modern English projects: the revival of soil amendment and composting and the attempt to establish a silk industry in colonial Virginia. Proponents of soil amendment did not recognize the earthworm as an ally in their project; proponents of the silk industry idealized the heroic (and chaste!) silkworm.

Numerous seventeenth-century English texts make the case for amending soil. They do so by promoting it as both old and new, as was so often the case with proposals for agricultural improvement in the period. For example, Gervase Markham's *The Inrichment of the Weald of Kent* (1649), a guide to "the true Ordering, Manuring, & Inriching of all the Grounds not only in Kent but in all of England," which went through numerous editions, argues that soil amendment is "not now newly discovered, but was the ancient practice of our forefathers many yeares agoe." Nevertheless, the practice had fallen into disuse by the time that Markham wrote and so needed to be "newly born and revived, rather than restored," in part through treatises on composting and soil amendment, which proliferate in the seventeenth century.[1] Proposals for amending soil emerged not only through observation and experimentation but also through research. Joan Thirsk traces the seventeenth-century vogue for composting to "one pregnant sentence" in Columella's first-century Latin treatise *De Re Rustica*, translated as *Of Husbandry*. This sentence proposes that those who do not keep animals, and so have the benefit of their manure, may gather "ashes and dirt of the kennels, sinks, and common sewers, straw, and stubble, and the other things that are swept out of the house" and ripen them in a "pit" to create a substitute for manure and an invaluable amendment for soil.[2]

In many ways, the composting that Columella and seventeenth-century writers such as Markham describe seems recognizable to us. It depends on wide-ranging collection, a dedicated spot or pit, careful management of moisture and heat, and patient waiting. Early modern writers understand that the compost pit performs the function of an animal's digestion, breaking down components and preventing the germination of seeds, for example. But they do not understand the role of microbial activity or of worms. Today, earthworms are the heroes of the compost pile; composters promote worms' beneficent and collective industry through "worm farms" and vermiculture. Writing in 1947, Albert Howard, sometimes called the father of compost, advised that "Nature has her own labour force—ants, termites, and above all earthworms. These carry the humus down to the required deeper levels where the thrusting roots can have access to it." Howard celebrates "the lowly earthworm" as "the great conditioner of the food materials for healthy crops." Earthworms "are actively at work," and their work is a productive form of consumption: "Actually the earthworm eats of the humus and of the soil and passes them through its body, leaving behind the casts which are really enriched earth—perfectly conditioned for the use of plants."[3] More recently, geologist David Montgomery, in his history of soil erosion and his proposals for soil regeneration, emphasizes the agency of worms: "Worms are like tiny livestock, eating organic matter and fertilizing a farmer's field. We need them there, wellfed and happy. Plowing is like setting off a bomb in their living room, first destroying their homes and then, when the bare soil at the surface has turned into a water-resistant crust, drying up their water well."[4] Regenerative agriculture, or agroecology, is sometimes called "ditching the plow," and Montgomery makes it clear here that one must ditch the plow to save the worms. One impediment to ditching the plow is its long history of standing as the crucial engine of agriculture and symbol of human dominion and civilization. The plow's ability to disrupt and destroy worm habitat and activity is one of the things that endeared it to early modern farmers and writers because they sought to eliminate rather than promote earthworms.

The idea that worm work produces soil is a relatively recent one. Late in his life, Charles Darwin wrote one last book, *Formation of Vegetable Mould Through the Actions of Worms with Observations on Their Habits* (1881). Depicting worms' digestion as productive, Darwin insisted that "all the vegetable mould over the whole country has passed many times through, and will again pass many times through, the intestinal canal of worms." Darwin's worms were workers, ploughmen, and historical agents: "It may be doubted whether there are many other animals which have played so important a part in the history of the world, as have these lowly organized creatures," he wrote. According to David Montgomery, Darwin was perceived as "a fool obsessed with the idea that the work of worms could ever amount to anything."[5] Nevertheless, while Darwin was wrong about some aspects of soil life, he was right about the crucial role of worms. For Jane Bennett, Darwin's ability to recognize the "small agencies" of worms and their big "accumulated effects" is an important chapter in the history of vital matter or the political ecology of things.[6]

Early modern writers recognized the earthworm as an effective agent. But they insisted worm work was destructive. The Book of Common Prayer funeral service reminded believers that humans must return to the dust from which they came, and vernacular and elite jesting and eloquent descriptions of decomposition assigned worms a role in that return. Although putrefaction had long been understood as generative, worms were not seen as agents in that spontaneous generation.[7] Their subterranean industry, it was thought, consumed and contaminated but did not produce. They were widely maligned as threats to health and agriculture, as Ian MacInnes has shown.[8] They were the farmer's adversaries rather than allies, underminers of agriculture rather than creators of its very foundation.

Thomas Moffett, for example, understands the earthworm as a consumer rather than producer of soil: "They breed of the slime of the earth, taking their first being from putrefaction, and of the fat moisture of the same earth they are again fed and nourished, and into earth at last are resolved." They might then be considered analogues of the human, bred of dirt and resolving back into it. But while Moffett is quick to find uses for earthworms as fish bait and ingredients in medicines, his assessment is largely negative. Since worms appear to be full of earth, Moffett opines that they eat it rather than excrete it. Observing that "earth-worms are not to be found in all soils alike, as in barren, sandy, stony, hard, and bare grounds, but only in fat, gravelly, moist, clammy and fertile," he thinks they are drawn to the fertile rather than helping to produce it.[9] In Moffett's account, the only valuable work worms do is helping humans to foretell rain.

Early modern recipes for compost do not advocate promoting earthworms. Instead, agriculture and gardening manuals offer suggestions on how to eliminate them as pests. John Maplet so consistently links worms to destructive eating that he calls moths "our Garment worme." Leonard Mascall, in *The Countrymans Recreation* (1640), advises that when one is planting fruit trees, "If there be wormes in the fat Earth or Dung, that ye put about your roots, ye must mingle it well also with the dung of Oxen or Kine, or flekt Sope-ashes about the Roote, which will make the wormes to dye, for otherwise they will hurt greatly the Rootes." *The Expert Gardener*, appended to this text, offers "divers remedies to destroy . . . Earth-wormes . . . and other Vermine," all "faithfully collected out of sundry Dutch and French Authors."[10] Markham's *Farewell to Husbandry* (1649) warns that worms, "being as it were the main citizens within the earth, are so innumerable, that the losse which is bred by them is infinite." They are "a secret hurtful vermine which is so innumerable, and lies so much concealed."[11] Seventeenth-century writers, then, had no problem imagining the "small agencies" of earthworms. They could even see them as citizens of the earth, incalculably effective but not to the good. Secret agents, early modern earthworms were not productive workers.

In contrast, the silkworm was an industry, a much-promoted colonial start-up, routinely called "silk-work." As is well known, James I loathed tobacco, which rapidly established itself as Jamestown's cash crop. He tried (unsuccessfully) to establish two other industries to compete with it, wine and silk.[12] Both proposed to capitalize on plants native to Virginia: the grapevines that every promotional account of Virginia describes as climbing up the trees and over the ground, and the Mulberry trees, some of which were already occupied by silkworms. In an attempt to launch these new industries, James and the Virginia Company sent experts, how-to books, and plant starts to Virginia, since the native plants (grapes and mulberries) that inspired these projects were quickly found wanting. Twice the king also sent "Silke-wormes seed of his owne store," since the first shipment "miscarried."[13] The texts sent to Virginia included John Bonoeil's *Observations to Be Followed, for the Making of Fit Roomes, to Keepe Silk-Wormes In* (1620) and, two years later, *His Majesties Gracious Letter to the Earle of South-hampton Treasurer, and to the Councell and Company of Virginia Heere: Commanding the Present Setting up of Silke-Works, and Planting of Vines in Virginia*. The first text promises "another booke which is to be printed" and does not really promote the silk industry so much as give detailed instructions for how to get on with "the ground-worke of the business." In an epistle at the front of the second book, *His Majesties Gracious Letter*, Bonoeil's fuller account of how to establish silk works, the Earl of Southampton explains that the Virginia Company is sending "store" of this text, "to bee dispersed over the whole Colony, to every Master of a Family one."[14] By the time Samuel Hartlib published his *A Rare and New Discovery . . . For the Feeding of Silk-Worms in the Woods* in 1651, he lamented not only that Bonoeil's text was insufficiently detailed but that the books had become "but few, wholly out of print, and very much desired."[15] This enormous, if failed, effort to promote silk works in Virginia enjoined the reader to industry (while downplaying how much work would actually be involved) and set the silkworm up as a model of this industry.

Moffett's lengthy verse appreciation of the silkworm preceded James's plan for establishing silk works in Virginia. In 1599, Moffett's *The Silkewormes, and Their Flies*, dedicated to Mary Sidney, begins in wonder at the remarkable power of "these almost thingles things." The primary question for Moffett's poem is how the silkworms acquired their skill: "What Artist taught their feete to spinne and weave: / What workman made their slime a robe for kings?"[16] Subsequent appreciations also celebrated the worms' artistry. While Bonoeil's didactic treatises focused on the details of preparing for the arrival of the seed worms, sent to swell the population of indigenous worms, and on the details of establishing silk works, later writers waxed eloquent about the worms as themselves model workers. Edward Williams describes "this admirable and natural Weaver" and "this profitable and industrious Spinner." He also recommends protection from heat and disturbance, so that nothing can disturb "the Worme in his curious operations." For Williams, the silkworm is not just a worker but an artist: "There is nothing in the world more proper then this curious atome of Nature the Silkeworme: to see this untaught Artist spin out his transparent bowels, labour such a monument out of his owne intralls, as may be the shame, the blush of Artists, such a Robe that Solomon in all his glory might confesse the meannesse of his apparell, in relation to the workemen, cannot but bring them to admiration."[17]

An account such as Williams's makes it possible for Margaret Cavendish to invoke the silkworm as a model for her own artistic process just a few years later: "Yet I must say this in the behalf of my thoughts, that I never found them idle; for if the senses bring no work in, they will work of themselves, like silkworms that spins out of their own bowels."[18] In contrast to the bee, proverbial for gathering, collecting, and transforming, the silkworm, Williams and Cavendish insist, creates wholly out of itself.[19] For Cavendish, this is an image of a solitary creativity, one that does not depend on external stimulation or nourishment. Yet the treatises describing sericulture, which became a gendered form of productivity, as Allison Bigelow has shown, suggest that silkworms needed a very particular diet as well as controlled circumstances.[20] What's more, this image that so appealed to Cavendish is an excremental one of artistic production. The earthworm's excrements or castings are essential to soil rejuvenation, although early moderns did not understand this. But praise for the silkworm dwells on its miraculous "bowels" and "entrails" and the gossamer slime they produce. While other fibers had to be spun, the silkworm presents thread ready to use. The contrast between source and product is part of the miracle of silk work. As one treatise dedicated to James I reminds the reader, "This Worme one of the abjects creatures of the world is ordained of God to clothe Kings and Princes."[21]

Itself a model of industry, the silkworm then makes just the right kind of work for human laborers who are otherwise compromised in one way or another. Hartlib's *A Rare and New Discovery*, as well as his retitled second edition, *The Reformed Virginian Silk-Worm* (1655), which present the fruits of Virginia Ferrar's experiments with silkworms, praise the silkworm not just as a superworker but as a creator of work in others. The work is attractive, Hartlib assures the reader, because it is so light that natives, children, and ladies can do it and thereby achieve what Bigelow describes as "the spiritual and economic joys of dignified work."[22]

At the end of Hartlib's *The Reformed Virginian Silk-Worm*, he offers a poem, "Homo Vermis" (Worm Man), which reminds readers that "wee all are creeping Worms of th' earth." Early modern naturalists justified their attention to "lesser life" by such analogies. To say that humans are "creeping earthworms" is to remind us of our fallen nature and our mortality, our affinity to filth, decay, lowliness, and corruption. But whatever work the earthworm does as a memento mori does not earn it much esteem. If, as Moffett's poem avers, "in smallest things that greatest wonders bee," this admiration focused on the silkworm, a model of how humans could improve their status and prospects through industry.[23] Only the winged creature, with its "worm story" of transformation, profit, and distinction, and its production of the garments that distinguished kings from peasants, earned recognition and admiration for its work. Associated with height, flight, metamorphosis, production, luxury, and profit, the silkworm modeled metamorphosis and uplift. In contrast, the earthworm would wait centuries to earn recognition as a worker and one on whose labors human societies depend far more than they do on silk work. However invested in soil amendment early moderns were, their quest to improve their soils was hampered by what they not only did not know but by the ways that their cultural associations with the earthworm impeded their knowledge and their observation, making it impossible to imagine the lowly and dirty worm as a central agent in creating fertile soils.

Notes

1. Markham, *Markhams Farewell*, sig. B2r–v, B3.
2. Thirsk, "Making a Fresh Start," 22. The quotation is from Columella, "Several Kinds of Dung," 91. On composting, see Dolan, "Compost/Compositions" and other essays in *Ground-Work*; and Dolan, *Digging the Past*, 14–44.
3. Howard, *Soil and Health*, 28, 29, 74.
4. Montgomery, *Growing a Revolution*, 103.
5. Darwin, 13, *Formation of Vegetable Mould*, 276–77; Montgomery, *Dirt*, 10–13.
6. Bennett, *Vibrant Matter*, 96.
7. Steel, "Creeping Things."

8. MacInnes, "Politic Worm." Even the work of worms as parasites is now being rethought. Studies that link soil health to the health of the human biome emphasize the work worms do for the soil and the human gut. Daphne Miller, for instance, argues that "geohelminths, worms that live as happily in the soil as they do in the human or animal gastrointestinal tract . . . tend to act like many other farm microbes, releasing protective substances and stimulating a counterregulatory, anti-inflammatory response. In other words, the worm and host are involved in a long conversation and are working for mutual benefit, since the worm is able to live indefinitely within the human intestine and the host gets a boost in immunity" (*Farmacology*, 79).
9. Moffett, *Theater of Insects*, 811, 812. On Moffett and the genesis of this text, see Harkness, *Jewel House*, 27.
10. Maplet, *Greene Forest*, sig. N6r; Mascall, *Countrymans Recreation*, sig. H2r.
11. Markham, *Markhams Farewell*, sig. H4v-5r.
12. Of silk works in particular, James hoped that colonists would "rather bestow their travel [travail or labor] in compassing this rich and solid Commodity, then in that of Tobacco; which besides much unnecessary expence, brings with it many disorders and inconveniences" (Bonoeil, *His Majesties Gracious Letter*, sig. A3v).
13. *Declaration of the State*, 11.
14. Bonoeil, *Observations*, esp. sig. C3v; Southampton, "To the Governour," in Bonoeil, *His Majesties Gracious Letter*, sig. (a)1v.
15. Hartlib, *Rare and New Discovery*, Epistle to the "Ingennous Reader."
16. Moffett, *Silkewormes*, sig. B1r.
17. W[illiams], *Virginia in Generall*, 3:30, 37, 38.
18. Cavendish, "True Relation," 59.
19. On apian metaphors, see, among others, Smyth, *Autobiography*, 132.
20. Bigelow, "Gendered Language." This essay is an invaluable account of the Ferrar family and the texts it produced, as well as the provenance and diction of other texts about sericulture.
21. Serres, *Perfect Use of Silke-Worms*, sig. K3v. On the dependence of fallen beings on animals for their clothing, see Shannon, *Accommodated Animal*, 127-73.
22. Bigelow, "Gendered Language," 272. Bigelow documents that illustrations and promotional texts described silk work as "light and easy" and thus suited to women, despite the fact that it was grueling, labor intensive, and required considerable skill, patience, and effort (292, 300).
23. "Homo Vermis," in Hartlib, *Reformed Virginian Silk-Worm*, sig. F2v; Moffett, *The Silkewormes*, sig. F2r.

Bibliography

Bennett, Jane. *Vibrant Matter: A Political Ecology of Things*. Durham: Duke University Press, 2010.

Bigelow, Allison Margaret. "Gendered Language and the Science of Colonial Silk." *Early American Literature* 49, no. 2 (2014): 271-325.

Bonoeil, John. *His Majesties Gracious Letter to the Earle of South-hampton, Treasurer, and to the Councell and Company of Virginia Heere: Commanding the Present Setting up of Silke-Works, and Planting of Vines in Virginia*. London, 1622.

———. *Observations to Be Followed, for the Making of Fit Roomes, to Keepe Silk-Wormes In*. 1620.

Cavendish, Margaret. "A True Relation of My Birth, Breeding, and Life." In *Paper Bodies: A Margaret Cavendish Reader*, edited by Sylvia Bowerbank and Sara Mendelson. Peterborough, ON: Broadview, 2000.

Columella, L. Junius Moderatus. "Of the Several Kinds of Dung." In *Of Husbandry*, book 2. London, 1745.

Darwin, Charles. *Formation of Vegetable Mould Through the Actions of Worms with Observations on Their Habits*. London: John Murray, 1881.

A Declaration of the State of the Colonie and Affaires in Virginia . . . By His Maiesties Counseil for Virginia. London, 1620.

Dolan, Frances E. "Compost/Compositions." In *Ground-Work: English Renaissance Literature and Soil Science*, edited by Hillary Eklund. Pittsburgh, PA: Duquesne University Press, 2017.

———. *Digging the Past: How and Why to Imagine Seventeenth-Century Agriculture*. Philadelphia: University of Pennsylvania Press, 2020.

Harkness, Deborah. *The Jewel House: Elizabethan London and the Scientific Revolution*. New Haven: Yale University Press, 2007.

Hartlib, Samuel. *A Rare and New Discovery . . . For the Feeding of Silk-worms in the Woods*. London, 1651.

———. *The Reformed Virginian Silk-Worm*. London, 1655.

Howard, Albert. *The Soil and Health: A Study of Organic Agriculture*. Lexington: University Press of Kentucky, 2006.

MacInnes, Ian. "The Politic Worm: Invertebrate Life in the Early Modern English Body." In *The Indistinct Human in Renaissance Literature*, edited by Jean E. Feerick and Vin Nardizzi, 253–73. London: Palgrave Macmillan, 2012.

Maplet, John. *A Greene Forest, or A Naturall Historie*. London, 1567.

Markham, Gervase. *Markhams Farewell to Husbandry: Or, the Enriching of All Sorts of Barren and Sterile Grounds in Our Kingdome, to Be as Fruitfull in All Manner of Graine, Pulse and Grasse, as the Best Grounds Whatsoever*. London, 1649.

Mascall, Leonard. *The Countrymans Recreation*. London, 1640.

Miller, Daphne. *Farmacology: Total Health from the Ground Up*. New York: Morrow, 2013.

Moffett, Thomas. *The Silkewormes, and Their Flies*. London, 1599.

———. *The Theater of Insects; or, Lesser Living Creatures*. In *The History of Four-Footed Beasts and Serpents*, by Edward Topsell. London, 1658.

Montgomery, David R. *Dirt: The Erosion of Civilizations*. Berkeley: University of California Press, 2012.

———. *Growing a Revolution: Bringing Our Soil Back to Life*. London: Norton, 2017.

Serres, Olivier de. *The Perfect Use of Silke-Worms and Their Benefit*. Translated by Nicholas Geffe. London, 1607.

Shannon, Laurie. *The Accommodated Animal: Cosmopolity in Shakespearean Locales*. Chicago: University of Chicago Press, 2013.

Smyth, Adam. *Autobiography in Early Modern England*. Cambridge: Cambridge University Press, 2010.

Southampton, Henry. "The Treasurour Councell and Company of Virginia, To The Governour and Councell of State in Virginia residing." In John Bonoeil, *His Majesties Gracious Letter*. Sigs. a1r–a2r.

Steel, Karl. "Creeping Things: Spontaneous Generation and Material Creativity." In *Elemental Ecocriticism: Thinking with Earth, Air, Water, and Fire*, edited by Jeffrey Jerome Cohen and Lowell Duckert, 209–36. Minneapolis: University of Minnesota Press, 2015.

Thirsk, Joan. "Making a Fresh Start: Sixteenth-Century Agriculture and the Classical Inspiration." In *Culture and Cultivation in Early Modern England: Writing and the Land*, edited by Michael Leslie and Timothy Raylor, 15–34. Leicester, UK: Leicester University Press, 1992.

W[illiams], E[dward]. *Virginia in Generall, but the South Part Therof, Richly and Truly Valued, viz.: the Fertile Carolana, and the No Lesse Excellent Isle of Roanoak*. London, 1650. In *Tracts and Other Papers, Relating Principally to the Origin, Settlement, and Progress of the Colonies in North America, from the Discovery of the Country to the Year 1776*, by Peter Force. 3 vols. Gloucester, MA: Peter Smith, 1963.

CHAPTER 8
LOCOMOTION
Creeping and Crawling

Keith Botelho

And God said, Let us make man in our image, after our likeness: and let them have dominion over the fish of the sea, and over the fowl of the air, and over the cattle, and over all the earth, and over every creeping thing that creepeth upon the earth.
—GENESIS 1:26

It was the Hexbug that initially got me thinking about insect locomotion. These autonomous toy bugs were released by the US company Innovation First late in the first decade of the twenty-first century. Each microrobotic creature mimics the movements of various insects (spiders, beetles, and the like), and the accounts of their movements described on their website are enough to give anyone the creepy-crawlies:

> The Scarab "is a high-speed, mechanical beetle-like robotic bug that **skitters** around on six angled legs;" "**propels** itself forwards and backwards, and is capable of popping from its back to its feet if placed upside down" and its legs and speed "make it easy for it to **scurry** away from obstacles in its path and flip over

if caught on its back"; the XL version "can move **super-fast or creepy slow**—guaranteed to give anyone a good spook!"

The Nano, a "micro insect," is said to "behave like a real bug" and is described as "**scaling** up tubes, around corners, and across the floor;—"a micro robotic creature that uses the physics of vibration to propel forward and explore its environment. . . . The industrious critter **traverses** the ground beneath it and quickly **navigates** through the most complex mazes. Possessing an uncanny sense of balance, it can even flip to its feet and zoom forward when turned on its back! When coming into contact with an object in its path, the energetic insect will switch directions and scurry away on a new path due to its persistent random behavior."

The Beetle "will travel in a straight line until it hits an object in its path, or hears a loud noise. Upon contact or noise, the bug reverses in a half circle, then moves forward again in a new direction." A "micro robotic creature that **crawls** around sensing objects in its path" that you can "watch as it **scurries** away."[1]

I have seven of these creatures currently on my desk as I write, and I turned each of them on to observe and handle. They truly seem to have a mind of their own, navigating one another with their antennas, bumping into the laptop, rerouting without hesitation. One twelve-legged bug even managed to escape under a mound of assorted notes and papers, vibrating and moving every which way. Collectively, these bugs on the desk of various shapes and sizes do in fact reinforce the notion that these are untamed creatures, moving in ways that are decidedly *not* human. The company boasts that the fascinating, animated behavior of these microcreatures fools animals and humans into thinking they are alive. When they are picked up, they even vibrate and crawl in the palm of your hand and occasionally flip over by themselves unprovoked, and you have the feeling that left unattended, they would indeed creep over your entire body.

Laurie Shannon, speaking of quadruped locomotion, points out the striking difference between such animals and human uprightness or erectness: "While we are anchored, looking up to contemplate the heavens, they run around, ignoring boundaries and escaping our grip."[2] If this acknowledgment of difference in four-footed beasts is off-putting, then might we see the six-legged arthropod's elusiveness as revulsion? Is what drives our fears of insects their uncanny movements, their suprahuman ability to scurry and swerve in ways unlike ourselves, marking them as decidedly not subhuman, or even lesser creatures, despite the size differential? Most people detest insects. As Eric Brown has rightly noted, insects are "popularly termed 'creepy' and 'crawly'—both derived from their locomotions and six-leggedness," thereby marking their "insectability" as Other.[3] And as the entomologist Jeffrey A. Lockwood has discussed in speaking about entomophobia, that is, the fear of insects, "When insects infest our minds—through evolution or enculturation—they bring with them not only the capacity to invade, evade, overwhelm, attack, perturb, and defy. They also bring an organic, viscid, ugly, soft, wriggling filthiness."[4] Perhaps it is our inescapable entanglement with insects in our daily lives that magnifies our loathing.

The science of insect locomotion has, according to George A. Bekey, provided inspiration for early projects in robotics since the 1970s. Insects, he writes, "have six legs, a fact that gives them clear stability advantages over four-legged animals. For this reason they have been studied extensively and used as models for the design of walking machines."[5] Furthermore, by looking to insect maneuverability and flight, scientists have been able to innovate with the development of drones, or unmanned aerial vehicles. Robert Wood remarks on the entomologically inspired RoboBee project, "Bees and other social insects provide a fascinating model for engineered systems that can maneuver in unstructured environments, sense their surroundings, communicate and perform complex tasks as a collective full of relatively simple individuals."[6] However, as Steven N. Fry notes, insects perform maneuvers much faster "based on completely different locomotion principles than their robotic counterparts."[7] Insects move to escape from threats, to find shelter or food, to migrate, or, as in the case of the forager bee's waggle dance, to communicate. Insects, with their coordinated muscle activity and skeletal muscles occurring in antagonistic pairs, can walk at somewhat high speeds relative to their small sizes.[8] Robert and Janice Matthews write in *Insect Behavior*, "Many insect locomotory activities appear extraordinarily impressive by human standards.... Their muscles are quite similar in almost all respects to our own, although the insect may possess many more individual muscles than a human does. Instead, many of the strange powers insects appear to have (as well as many of the problems they face) are the consequence of a simple physical relationship between surface and mass. As the size or mass of any object diminishes, the relative amount of its surface increases."[9] They continue: "Although most insect legs are adapted for walking, climbing, or running, some are modified in ways that aid other forms of locomotion. The ability to leap or jump appears to have repeatedly and independently evolved in insects of all sizes, particularly as an escape reaction."[10] Insects are sometimes seen as preternatural in their movements, yet their agility—a product of their wings, limbs, and sensory preceptors—makes them adept at rapid locomotion, particularly when in danger.[11]

What does it mean for humanity to become insect-like? The Audubon Insectarium in New Orleans allows visitors the opportunity to "shrink to the size of a bug with gigantic animatronic insects" in the Underground Gallery. Despite such attempts for humans to imagine insect life from the perspective of the bug itself, it is difficult for humans to even begin to contemplate such a transformation in terms of scale (even as a number of science-fiction texts and films have explored these possibilities), given our commitment to anthropocentrism. Yet as the study of insects became widespread in Europe in the sixteenth and seventeenth centuries, many turned to speaking of the human in such terms. For instance, in Marlowe's *Edward the Second*, when Pembroke sees Edward's beloved Gaveston sit by the King, he asks, "Can kingly lions fawn on creeping ants?"[12] It is here that we can see how four-footed beasts are routinely elevated above insects, particularly in this instance the ant, a conventional image for favorites perhaps tied to notions of not yielding anything worthwhile for anyone beyond one person; but more important, the human acting ant-like is also dangerous and destructive. In his November 1620 sermon preached at Lincolns Inne, John Donne aligns humans with insects, saying, "And shall we that are wormes, but silke-wormes, but glow-wormes at best, chide God that he hath made slow-wormes, and other venomous creeping things? shall we that are nothing but boxes of poison in our selves, reprove God for making Toads and Spiders in the world?"[13] Such a move to metaphor becomes a commonplace in religious texts of the period, where humans become (positively or negatively) aligned with insects and their behaviors.

If we look to Shakespeare as our test case, we can see that the acts of creeping and crawling come in other names. I focus on four in particular:

slink, sneak, steal, stalk. Slink, meaning "moving in a stealthy or sneaking manner," applies to both humans and animals and appears only three times in Shakespeare.[14] Lorenzo in *The Merchant of Venice* tells Graziano that "we will slink away in supper-time, / Disguise us at my lodging" (2.4.1–2), and Rosalind tells Celia in *As You Like It* to "Slink by, and note" Orlando (3.2.230).[15] Both instances are moments of stealth, potentially cueing an act of crawling in a secretive manner. *Sneak*, used only twice in Shakespeare, means "to creep or steal furtively; to slink, skulk," particularly if afraid or ashamed to be seen, as Vincentio says to Lucio in *Measure for Measure*, who is attempting to leave the scene: "Sneak not away, sir; for the friar and you / Must have a word anon" (5.1.350–51).[16] *Steal*, meaning "to withdraw oneself secretly or quietly" or "to go or come stealthily; to walk or creep softly so as to avoid observation," appears over eighty times in the plays.[17] For instance, Prince Harry asks Poins in *Henry IV, Part 2*, "Shall we steal upon them, Ned, at supper?" to which Poins replies, "I am your shadow, my lord; I'll follow you" (2.2.136–37); and Lysander tells Hermia to "Steal forth thy father's house to-morrow night" in *A Midsummer Night's Dream* (1.1.164). These selective examples showcase the necessity of escape, of moving in a way that is not natural for humans. The word *stalk*, meaning "to walk softly, cautiously, or stealthily," appears in the opening scene of *Hamlet*, when Bernardo says of the Ghost of Hamlet's father, "See, it stalks away!" (1.1.48).[18] Such stalking calls to mind the Old English word *scriðan*, generally translated as "to stalk or creep," as when Grendel in *Beowulf* is said to stalk the moors seeking to wreak havoc upon the mead-hall. The monstrosity and terror that ghosts and creatures like Grendel bring forth is similar to the dread brought on by the earth's nonhuman creeping creatures, marking the Ghost in *Hamlet* as perhaps best aligned with beastly locomotion as any character in Shakespeare.

Benvolio in *Romeo and Juliet* even speaks of Romeo in insect-like locomotion terms when he describes Romeo's trying to break the quarrel between Mercutio and Tybalt: "'Hold, friends! friends part!' and, swifter than his tongue, / His *agile* arm beats down their fatal points, / And 'twixt them rushes." He later reports that as Tybalt fell "did Romeo turn and fly" (3.1.159–61, 168; emphasis mine). Romeo's agility (in fact, this is the only instance of *agile* in the canon), his ability to move about and between, his turning and escaping as he comprehends danger, interestingly links him to nonhuman, and decidedly insect, locomotion.

Such agility is about making the body and limbs move, perhaps best expressed as a movement via creeping and crawling.

There are humans, of course, who eschew their two legs as means of transport and embrace getting on the ground to creep and crawl. On the Shakespearean stage, one does not have to look far to encounter characters who resort to animal ways of locomotion. A character in a play that creeps or crawls is in contact not with the ground but with the floorboards on the stage, similar to that "smallest monstrous mouse that creeps on floor" that Snug in *A Midsummer Night's Dream* says makes women tremble (5.1.215). Falstaff's creeping in *The Merry Wives of Windsor* is meant to make a mockery of his size, first creeping into a buck basket before Mistress Page later suggests he creep into the kiln-hole and Falstaff figures he could creep up into the chimney to avoid Ford (3.3.140; 4.2.36, 55). In *The Tempest*, Trinculo says he will "creep under [Caliban's] gaberdine" to shelter himself from the storm, which involves him lying on the ground (2.2.35–36). And Hermia in *A Midsummer Night's Dream*, after earlier having a dream of a crawling serpent on her breast, comes onstage crawling: "I can no further crawl, no further go. / My legs can keep no pace with my desires" (3.3.32–33).[19] In these cases, the human acts of creeping and crawling, no longer on two legs to propel them, mimics creaturely ways of movement.[20] It is worth considering these examples, then, and asking if there is something inherently comedic, or even unsettling, about moving along on the ground.

Modern Shakespeare performances reveal moments of creeping and crawling, of characters reverting to animal-like movement, although insects do not often seem to be the inspiration. Martin White recounts director Trevor Nunn's production of *Titus Andronicus* in 1972, where, according to the *Guardian*, Janet Suzman as Lavinia entered in 2.4 like "a pitiable, hunched grotesque crawling out of the darkness like a wounded animal."[21] In a review of *A Midsummer Night's Dream*, Alan Dessen recounts, "I have seen actresses playing Helena go into a dog-like posture for her spaniel speech to Demetrius (2.1.202–10), but a gangly and very entertaining Lucy Briggs-Owen, when given a signal by Demetrius, went so far as to creep across the floor and retrieve his shoe in her mouth."[22] In another review, of the 2008 Royal Shakespeare Company *Hamlet* starring David Tennant, Dessen describes how the king in the final scene tried unsuccessfully to crawl across the stage to take Gertrude's hand.[23]

And Michael Shurgot recounts a powerful *Othello* in Seattle during the 2014–2015 season where the actress playing Emilia, after having been stabbed by Iago, "crawled to the bed to die with her mistress."[24]

It is not a surprise, then, that modern performances often showcase characters engaging in various acts of creeping and crawling. Stage actors, in fact, are often trained in movement and the physicality of bodily expression. Vanessa Ewan and Debbie Green, in their *Actor Movement: Expressions of the Physical Being*, encourage connection with the body, and one section, "Working In and Out of the Floor: Shifting Sensibilities," includes an exercise called "Creep to Crawl to Stand to Rise." The idea is to "offer the experience of suspension and propulsion," asking the actor to move on all fours and "to move in opposition, opposite thigh to arm, finding the power in the legs to propel the body, to be able to move independently and yet always in connection with your intention."[25] This grounds actors quite literally, feeling the ground below them, forcing them to think about movement and propulsion and the interconnectedness of the body's parts. Jackie Snow, in *Movement Training for Actors* for London's Royal Academy of Dramatic Art, notes that actors are encouraged to study animals, particularly with how they contact the ground: "Hooves could be likened to women in high heels, flat feet of bears could be those of an old man, the webbed feet of the duck could be the feet of a waddling woman. The slow motion of a three-toed sloth or chameleon could be ideal for a spy; the movement from relaxation to alert, defence to attack, is really good for an army or someone running away."[26] Later she encourages students to research animals and practice "qualities such as walking, breathing, weight distribution, breath, muscle use, how they stand, leap, trot or fly."[27] Of the animals studied in Snow's book, however, none are insects. What might it mean if actors actually studied insect locomotion, and how could that affect character movement on stage? One need not be playing Mosca to consider the movement of insects, after all.

Notes

1. See https://www.hexbug.com for a complete listing of the company's product line and to see their robotic bugs in action.
2. Shannon, *Accommodated Animal*, 83.
3. Brown, "Introduction," xi.
4. Lockwood, *Infested Mind*, 48.
5. Bekey, *Autonomous Robots*, 291.
6. Wood, "Flight of the RoboBee."
7. Fry, "Experimental Approaches," 1.
8. Chapman, *Insects*, 255.

9. Matthews and Matthews, *Insect Behavior*, 95. Discussing the walking sequence of insects, they write, "First, no leg is raised until the leg behind it is in a supporting position. Second, the movements of the two legs of a segment alternate. A pattern of alternating triangles of support is commonly observed: with never fewer than three legs on the ground, an insect can stop at any point without losing stability. Stability is also enhanced by the fact that the insect body is slung between the legs in such a way that the center of gravity is low.

"Walking is done by moving the three legs contacting the ground backwards while the other three legs are raised and moved forward. This propels the insect's body forward, and when the raised legs are all the way forward they lower and make contact while the legs that were down are raised and the whole pattern repeated" (96).
10. Ibid.
11. Cameron, *Cockroach*, 21
12. Marlowe, *Edward the Second*, 4.15.
13. Donne, "Preached at Lincolns Inne," https://contentdm.lib.byu.edu/digital /collection/JohnDonne/id/3156/rec /3. Catherine Wilson reminds us that in the Renaissance "the term 'worm' refers to creeping or crawling animals generally" (*Invisible World*, 154).
14. OED, s.v. "slink, v.," 1a.
15. All references to Shakespeare's plays are from *The Norton Shakespeare* and are provided parenthetically by act, scene, and line number.
16. OED, s.v. "sneak, v.," 1.
17. Ibid., s.v. "steal, v.," 8, 10a.
18. Ibid., s.v. "stalk, v.," 1a.
19. Creeping and crawling are also implied in the gulling scenes in *Much Ado About Nothing*, where the script allows Benedick and Beatrice to move about the stage to note what others are saying. In Shakespeare, creeping things often imply animals, but hours, wind, shadows, and sounds are also said to creep, not to mention the school boy "creeping toward school" in *As You Like It*.
20. Pride in Marlowe's *Doctor Faustus* aligns himself with insects when he announces, "I am like to Ovid's flea; I can creep into every corner of a wench" (7.110–11).
21. White, *Renaissance Drama*, 191.
22. Dessen, "2011 Gallimaufry," 39.
23. Dessen, "Eyeballs and Icicles," 61.
24. Shurgot, "Seattle Shakespeare," 133.
25. Ewan and Green, *Actor Movement*, 30–31.
26. Snow, *Movement Training*, 123. She continues: "Animal study is also a very good way to teach the students to observe as an actor; to look at minute detail and to discover ways to make it look as if they are using four legs, legs that turn inside out, arms that are wings and necks that are six feet long, without actually having these actual physical attributes."
27. Ibid., 129.

Bibliography

Bekey, George A. *Autonomous Robots: From Biological Inspiration to Implementation and Control*. Cambridge, MA: MIT Press, 2005.

Brown, Eric C. "Introduction: Reading the Insect." In *Insect Poetics*, edited by Brown, i–xxiii. Minneapolis: University of Minnesota Press, 2006.

Cameron, Ewen. *The Cockroach*. London: Heinemann, 1961.

Chapman, R. F. *The Insects: Structure and Function*, 5th ed. Edited by Stephen J. Simpson and Angela E. Douglas.

Cambridge: Cambridge University Press, 2013.

Dessen, Alan C. "A 2011 Gallimaufry of Plays: Shakespeare, Heywood, Marlowe, and Massinger." *Shakespeare Bulletin* 30, no. 1 (Spring 2012): 37–47.

———. "Eyeballs and Icicles, a Swimming Pool and a Dummy: Shakespeare and *The Revenger's Tragedy* on Stage in 2008." *Shakespeare Bulletin* 26, no. 4 (Winter 2008): 53–64.

Donne, John. "Preached at Lincolns Inne." The Collected Sermons of John Donne. BYU Library, Digital Collections. https://contentdm.lib.byu.edu/digital/collection/JohnDonne/id/3156/rec/3.

Ewan, Vanessa, and Debbie Green. *Actor Movement: Expressions of the Physical Being*. London: Bloomsbury, 2015.

Fry, Stephen N. "Experimental Approaches Toward a Functional Understanding of Insect Flight Control." In *Flying Insects and Robots*, edited by Dario Floreano, Jean-Christophe Zufferey, Mandyam V. Srinivasan, and Charlie Ellington, 1–14. New York: Springer, 2010.

Greenblatt, Stephen, Walter Cohen, Jean E. Howard, and Katharine Eisaman Maus, eds. *The Norton Shakespeare*. New York: Norton, 1997.

Lockwood, Jeffrey A. *The Infested Mind: Why Humans Fear, Loathe, and Love Insects*. Oxford: Oxford University Press, 2013.

Marlowe, Christopher. *Doctor Faustus*. In *The Complete Plays*, edited by Frank Romany and Robert Lindsey, 341–95. London: Penguin, 2003.

———. *Edward the Second*. In *Christopher Marlowe: The Complete Plays*, edited by Frank Romany and Robert Lindsey, 397–505. London: Penguin, 2003.

Matthews, Robert W., and Janice R. Matthews. *Insect Behavior*, 2nd ed. London: Springer, 2010.

Shannon, Laurie. *The Accommodated Animal: Cosmopolity in Shakespearean Locales*. Chicago: University of Chicago Press, 2013.

Shurgot, Michael W. "Seattle Shakespeare Company 2014–15 Season." *Shakespeare Bulletin* 35, no. 1 (Spring 2017): 119–33.

Snow, Jackie. *Movement Training for Actors*. London: Methuen Drama, 2012.

White, Martin. *Renaissance Drama in Action*. Abingdon, UK: Routledge, 1998.

Wilson, Catherine. *The Invisible World: Early Modern Philosophy and the Invention of the Microscope*. Princeton: Princeton University Press, 1997.

Wood, Robert. "Flight of the RoboBee." National Science Foundation, June 7, 2016. https://www.nsf.gov/news/news_summ.jsp?cntn_id=138802.

CHAPTER 9
COMMUNICATION
Tettix

Lowell Duckert

A sub-sonic war of noiseless passions, played out in the echo-chamber of the body. A war of unreliable and perilous sensation. A war without taboos or scruples. Or, of course, end.
—TIM EDGAR WITH HUGH RAFFLES, *Insect Theatre*

The parasite is always an exciter.
—MICHEL SERRES, *The Parasite*

"Cicada mania" gripped the mid-Atlantic United States in the summer of 2016. After a seventeen-year-long wait, Brood V emerged from the ground, emitted its cacophony of copulation, and died, thereby initiating another life cycle anew. Entomologists have studied the various bioacoustic cues with which insects converse; a cicada, for instance, clicks when its membraneous tymbals oscillate.[1] This brood annoyed their human neighbors for nearly a month, communicating what Jeffrey Lockwood calls "the infested mind."[2] Moments of entomophilia, or the "infatuated mind," could balance the boisterousness: people ate cicadas, recorded sounds, and uploaded photos onto social media. In most of these conversations, however, cicadas were periodical creatures (*Magicicada*) that invaded human space only to disappear, mundanely, at a predetermined time. Humans, not to fear, could simply set their watches (to a *click*) for the next onslaught of *them*. And while the platforms of social media insinuated insective participation, these lesser things were only temporarily "social" at best: little beasts digested literally into the body politic or translated metaphorically into a miniature metaphor comparing insect behavior with human culture. (The circle of life is small.) But relations cannot be so easily quieted.

Talking to a colleague that summer outside my building about this chapter, bemoaning the fact that I still had not found a point of entry, I suddenly felt one: a cicada accidentally touched my lips, perhaps mistaking the vibrations of my vocal chords for a mating call that I had inadvertently ventriloquized. *I liked it*, I admit: for its chancy quality, for exposing the erogenous contact zone of inhuman affect into which I had suddenly flown. Whether the insect was purposefully trying to speak to me, the excitement of oral contact opened up a magical space of speaking. The violent outcomes of "click bait"—the logic of trap and chase—gave way to interminable pursuits in and of pleasure. Mites make *mights*, I mused. What other kinds of magic might the periodical cicadas and their insectan kin perform, even if their meaningful cues exist outside human comprehension? How might the cicadas' anticipated noise amplify the unceasing human-insect dialogues occurring every day—including the event that is *this* writing—vocalizing ontological, epistemological, and ethical questions on the edges of wing and lip? How can nonhuman clicks and their cliques intensify the "commune" (*communis*) within "communication" (*communicare*), charge political speaking with doing, all by marching to drummed rhythms beating in insect time?

In his Foreword to Vinciane Despret's *What Would Animals Say If We Asked the Right Questions?*, Bruno Latour advises that we "experiment on ourselves about our own ethical reactions," shifting attention from anthropomorphism to *metamorphosis*, since "animals seem to be able to tell quite a lot of moral tales that would bring immense benefits if humans were allowed by *their* scientists to hear them."[3] Stretching my introductory talk experiment into the present, my question is not whether insects can speak but why they have been prevented from doing so and, more important, what they would say when asked the "right" questions.

The segregation and concomitant denigration of sonorous animals based on their spontaneous, emotive voice as opposed to humanity's voluntary, rational "speech" dates back to Aristotle's *Politics* (fourth century BCE). Later authors adjusted this trilogy of sound, voice, and speech—a reliable species order of difference—ranking creatures according to so-called scientific echelons of "anatomy" or "mind." Take Ben Jonson's *Timber: or, Discoveries*: "*Speech* is the only benefit man hath to express his excellencie of mind above other creatures. It is the Instrument of Society.... Language most shewes a man." Not just mammals contributed to this debate; stentorian insects, in fact, had much to say. Jonson would know: the "Apologetical Dialogue" to his play *Poetaster* (1601) complains of "screaming grasshoppers / Held by the wings, [who] fill every ear with noise."[4]

My aim is not only to refute this trenchant and talkative boundary between human and nonhuman, which has been thoroughly tackled already—most notably by Jacques Derrida's "And Say the Animal Responded?" and a host of early modernists before me—but redefine the categories of speaking subject (the human) and silenced object (the nonhuman) altogether.[5] An actor-network approach to "articulation" tracks how insectan "actants" enact "translations" upon their environments.[6] I find that language, however conceived, detrimentally dominates our questions of communication; logos has been the loudest speech impediment historically. I avoid endowing dumb insects with language and its enviable qualities; moreover, I refuse to classify these terms of communication.[7] Putting pesky terms like "speech" into scare quotes is not problem solving either, only dialogue delimiting. Like caged (") grasshoppers (") singing at the human's command, these quotation marks are entirely quote constraining, configuring their captives as mute even if expressive. Instead, I second a different complaint about insects done in little talks. "Speaking only counts if it means speaking to us and in our language," Laurie Shannon laments, for "just being is good enough to certify a singular human self, but animal others face the further hurdle of *being understood*."[8] Logos has aided assertions of the anthropo- over the arthro- since antiquity, which is ample reason to let go of its hold on criticism and skirt arguments over language as either a breaker or bolsterer of human-nonhuman distinction.

Animal critics, to be clear, have crucially queried the species-ism of language; now, the embodied cues of lesser things might cue us in on the logocentrism still used to debate anthropocentrism and sponsor more expansive vocabularies conveying the nonlinguistic signals with which humans and nonhumans converse.

Cicadian Rhythms

The Russian poet Osip Mandelstam reminds us that a "quotation is not an excerpt . . . [it] is a cicada. It is part of its nature never to quiet down."[9] This chapter seeks to translate what was communicated while talking *with* my mouthy cicada. Even as it depends (at times) on sound "cues," insectan, obstreperous articulation loosens our dependence on the linguistic/verbal as well as the acoustic/aural in order to excite other expressive senses (touch, sight) and raise the onto-epistemological issue of relationality itself. But I might be caught in a bugging quandary: How am I to write, in language, about non- and extralinguistic intimacy with an insectine other? In a word: *tettix*. To think with insects, literary or not, is to think inevitably on language. The Greeks gave us onomatopoeia, literal "word making," in insect action: "cicada" comes from *tettix*, the bug's unquiet click. This translation marks a magic moment when language took the clickety turn; moreover, this ancient example insists on detailing the embodied passions by which words continue to be made: onomatopoeic references just described as well as the "subsonic" vibes that are never silent ("noiseless") or merely imitative ("echo") but mutually transformative by virtue of being felt in the body's corporeal "chamber."[10] "There is something about vibration," Elizabeth Grosz writes, "even in the most primitive of creatures, that generates pleasurable or intensifying passions, excites organs, and invests movements with greater force or energy."[11] Tettix talks in what I call "cicadian rhythms"—a cross-species current that is not solely confined to metaphysical aeries of abstraction,[12] but is a physical vector of infinitely variable force, a translatable energy of imprecise duration and periodization that elevates the lesser of size into sizable interlocutors. Entomological rhythms (from Greek *rhein*, "flow") enfold macro- and microscales; check inferior/superior, "primitive"/advanced positions; and communicate potential for an invested politics through excitable art. Despite their given name, "cut up into segments," insects sing the body eclectic, one wholly indivisible from its environment. Garrulousness is the only given.

Our foray into insectiferous transcription will be Thomas Moffett's *The Theater of Insects: or, Lesser Living Creatures* (1634/1658), a noisy text for more reasons than the "stridulous noise" of cicadas it detects.[13] Its entomological and etymological examples link our present fascination (or mania) with insect communication to early modern concepts. By establishing a transhistorical and theoretical conversation about conversation, I explore what communication is, does, and can be in our eco-cosmopolitical theaters. Infectious formication, a sensation like insects crawling over the skin, is the celebrated effect I am after; communes that endure catastrophic times through unexpected conversations—rather than the imperturbable balance of conservation—the buggy bargains I solicit.[14] Where to begin this peaceful campaign in search of a no less "perilous sensation" to be shared between both greater and lesser living things? With a conversation begun not long ago, a communing—how else?—done in six ways.

Parasite

[*Moth:*] Hail!
—A MIDSUMMER NIGHT'S DREAM (3.1.183)

The earliest English entomologists heeded the tettix's call when they translated Aristotle's "horns of insects" (Greek *keraioi*) into "antenna" (from Latin *antemna*, "yard of a ship"). *Insects instigate trips.* Michel Serres mentions that the French word for "parasite" signals at least three meanings: a biological eater, a human (social) parasite, and noise (static). What the parasite communicates, by extension, is relationality in excursus; it is absolutely relational, *para-*, next to, "[having] a relation only with the relation itself."[15] Each parasite tries to overtake its predecessor, each spurred ever onward by a third, "[a] parasite, physical, acoustic, informational, belonging to order and disorder, a new voice, an important one, in the contrapuntal matrix." Subjects and objects excitedly switch positions, muddling the ontological chain of command between host and interrupter. Because systems incorporate rather than suppress the "chance, risk, anxiety, and even disorder" that constitute them, no network can ever be bug-free. The parasite is what is (always already) inside.

In 1947, Grace Hopper famously discovered the first computer "bug"—a moth—in the relay of her Harvard Mark II. Parasitical analysis dodges the debugging of systems; it prefers the mystery of mis/communication, a dialogic programming of passing through, an interpellation—hail!—with the possibility of enjoying a little buggery along (*para-*) the way. A mothy matrix, of many words and morals, invents new systems precisely because of its disequilibrium. Refuse to "restore" harmony to ecosystems, Serres counsels; we are better off allowing for disputability, error, and disruptions: "One must write . . . of the interceptions of the accidents in the flow along the way between stations—of changes and metamorphoses." The shape of such noisy flows, the crazed crossings of creaturely things, is left to the *-sited* to extrapolate. (Serres quotes La Fontaine's animal fables extensively, including "The Cicada and the Ant.")

Recent studies of insectic ecopoiesis resonate with the tumultuous metamorphosis Serres describes. Eric Brown's impressive volume *Insect Poetics* examines "insects as poetry, insects as poets, and finally insects as poems." He situates "literature . . . itself [as] an 'insective' enterprise" and strains to hear "the ways in which insect poetics and the natural world are cognate—neither ever resolved before us in their entirety, both chaotic and controlled at once."[16] Dwelling on this turbulent (Serresian) order, Bertrand Gervais admits, "I must let the text live in me to understand it." His intrepid insectological reading practice differs from my flight path, however, in terms of purpose: "To understand a text means to tame it, to work to decipher it; it means to listen to it, not as we would hear another person's words, in a simple act of communication, but as we listen to the cicada's song or the humming of a mosquito. There is no equality between the reader and the text; there is only a distance that the reader tries to reduce."[17] Drawing closer to cicadas' complex calls is not an attempt to decode ("decipher") necessarily; it may mark an inclination to cohabit the insectan obscure, transmit parasitical missives of mis- and disunderstanding, span human-insect "distance," transduce gregarious gestures: *bug on, bug in, bug out.* "Tame" is as it sounds: a reductive domestication, the policing of interference, a gag disguised as a stopgap. In my estimation, a "close encounter of the third kind"—from which Gervais takes his title—more accurately communicates the "third" that is intrinsic to the Serresian "kind" of relationality. A parasitical poetics announces the insectary intimacy known as reading and writing through the creative-collaborative noise it makes and on which it simultaneously feeds. The parasite asks—persistently, if pestilently—what stories will be il/legible in the future, whether or not the talking tettix book of becomings will remain truly open-ended.

Gloss

And so does Moffett's *Theater*, I hear. I turn now to this unlikely *talking* point despite the fact that, plainly speaking, the words he uses to dramatize communication appear to reinforce a too-human circular commentary in which an autonomous author makes pinned corpses converse. Aggrandizing himself as a speaker *to* obedient objects, Moffett masterfully performs the human via an entomological didactic discourse—humanism—that re/establishes humanity's authority over insects. "Speak" is ubiquitous, but it refers almost unfailingly to the "I/we/they" of human authorities. He and his classical predecessors help guide the reader; pointed phrases like "now we shall bend our discourse to speak of winged solitary insects" . . . "now let us proceed to speak" do not entail a "bend[ing]" of the ear or body to better listen in a multisensorial sense, but a private chat between less knowledgeable noviciates and their learned mentors. "Language" operates in the same way; it often denotes the original source material (passages in Greek) or lexical translations (as in Polish).

Thus, two of the most weighted words in the human-animal critical debate—*language* and *speak*—follow the above-mentioned historical trends. There is hardly any histrionic "excitement" on his stage; "passions," when present, are of an intellectual sort to be shared with other male minds: "(to speak in *Plinies* language)" . . . "I have mended [my contributors'] method and language" (sig. Ffff5v). As Moffett's preface pronounces, small voices provide larger lessons in vocational craftsmanship. He extends an invitation to praise a human creator's (his) and a holy Creator's (God's) skill. Hark the angelic insects singing in the

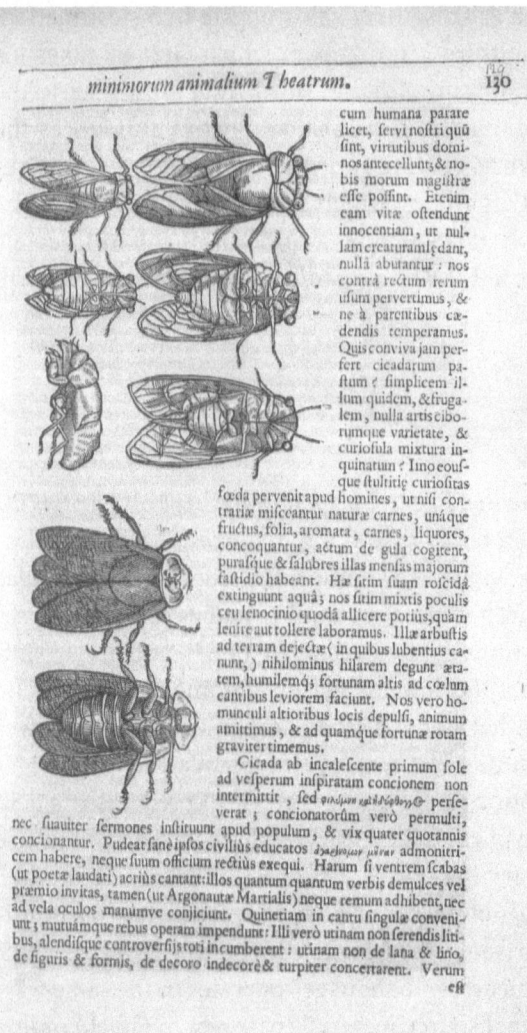

Figure 2.9.1 From Thomas Moffett, *Insectorum sive Minimorum Animalium Theatrum* (London, 1634). Call #: STC 17993b. Used by permission of the Folger Shakespeare Library under a Creative Commons Attribution-ShareAlike 4.0 International License.

opening pages, for they herald eternal wisdom for human ears: "Would you have a Musician? hearken to the Grashopper, which is alwaies filled with singing... and by her most pleasant melody challengeth the Nightingal. Would you hear a Trumpeter? hold your ear to the Bee-hive, hear the humming noise: hearken a little to the Gnat, in whose small beak the great Master workman hath formed that horrid and clanging sound of the Trumpet" (sig. Ffff6r). We are meant to marvel throughout at the tiniest "mouthes," peering into them to find the "Art and Excellency," the "workmanship" of God.

Yet there are several instances in which Moffett cannot wholly—godly—gloss over the reciprocal vibes affecting bugs' and humans' lives. He suggests one such "[c]ould have" on the next page: "If men should deny that [insects] contribute very much to feed, and fat, and cure many other creatures, Birds and Fishes would plead for them, and the brute beasts that feed on grass would speak in their behalf" (sig. Ffff6v). This "speak[ing] in their behalf" is a multispecies appeal as much as it is an argument for ecological interconnectedness (everything "contribute[s]") or utility (insects "feed" those higher on the great food chain of being). As a moment of conversational curiosity, the preface's "ple[a]" also betrays a parasitical point of prepositional contact: to "speak *in*" and "for" the other's behalf intertextually, even if posthumously. Moffett himself is not exempt; regardless of his ponderous "how unspeakable is the [insects'] perfection?" he has been perfectly parasited; he has been permitted to speak—theatricalize, that is—by his insect subjects (sig. Ffff5v). And while extremely rare, his use of "communicate" apprehends such physical vibrations of parasitical envelopment. Hornets dole out duties "in communication of labour," but so do bees, that "communicate some portion [of honey]" to the drones. Both honey's sticky matter and the hive's abstract order are equally "communicate[d]" across bodies. Sizing up Moffett's *Theater*, paying greater attention to the speech-enabling parasitism of lesser things in stature, troubles anthro- and logocentric dictation. Rearticulating terms about communication—*glossing* a more-than-human dictionary by speaking with others "in" their "behalf"—speaks insective volumes about the various kinds of communication, those embodied acts of transmission and transferal, that (will) come.

Dissect

Would that the communion call was so easy. The violence of communication is far too prevalent in this *Theater* of "war." Moffett notes noisome moments of material translation; humans disabled by toxic transfusions abound. Poisonous spiders "by only touching doth communicate . . . venome" (1059). Unintelligible speech often identifies a clear case of parasitism; one symptom of being infected by "broad Worms," tellingly, is that human hosts "put forth their tongues... they speak strange words... their voice is interrupted" (1111). Slurred symbiosis is the sure sign of the parasite, language's interruption marking a hijacking of body and mind, a halt of logos, or, conversely, a logorrhea: words out, tongues out. In any event, the lesser beastie commands the greater beast to megaphonically speak for *it*. And a healthy body, once cured, prognosticates a hearty dialect.

The most obvious problem with this syllogism of health is that it benefits the human doctor/ed; exploring the open somas of insects seldom counts as an assault. In this medical arena, the killing of the cold-blooded is a warm-blooded privilege. Bodies wither under Moffett's, and mankind's, scientific sovereignty. Windpipes are sliced open as the "cut into" (of "dissect") meets the "cut apart" (of "insect"). Theodore de Mayerne's "Epistle Dedicatory" relishes this opportunity to penetrate the secret voice of cicadas: "What a most pleasant spectacle will this be when the artificial hands carefully and curiously guide the most sharp pen-knife, and very fine instrument by direction of the sight! To behold the pipe of the Grasshoppers [cicadas] that live upon dew, and the organs of the shrill sound they make, that in the heat of the Dog-daies importunately beats upon the ears of travellers" (sig. Ffff3r). The keen incision reflects the entomologist's incisive mind, and Mayerne describes in precise detail how the "Drum" of the cicada's torso operates: "which being beaten" by the wings, "beat[s] against the rough-cast walls of the hollow place" (sig. Ffff3r). Sounds beating on bodies and soundless bodies beaten, a drumroll ceased by the surgeon's steady hand: there is little pause for a recognition of shared anatomy here (in "pipes," perhaps).

Moffett will repeat this procedure in his seventeenth chapter, "Of Grashoppers and Krickets" (989), the noisiest, by my count, and yet simultaneously the most silencing. At first, his tiny experiments seem interested in collapsing human-insect difference: "For you must not think that in Man only the Art of the great Artificer is so great, as I have explained before, but what creature soever you would dissect, you shall finde the like art and wisdom to appear in it" (sig. Ffff5r). But any discovered similarities ("like art") end up disassociating bodies, not confusing them; a cut into the lesser "creature['s]" exoskeleton segregates in order to hierarchize. The moment of "dissect[ion]" is meant to sever the human from what it is not. Uncertainty, in general, is answered with more slicing. Both his and Mayerne's mislabeling of cicadas as grasshoppers, while erroneous in retrospect, reveals Moffett's exhaustive attempts at taxonomy. (Perhaps due to their rarity: the New Forest cicada is the only species native to England.) The disordered class of *insecta* must be expertly arranged lest the grasshopper—or was it a cicada?—gets away.

So he severs on: targeting the physiological source of cicadas' noise—it is the inner membrane that "breaketh forth a stridulous sound"—he separates them, presciently, from crickets, locusts, and true grasshoppers (of the order now known as orthoptera; 992). Satisfied with his dicey work, he uses the same method to distinguish the "great[ness]" of "Man" from the slightness of women. "The reason why the female Grashoppers sing not at all," he explains, is "because they want that space between the thighs." Vivisection supports silence's golden, and gendered, rule: "Nature certainly intended by denying a voice to the females of these Grashoppers to teach our women that lesson.... *What ornament silence brings to the female sex*" (992). This long-awaited moment of species assimilation is a misogynistic one: humans, at least their genitalia (or lack of them), are likened to insects' organs in order to cleave, doubly and definitively, humans from insects and humans (men) from humans (women). An anecdote from Edward Topsell's *The Historie of Four-Footed Beasts and Serpents* (1658), with which Moffett's work was bound, augurs these distressing associations. "*Allens* wife," we are told, thirstily took a harmless looking tankard, "and suddenly a Wasp in her greedinesse passed down with the drink."[18] The wife's throat swells shut; she dies. In these suffocating theaters of sundering scrutiny, the joy of the "Wor[m]"—the "greedinesse" of parasitical communication "broad[ly]" defined—meets a tragic end. There must be better "wisdome" to learn than this, though. Lost in English translation from its original European locales, tettix communicates how the ento- and etymo- escape the logical. Confronting the graphic consequences of human-nonhuman dissection at the points of men's "pens"—for cicadas and grasshoppers, for women and wasps—is an impulse to discover mutually beneficial forms of conversation built on assemblage, not autopsy.

Tickle

How to open up these one-way insecticidal translations to the possibilities of interspecies pleasure? Bees' buzzes are universally pleasing. In the first line of his beginning chapter, Moffett reports on bees "procreating ... for the pleasure of the ears" (889). But even in the apiarist's absence, Moffett ably interprets bees' hushed hums as a human civics lesson: "The Captain of the watch flies about and makes a buzzing, as it were commanding them to their rest; after which signal given, they are all so husht and still, so subject are they to their rulers and governors, and at their beck and nod are presently quach't" (896). The method that produces this "watch-word" is debatable, their "murmur [being] a matter so exceeding intricate and obscure" (893). The question is not *if* bees communicate but what "rule" humans may emulate; nevertheless, he needs these interrelationships to thrive if he is to proceed. Moffett navigates a pulsing soundscape to get near his educational sources; he must simply put and keep his ear beside the busy hive. Not always does he strive to comprehend; in his inconclusive investigations, the sounds are dulcet enough that "the English call it singing." The bee-flies "are the *Sirenes* of both kindes," he marvels, "because they seem to have a kind of articulate or significant voice, or perhaps as that sea Monster ... with his pleasant noise and buzzing he doth as it were tickle and charme the ear and not unfitly" (930). The "charme" is pure attraction; despite monstrous warnings, the "beat and flutter" pulls him heartily toward insectan odysseys and presses him voyeuristically up against the nest. The "shrill" is a thrill.

Interspecies seduction resounds in his chapter on cicadas by another name: "In a word, there is none to whom the musick of the Grashopper can seem harsh or unpleasant. ... Of all the Insects making a stridulous noise, the Grashopper challengeth the chief place, and by greater right, too" (992, 989). Cicadas live not on dew—popular know-how at the time—but by singing. At work in the heat of the day, their "melodious noise" motivates human labor, since "musick is a kinde refreshment and recreation to the fainting spirits and tired brain" (991). Shared labor provokes a call-and-response dynamic. Cicadas spur the mowers; the harvesters affectively answer back: "If once [cicadas] hear the reapers making merry, talking and singing, (commonly at noon) then they sing so loud as if they strove who should sing loudest, together with them"

(993). A multispecies symphonic competition of the strident: all to please, parasitically, all passengers together. And there is an even more touching response he communicates: in a complicated simile, Moffett compares inconsistent preachers with insects who sing sweetly without intermission: "These [cicadas] if you scratch or tickle their belly (as Poets which were commended) sing more shrill; but those [men] speak them as fair as possible may be" (991). (The moral: cicadas do not like flattery.) But in order to prove the point that "Grashoppers are a friend each to other," unlike vainglorious man, he must "tickle" tiny stomachs (991). Increasing the pitch of arousal amplifies a transspecies desire, a queer love of disquietude, the commencement of cicada-man's cocooning. Might there have been more communicated by this stroke? Moffett's scratch stokes an eroticized entomophilia; his crooning curiosity lingers: "And such creatures as you cannot possibly dissect," he writes in his preface, "will make you to admire the more, the smaller they are" (sig. Ffff6r). Change the pleasurable station: you do not need the pen's "knife" to feel sharp wonder.

Compose

Let there be gall enough in thy ink.
—TWELFTH NIGHT (3.2.49)

A penultimate point in bookish parasitism: the *Theater*'s manuscript, Mayerne complains, "lay for some years in my Study cast aside in the dust among Worms and Moths . . . those beasts that are the greatest enemies to the Muses & their darlings" (sig. Ffff2r). Such discomposure un/intentionally places the human in the prime compositional position, however. Counting the semiofficial collaborators present in its chewed pages—Thomas Penny (ca. 1530–1589); Swiss naturalist Conrad Gessner (1516–1565); Edward Wotton (1492–1555); Moffett (1553–1604); his apothecary, Mr. Darnell; and finally the French physician Mayerne who published it for the first time, in Latin, as *Theatrum Insectorum* (1634)—highlights human authority under parasitical attack and, as a result, nervously reinscribes the entomologists' already shaky authorship.[19] Contrary to Mayerne's opening condemnation, Moffett's insects are far less foes than they are raucous authors with whom he writes. A parasitical take on complicit coauthorship reroutes anxieties over first (second, third) place into multispecies insectariums—such as the *Theater*—in which writers forgo ventures in anthropocentric placehood for an investigation into who eats (writes) whom.

If this companionate kind of composition risks sounding insectually abstruse, I would put "gall . . . in thy ink." Galls are responsive plant growths produced in the presence of herbivorous insects; harvested (and prized) for millennia, the tannic acid found within oak provided a principal component of ink. The *Theater* is not an explicitly galled text—Moffett's press would have probably been oil based—and yet the event of inking raises issues of parasitical precipitates nevertheless.[20] The cicada's undying association with resurrection—its cast skin—also considers the survivability of insects' effects known as *texts*. Revisiting the noisy composition of Moffett's book displays how insect actors continually communicate their material-metaphorical eagerness of enmeshment. The Roman poet Lucretius mentions cicadas in his chapter of *De Rerum Natura* (first century BCE) devoted to the senses. It is the nature of things, he argues, including words, to shed their images: these films, once perceived, convey the form and likeness of the original, "As commonly cicadas doff the shiny shirts they've worn / In summertime."[21] Moffett was well acquainted with this line; he cites it when discussing cicadas' song: "Amongst all the insects there is none like it, accounted so sweet amongst the Ancients . . . and it may be *Lucretius* therefore called Grashoppers *Teretes*" (991). *Teretes* is a multifaceted word; it may mean "smooth," "shapely," or "well turned." The allusion here is arresting: letters and likenesses lie sprinkled on Moffett's pages like Lucretian exoskeletons, voicing their more-than-musical (and phonic) eco-phenomenological force in stride. Even if a kind cicada helped the mythological figure Eunomis win a harp contest after his C string broke, noise de/territorializes in major and minor keys; there is no harmonious inner chord that precedes relations.[22] "C" is for circumscribed cicada (staved music) and improvisational composer (deviant noise) at once.

A rhythmic *teretes* communicates insects' parasitical impression waiting to strike its readers, turning us, smoothly listening, on to smooth spaces and feelings. The *Theater*'s co-composition—its vibrant entomography—enjoins us to pursue these sites of insect media (books) and mediation (bodies).²³ In what shapes did insects leave their fellow authors as they noisily worked? Mayerne had hoped that "these lines that I have written may speak"; with a click-clack, they do. Moffett kept two crickets in a box to test whether "besides air and sound [they] have nothing in them" (996). The male eats the female, then dies two days later. Did his captives sing out as he penned his dramatis personae? Did their "melodious noise" merely encourage his literary labors, or did their "stridulous noise" strum a sympathetic chord? Whatever was communicated became his commune "Of Grashoppers and Krickets," which now, significantly, comes to us. Poly-legged letters of mine-not-mine: what else, more or *less*, can be communicated?

Compromise

So let us say the cicada replied in this sixth leg, not ask whether it did. And let us ask *again*. Let us pose more "experiments" on ourselves according to the communicative method I have dispatched—through Moffett's *Theater*, by way of a cicada's click—in six ways (and counting). Others have tried to reinvigorate these vibrational rhythms: Jacob Garret, Moffett indicates, was so enthralled with crickets that with "the wings pluckt off and rubbed together, [he] very cunningly imitate[ed] them" (995). But we can bug better than this; plucking wings is becoming-cricket at the expense of the other. Taking wing need not take life. It must be said that attending to nonlinguistic vociferousness attuned to the insect does not mean that we should neglect actual silencing. Heeding the animal's affective address—what Tobias Menely calls "the animal claim"—necessitates "accounting for the communicative conditions in which we find ourselves answerable to the clamor of other beings who are like ourselves passionate and finite."²⁴ The entomological project I imagine enfolds both humans and nonhumans by stressing the endless wires of communication stretching across their antennal trips. If rhetorical eloquence has been a marker of humanism, the humanist Moffett's passionate "noyse" and other sub/sonic signifiers problematize the human but might also make us a little more humane. It might make us "compromise": not to lay down arms reluctantly in a never-ending war but to "send forward together" (*com-, pro-, mittere*), to take up plights "in . . . behalf."

Insects call out the inequalities between readers and texts at large and in small. Any improvisational matrix of compromise must include them: insect-borne illnesses (malaria); the injustices of class waged by capital (agribusiness) or kingdom (pesticides); misdirected monarch butterflies and colony collapse disorder (CCD); and even the terror of "entomogenic climate change." "Listen," Hugh Raffles requests near the end of *Insectopedia*, "It's the sound of global warming. It's getting even louder."[25] Lockwood, listening in, coins "entomapatheia": the psychologically healthy state of "benign indifference toward insects." But tolerant detachment is difficult to translate into political effectiveness during entomo- and anthropogenic times.[26] Extinction is the true sound of silence; Moffett, centuries before, illustrates how easily indifference can align with differentiation. Grasshoppers will not sing in certain regions, he presumes, because, "like the people of the Jewes, they refuse to sing their native Songs in a strange Countrey; who being cast out of their own habitation, seek means to die rather than waies to live" (993). We do not just need to delegate homes for creatures—called the *oikos*, the *polis*—but draft them in compromise.

Hopeful "waies" are already here; insect designs are already at work. Moffett felt its magic: in August 1586 he and Penny were hosts at the Countess of Somerset's house when "(after a great clap of Thunder) under the next ceiling between the joysts, we heard a great noise, as it had been an alarm of war, and as we thought the floor did rebound with the noise" (899). Bees had been living there "30 years together," the unsuspecting human inhabitants learn, *together* with noble company. The house of ecology absolutely hums at all times. During un/predictable parasitisms—from weather, "war," and what else—communicative creatures interrupt each other to share scares but also their joys. Spending unquiet time with an insect is just this ambience of resilience. When we listen to listening many "waies," we hear an insect's voice—Moffett's, mine, yours, "excited" all—passionately communicating possibilities. I know something clicked for me that summer day; it sponsored several speculative translations written down in tettix: "Although I am an Insect very small, / Yet with great vertue am endow'd withall" (995). Close encounters with insects keep the lines of communication open.

Notes

1. Raffles, *Insectopedia*, 328.
2. Lockwood, *Infested Mind*, 144.
3. Latour, "Scientific Fables," xi, xiv.
4. Jonson, *Works*, 9:196, 2:515.

COMMUNICATION | 157

5. Derrida, "And Say." See also Wolfe, "Shadow of Wittgenstein's Lion." Helpful works I recommend consulting are Cummings, "Pliny's Literate Elephant"; Fudge, *Brutal Reasoning*, especially chap. 5, "A Reasonable Animal?"; Senior, "When the Beasts"; Serjeantson, "Passions and Animal Language"; and Sorabji, *Animal Minds*, chap. 7.
6. See Latour, *Pandora's Hope*, chap. 2. Jacob Smith is in the same groove, albeit with lac insects and the shellac industry, in *Eco-Sonic Media*, chap. 1.
7. Consider bees' "waggle dance," Austrian ethologist Karl von Frisch's (1886–1982) phrase for specialized motions indicating distance and direction to other members of the colony. See Zuk, *Sex on Six Legs*, chap. 6; and Raffles, *Insectopedia*, 171–200, for a pitiable summation (to which I am sympathetic): we are "so trapped in language" (200).
8. Shannon, *Accommodated Animal*, 15–16.
9. Quoted in Hollingsworth, *Poetics of the Hive*, ix.
10. Edgar with Raffles, *Insect Theatre*, "The World Vibrates."
11. Grosz, *Chaos*, 33.
12. See Lauck, *Voice of the Infinite*, for "the message that Spirit moves through all creatures and that insects are messengers and guides of the beneficent powers of creation" (xviii).
13. Moffett, *Theater of Insects*, 989. Subsequent references to *Theater of Insects* appear parenthetically by page number.
14. "Acknowledging and celebrating affect is important," Jamie Lorimer cautions, "but it is not a simple solution for conservation after the Anthropocene" (*Wildlife in the Anthropocene*, 188).
15. Serres, *Parasite*, 39, 6, 14, 11.
16. Brown, "Reading the Insect," xv, xix, xviii.
17. Gervais, "Reading," 194.
18. Topsell, *Historie of Four-Footed Beasts*, 656.
19. See Neri, *Insect and the Image*, 45–73.
20. See Berenbaum, *Bugs in the System*, 127–33.
21. Lucretius, *Nature of Things*, 4.58–59.
22. See Kritsky and Cherry, *Insect Mythology*, 10–11.
23. See Parikka, *Insect Media*.
24. Menely, *Animal Claim*, 205.
25. Raffles, *Insectopedia*, 318.
26. Lockwood, *Infested Mind*, 165–76.

Bibliography

Berenbaum, May R. *Bugs in the System: Insects and Their Impact on Human Affairs*. Reading, UK: Helix Books, 1995.

Brown, Eric C. "Reading the Insect." In *Insect Poetics*, edited by Brown. Minneapolis: University of Minnesota Press, 2006.

Cummings, Brian. "Pliny's Literate Elephant and the Idea of Animal Language in Renaissance Thought." In *Renaissance Beasts: Of Animals, Humans, and Other Wonderful Creatures*, edited by Erica Fudge, 164–85. Champaign: University of Illinois Press, 2004.

Derrida, Jacques. "And Say the Animal Responded?" In *Zoontologies*, edited by Cary Wolfe, 121–46. Minneapolis: University of Minnesota Press, 2003.

Edgar, Tim, with Hugh Raffles. *Insect Theatre*. London: Black Dog, 2013.

Fudge, Erica. *Brutal Reasoning: Animals, Rationality, and Humanity in Early Modern England*. Ithaca, NY: Cornell University Press, 2006.

Gervais, Betrand. "Reading as a Close Encounter of the Third Kind: An Experiment with Gass's 'Order of Insects.'" In *Insect Poetics*, edited by

Eric C. Brown. Minneapolis: University of Minnesota Press, 2006.

Grosz, Elizabeth. *Chaos, Territory, Art: Deleuze and the Framing of the Earth.* New York: Columbia University Press, 2008.

Hollingsworth, Christopher. *Poetics of the Hive: The Insect Metaphor in Literature.* Iowa City: University of Iowa Press, 2005.

Jonson, Ben. *The Works of Ben Jonson.* Edited by William Gifford. London: Bickers and Son, 1875.

Kritsky, Gene, and Ron Cherry. *Insect Mythology.* San Jose, CA: Writers Club Press.

Latour, Bruno. *Pandora's Hope: Essays on the Reality of Science Studies.* Cambridge, MA: Harvard University Press, 1999.

———. "The Scientific Fables of an Empirical La Fontaine." Foreword to *What Would Animals Say If We Asked the Right Questions?*, by Vinciane Despret, translated by Brett Buchanan. Minneapolis: University of Minnesota Press, 2016.

Lauck, Joanne Elizabeth. *The Voice of the Infinite in the Small: Re-Visioning the Insect-Human Connection.* Boston: Shambhala, 2002.

Lockwood, Jeffrey. *The Infested Mind: Why Humans Fear, Love, and Loathe Insects.* Oxford: Oxford University Press, 2013.

Lorimer, Jamie. *Wildlife in the Anthropocene: Conservation After Nature.* Minneapolis: University of Minnesota Press, 2015.

Lucretius. *The Nature of Things.* Translated by A. E. Stallings. London: Penguin, 2007.

Mayerne, Théodore de. "Epistle Dedicatory." In *The Historie of Four-Footed Beasts and Serpents*, by Edward Topsell. London, 1658.

Menely, Tobias. *The Animal Claim: Sensibility and the Creaturely Voice.* Chicago: University of Chicago Press, 2015.

Moffett, Thomas. *The Theater of Insects: or, Lesser Living Creatures.* In *The Historie of Four-Footed Beasts and Serpents*, by Edward Topsell. London, 1658.

Neri, Janice. *The Insect and the Image: Visualizing Nature in Early Modern Europe, 1500–1700.* Minneapolis: University of Minnesota Press, 2011.

Parikka, Jussi. *Insect Media: An Archaeology of Animals and Technology.* Minneapolis: University of Minnesota Press, 2010.

Raffles, Hugh. *Insectopedia.* New York: Vintage Books, 2010.

Senior, Matthew. "'When the Beasts Spoke': Animal Speech and Classical Reason in Descartes and La Fontaine." In *Animal Acts: Configuring the Human in Western History*, edited by Jennifer Ham and Senior, 61–84. New York: Routledge, 1997.

Serjeantson, R. W. "The Passions and Animal Language, 1540–1700." *Journal of the History of Ideas* 62, no. 3 (2001): 425–44.

Serres, Michel. *The Parasite.* Translated by Lawrence R. Schehr. Minneapolis: University of Minnesota Press, 2007.

Shakespeare, William. *The Norton Shakespeare.* 2nd ed. Edited by Stephen Greenblatt, Walter Cohen, Jean E. Howard, and Katharine Eisaman Maus. New York: Norton, 2008.

Shannon, Laurie. *The Accommodated Animal: Cosmopolity in Shakespearean Locales.* Chicago: University of Chicago Press, 2013.

Smith, Jacob. *Eco-Sonic Media.* Oakland: University of California Press, 2015.

Sorabji, Richard. *Animal Minds and Human Morals: The Origins of the Western Debate.* Ithaca, NY: Cornell University Press, 1993.

Topsell, Edward. *The Historie of Four-Footed Beasts and Serpents.* London, 1658.

Wolfe, Cary. "In the Shadow of Wittgenstein's Lion: Language, Ethics, and the Question of the Animal." In *Zoontologies*, edited by Cary Wolfe, 1–57. Minneapolis: University of Minnesota Press, 2003.

Zuk, Marlene. *Sex on Six Legs: Lessons on Life, Love, and Language from the Insect World*. Boston: Houghton Mifflin Harcourt, 2011.

CHAPTER 10
SWARM
Song of the Swarm

Derek Woods

Homer and Virgil write that bees swarmed around the mouth of the infant Plato, presaging his "mellifluous" (honey-like) speech.[1] This image captures a tension at work in the history of rationality from Plato to Derrida. Idealist reason associates rationality with voice rather than writing; voice gives a presence to self and other that writing disrupts. The philosopher's mouth expresses the purity of reason through airy immaterial speech. But these Platonic bees draw attention to his embodied mouth through their proximity and their metonymic honey that figures his eloquence.

I open with Plato's mouth bees to discuss the relation between the concepts of swarming and communication—communication among humans, among bees and other social insects, and between humans and bees. There are many social insects in addition to bees, such as termites, ants, locusts, and wasps. Taking the notion of the swarm at a certain level of abstraction, we can say that all social insects swarm. Not all bees are social, however, and from a biological and ethological perspective, there are many differences among social insects—or in biological jargon, *eusocial* insects—the ones for which sociality confers evolutionary fitness.[2] In literary history, the examples that get the most attention are doubtless ants and bees. In this chapter, I stay with bees because of their importance in Renaissance culture, their role in twentieth-century debates about animal communication, and their continued importance as canaries in the coal mine of ecological decline.

The image of bees swarming the mouth of Plato captures a paradox of the swarm concept through its distinctive mixture of order and disorganization, purposefulness and indirection. As a feature of the concept (and not a bug), this paradox appears across texts from multiple genres, fiction and nonfiction. In the BBC's science-fiction series *The Black Mirror*, for example, one episode imagines a swarm of artificial bees coordinated by central computers. Designed by a high-tech firm for the British government to replace extinct pollinators, these digitally controlled bees replace analog insects as the nation's primary pollinators. Unfortunately, an antagonist appropriates them for terrorist activities, murdering people who have been trolls on social media and inviting analogies (mediated by the swarm concept) between bee behavior and networked human sociality. The inventor of this pollination system argues that this hack is impossible. There are too many bees to control individually; once set in motion, they self-organize beyond central control. The paradox of swarming comes from this tension between control by a subject and order that emerges from interaction among simple elements.

This chapter addresses the concept of the swarm and the topos of bee communication. The swarm concept is the set of principles we can derive from empirical observation and historical accounts of swarming. Literary writers often do just this, abstracting the swarm from lifeforms such as bees and using it to describe other phenomena. Henri Michaux uses swarming to describe the experience of mescaline: "there is a crowd, a swarming of what is possible."[3] In an example from Jorge Luis Borges's story "The Garden of Forking Paths," the narrator writes his momentary experience of the co-presence of all possible historical trajectories as a "swarming sensation."[4] In this respect, *concept* is already the wrong term, since the swarm disseminates across numerous figurative uses. Even so, philosophers, scientists, and other theorists have long worked to think the swarm in general, understanding it in organicist terms or as a cybernetic system. Working in different but overlapping discourses, scientists and engineers use the swarm concept in both modeling and design. Scientists, for example, use models developed for insect swarms, schools of fish, and flocks of birds to understand other kinds of group behavior: molecules interacting in a fluid and humans interacting in a crowd, or even the complex behavior of markets.[5] And engineers mimic swarming by creating groups of simple robots and programming them to learn new behaviors—to exceed their programs—by interacting with one another in patterns without central control.[6]

By contrast, the topos of bee communication is more closely tied to a single life-form, which is not to say a single species. *Life-form* should not be synonymous with *species* or with concrete living individuals. Life-forms are a set of partial abstractions: they avoid some of the metaphysical pitfalls of higher-level abstractions such as "life" and "the animal."[7] For this chapter, *life-form* refers to the most common levels of abstraction at which social and cultural communication comes to circulate (and archive) the totality of biodiversity.[8] Communication trades in lizards, ants, bears, and bees, but often without our conscious recognition that we are not talking about concrete species. Insofar as these life-forms are easily grasped through the help of unconscious cultural memory, we might think of them as *life-form topoi*. In rhetoric, *topoi* are "commonplaces," or familiar subjects through which speakers can establish consubstantiation with their audiences. I return to the theory of life-form topoi in the chapter conclusion.

The bee topos can be addressed by comparing two forms of communication about communication (or second-order communication) separated by four hundred years: Renaissance and contemporary accounts of how bees message one another to make swarm life hold together. The two historical cross sections are accounts of bee song in works of Renaissance natural history from Edward Topsell, Moses Rudsen, and Charles Butler to entomologist Karl von Frisch's famous twentieth-century work on the bee dance language. It would be simple to arrange these two cross sections according to the difference between Foucauldian historical epistemes, or epistemological structures separated by breaks in the flow of history. On the one hand, Renaissance writers are happy to explain the social life of bees in anthropomorphic terms, describing kings, queens, soldiers, and the songs they sing to one another. They embrace the analogy between humans and bees, writing what Foucault calls "The Prose of the World."[9] On the other hand, the swarm behavior of bees has lent itself to arguments that, although they seem "postmodern" in their embrace of the episteme inaugurated by cybernetics and information theory, they are perhaps extensions of the same modernity that would consider the idea of bee language absurd.[10] As critics of Foucault like to point out, ample historical continuity accompanies these epistemic breaks, so that each archaeological stratum is porous, with tunnels that open onto other layers as well. Some tunnels are life-form topoi. Their transhistorical continuity comes from the persistence of the species that make life-forms, as partial abstractions, possible in the first place.

The Swarm Has No Face

How do social insects communicate? What organizes them if not central control? If they have no leader, how do they know where to go and what to do? The crux of these questions is not intelligence or brain size. We can imagine different arguments about the intelligence of nonsocial insects. They work through instincts determined by their genes, or they have individual minds and intentions after all. Swarms complicate the question because they also divide labor, coordinating their actions to accomplish tasks that seem to require communication. Since it is difficult to argue that such complex behavior is simply programmed by the genes of each individual, the swarm concept is central to work in science and philosophy concerned with emergent complexity—properties produced by the interaction of comparatively simple units but irreducible to them.

As Eugene Thacker notes in "Swarm Life," there are two dominant explanations of swarming before the information era: the idea of a swarm leader or insect sovereign and the notion that the swarm is a single organism.[11] In *Historia Animalium* Aristotle relies on sovereignty to explain the order of the swarm: "They say that, if a swarm goes astray, it will turn back upon its route by the aid of scent and seek out its leader. It is said that if he is unable to fly he is carried by the swarm, and that if he dies the swarm perishes; and that, if this swarm outlives the king for a while and constructs combs, no honey is produced and soon the bees die out."[12] For Aristotle, swarming requires a leader for motion, production, and fertility. In this account of the relation between subject and swarm, the swarm has a face: orders flow in one direction, from the leader to its otherwise directionless underlings.

Thacker's account of swarming jumps from the medieval period to modernity, skipping the Renaissance. I add a swarm concept before arriving at his second pre-cybernetic one. Renaissance accounts of swarming bees often do follow the logic of sovereignty at work in Aristotle. Yet some examples resemble more modern accounts in which the sovereign has no particular power. In *A Theatre of Political Flying Insects*, Samuel Purchas includes an encomium to bees: "One drop of water hath no power, one spark of fire is not strong, but the gathering together of waters called Seas, and the communion of many flames do make both raging and invincible elements. And *una Apis, nulla Apis*, one Bee is no Bee, but a multitude, a swarm of Bees uniting their forces together, is very profitable, very terrible, very comfortable."[13] In this passage, which contradicts Butler's overall orientation to sovereignty, the swarm is already a kind of emergent property. Quantitative difference turns over into qualitative difference. The repeating list of bee properties appears following the use of *multitude* as a general term for what reductionism would otherwise reduce away.[14] But the qualitative difference of the swarm loops back to change the definition of the bee in a way difficult not to read anachronistically, as an example of what complexity theorists call *downward causality*. Since one bee is no bee, our image of the individual bee with its fuzzy, yellow-and-black body, six legs, and two wings is misleading. For Butler in this passage, there is no such thing as an individual bee. Relations within the multitude define what it means to be a bee, so that a swarm concept overcomes the image we would most likely associate with Butler's topic. Already in this example, as Thacker would argue, the swarm has no face.[15]

Thacker's second concept explains the swarm in organicist terms. In this explanation, Rudsen's multitude becomes a superorganism that unifies the smaller-scale organisms of the swarm but uses a similar emergentist logic. For example, in *Creative Evolution*, Henri Bergson asks, "When we see the bees of a hive forming a system so strictly organized that no individual can live apart from the others beyond a certain time . . . how can we help but recognize that the hive is really, and not metaphorically, a single organism, of which each bee is a cell united to the others by invisible bonds?"[16] Bergson's effort to escape from metaphor through synecdoche matches a contemporaneous swarm description from the entomologist William Morton Wheeler, a contemporary in both historical and philosophical terms with organicists such as Alfred North Whitehead and C. Lloyd Morgan. In a 1911 article titled "The Ant Colony as an Organism," he compares the colony to a cell or a human body, making it a unitary whole that maintains its identity in space and resists dissolution.[17] Bergson and Wheeler consider the insect collective a whole that cannot be reduced to the sum of its parts—a formulation traceable at least as far back as Aristotle's *Metaphysics*. Though lacking any sovereign agent, these swarms have a centralizing, centripetal motion: the whole unifies the parts without explaining their relative independence as bodies.

"It is rarely mentioned that Norbert Wiener's first published paper was on ants."[18] In postwar swarm descriptions influenced by cybernetics, the conceptual framework is no longer organicist, instead emphasizing distributed information processing, emergent complexity, and self-organization. Once again, an element of emergentism is often in play, but the model is technological and computational rather than organic. As John Johnston shows in a discussion of artificial life research, despite the limited cognitive abilities of individual insects, their collective self-organizing activities make for impressive distributed problem solving.[19] Particularly in these post-cybernetic swarm theories, the social insects are a privileged example. New emphasis falls on the location of the intelligence in question. In *Swarm Intelligence*, for example, Russell C. Eberhardt, Yuhui Shi, and James Kennedy are clear on this point, opposing "the view that an isolated individual is an information processing entity and that thinking or cognition occurs inside an individual's head."[20] Bergson's "invisible bonds" become an intelligence of greater complexity than the individuals composing it. In the cybernetic swarm concept, however, the centrifugal motion that accompanies the centripetal inturning proper to the organism in its self-production, combined with the swarm's divisibility, rules out holistic unity. The swarm is fundamentally not analogous to an individual organism, especially not a lifeform with a head and front-to-back bilateral orientation. Returning to Thacker, the swarm "confronts the human subject with tensions . . . between networks and the self."[21]

"The English Call It Singing"

Joseph Campana argues that in Renaissance Europe, especially England, no species of charismatic, allegorical, or analogical megafauna "had such power to focus the entanglements of human and nonhuman creatures as the bee, which occasioned not only a series of reflections on sovereignty and the commonwealth but served as a kind of sovereign creature."[22] For Mary Baine Campbell, "the topos of the beehive... points backwards in time to the earliest Western literature"; "bee polities of the seventeenth century, in socially and politically unstable Britain especially, belong to a discourse that is... philosophical and fictional, allegorical and biological at once."[23] With their capacity for organized labor, bees were a major terrain for allegory and analogy concerning human social order. They remain so in later works such as Bernard Mandeville's *Fable of the Bees* and Marx's *Capital*, where the worst of architects is (in)famously better than the best of bees.[24]

Renaissance natural history shows diverse views about swarming. Bees might have a certain capacity for individualism that they subject to the social contract. They might be controlled directly by the singing voice of their queen, to the extent that they die if they fly out of earshot. In *The Theater of Insects*, Thomas Moffett holds bees in very high regard: "If we should go about to set forth at large their ingenious disposition, cunning, workmanship, industry, and memory, we should not with *Virgil* the poet yield them only to be endued with a small portion of divine inspiration, *but even wholly to be possest with a rational soul*, and (to erre with *Pythagoras*) to have the understanding of the most ingenious man infused into them by a... [metempsychosis, reincarnation]."[25] Adding to this argument about apian interiority, Moffett describes the communicative singing of bees, distinguishing mind from communication:

> As they fly they make a buzzing or humming noise, which according as they begin to fly or cease, is heard or not heard; which sound whether it proceed from their mouth, or from the motion of their wings, *Aristotle* and *Hesychius* do much contend about. *Neither was I ever so quick sighted, as to determine of a matter so exceeding intricate and obscure.* But the Fifes, and Cornets, seem to make that *sound or noise*.... The English call it singing; and that they make their *signal or watch-word* when they are to watch, when to sleep, when to go to work.[26]

Both passages suggest a relation between subject and swarm, which, as we saw above, is a feature of more abstract swarm descriptions as well. In the first passage, Moffett explains how something like rationality (here Plato's mouth bees are relevant again) finds its way into the tiny bodies of these foraging architects. In the second passage, Moffett describes his own trouble observing the swarm to locate the source of the bee's song, invoking the difficulties of scale and speed that attend the observation of swarming insects. The second passage also superimposes a reading of bee communication as song with a reading of their communication that echoes the role of the signal/noise distinction in information theory. The notion that bees' "sound or noise" is a "signal" or "watch-word" suggests a society regulated by communication—their songs have a clear social function.

Add to this the notion that "they," as Moffett writes, make their signal collectively. The tightly knit collectivity of swarming means that one bee is no bee in this sense also: different from human communication, bees can produce a sign only through collective singing, never through utterance on the part of a subject. Imagine that vocal harmony was required to say "hello." Perhaps Moffett is arguing that the human rational soul does not reincarnate *in* individual bees but rather *among* them, as the "invisible threads" of the superorganism.[27]

In order to explain how bee communication might ground the swarm's counterintuitive capacity for order, other Renaissance natural historians insist on continuous contact with the voice of the king. In *A Further Discovery of Bees*, Moses Rudsen argues that bees must have a very good sense of hearing, which serves as the channel by which the king controls the swarm: "They hear their King-Bee upon all occasions, and the several *signal notes* for preparing to swarm, otherwise what means the ringing of pans to stop the Swarm from flying away? but to confound their hearing of their Leader's voices and notes."[28] In this account, which offers a different distinction between signal and noise, the worker bees must be in continuous auditory contact with their king. Any break in the data leads to disorder and confounds the king's purpose. Livestream control music asserts the logic of sovereignty by removing any possibility that the workers might organize their own movements from below.

Once again, we should look back to the paradox at work in the image of bees swarming around the mouth of Plato. As a form of control, Rudsen's example extends the sovereignty of the voice to the exclusion of any spatial or temporal mediation. No absence, gap, or break in communication is possible without creating disorder in the swarm.

In *Feminine Monarchie*, Butler describes the "bee's musicke" in greater detail. He even offers musical notation for the song of the swarm:

> They sing both in triple time: the princess thus with more or fewer notes, as she pleaseth. And sometime, she taketh a higher key, especially toward [the swarm's] coming forth, and . . . tuneth the rest of her notes in C. . . . So that when they sing together sometime they agree in a perfect third, sometime in a *Diapense*, & (if you respect the termination of the base) in a *Diapaso*. With these tunes answering one another, and some pauses between, they go solemnly round about the hive. This they continue daily until their swarming, but you may hear them best in the mornings and the evenings.[29]

This passage is a more concrete account of bee organization than Moffett's. Butler provides another reason that one bee is no bee in Rudsen's and Moffett's analyses. In order to create the song that seems here to have some function in the process of "swarming" (which in its more particular, apiological sense refers not only to insect sociality but to the bee collective's journey to find a new hive site), the bees must harmonize, "answering one another" with "pauses between." Once again, the meaning of the sign seems complete and functional only when the bees sing it collectively. Different from Rudsen's sovereign voice of control, Butler's interest in pauses suggests that the songs are intermittent, their meaning dependent on periods of silence.

If Plato's rejection of writing as a philosophical medium relies on the self-presence of the voice, Derrida's critique of this idealism, as it persists in Edmund Husserl's phenomenology, features the division of the present moment by the passing of time. For a melody to take shape as a temporal object requires the retention of past notes and the anticipation of future ones. In a similar way, the undivided present moment that would ostensibly endow a subject with self-identity is something closer to a constant division between the past and the future. If the swarm's correlate of this subjective presence is hearing the king's voice "on all occasions," in Butler's account of signification's collective character the pauses break the temporal continuity at work in Rudsen's song of the swarm. Also in Butler's references to the variation of solar time, the temporality of bee communication undermines the concept of sovereignty on which much English Renaissance writing about bee communication rests.

Von Frisch and the Re-Mark

Reading von Frisch raises the question of how we observe nonhuman communication by using our own communication (in a kind of multispecies second-order communication) to distinguish it. The differences and similarities between the early modern texts read here, combined with von Frisch's modern account of nonhuman communication, position the swarm, and the bee topos in particular, as a strange site for a modernity that many consider to be nearing its end. If bee life was once an image of more perfect sovereignty, it functions now as a gap within modernity understood in terms of the epochal separation of nature and society and the cybernetic models of communication through which many of von Frisch's contemporaries came to understand his work. If generalizations of the swarm concept, which model everything from intelligence to markets, are a valedictory postmodern fold in this cybernetic modernity, bee communication as a specific topos remains more difficult to explain in terms of the still-powerful cybernetic episteme.

Through his methods, often richly described, von Frisch observes communication in process in order to distinguish it *as* communication. His books on bee communication include careful accounts of his experimental and observational work. Perhaps *work* is not the best word here, since much of it seems very enjoyable. Von Frisch is more of an experimentalist than a natural historian. *Bees* records days spent around hives in meadows, arranging sugar water, honey, colored bits of paper, vases filled with flowers, and cards "scented with lavender oil."[30] His experimental apparatus reads like an extension of the idyllic suite of objects and sensations that already surround bees as a literary life-form.

Von Frisch set out to show that the bee dance is a language in a replicable way that would compel other scientists to agree. Over the course of a long debate with behaviorists, it became clear that many disagreed about whether he was observing language or a pattern of mechanical stimulation and response.[31] Even von Frisch's work shows some ambivalence about this question. On the one hand, he argues in no uncertain terms that bees can communicate. On the other hand, he often uses "language" in scare quotes when referring to the dance. He never settles on a single positive term for this behavior.

One of von Frisch's innovations is to construct "observation hives"—hives with windows that allow him to watch what happens in the dark space where bees carry out their dance: "I was curious to learn how bees could tell their fellows about the presence of food at a new location. But it is not possible to observe what happens as the bees crawl about between the honeycombs inside an ordinary beehive. I therefore constructed an observation hive in which the honeycombs were arranged edge to edge to so that they formed a large comb, the surface of which could be watched through glass windows" (69).[32] With this design, von Frisch works to make a phenomenon that is fundamentally radial—the hives and honeycombs are roughly round; the swarm seems to move in all directions at once—into something observable by a bilaterally symmetrical mammal with a distinctly directional face.[33] Put differently, the observation hive returns us to the relation between subject and swarm and to Moffett's comments about the difficulty of observation. For Donald R. Griffin in a foreword to von Frisch's *Bees*, the Austrian apiologist "has told us what to look for in the seething turmoil of bees creeping over the honeycomb. . . . His insight has made order where there seemed to be utter chaos" (ix).

Among these conclusions is the claim that "the language of bees is on a higher level than the means of communication among birds and animals with the exception of man."[34] The dance language uses conventional signs to communicate information about food sources. As von Frisch's student Martin Lindauer went on to learn, bees also use the dance to communicate about the location of a future hive, establishing consensus, through swarm intelligence, about the possibilities presented by scouts.[35]

Von Frisch's experiments can be interpreted using Derrida's concept of the "re-mark": an inscription that distinguishes language as language, meaning as meaning. Timothy Morton offers a useful shorthand for the re-mark when he points to the speech bubbles that cartoonists use, especially speech bubbles filled with symbols for cursing or squiggles that refer to unintelligible mumbling.[36] In these examples, the re-mark is the only thing that tells us for certain that *these* marks on the page count as a signal.

How does von Frisch use the re-mark to distinguish bee communication? He begins by writing on the bodies of the bees themselves:

It was . . . necessary to number every bee we wished to study, so that it could be recognized individually among the mass of other bees on the honeycombs. For this purpose I painted the bees with small spots of five different colors; a white spot on the front of the thorax stood for the number 1; a red, for 2; a blue, for 3; a yellow, for 4; and a green, for 5. . . . By employing combinations of these colors I could apply any two-digit number; and spots to indicate the hundreds were painted on the abdomen, so that I could number as many as 599 bees at one time. . . . When a foraging worker comes to this feeding place she is marked with a colored spot while she is sucking up the sugar, so that we can recognize her later in the hive. (70–72)

Von Frisch creates re-marks that allow him to distinguish messages. He observes that "a few minutes after the start of the round dances in the hive new bees appeared simultaneously at all the dishes regardless of their direction. The message brought by a bee as she performed the round dance seemed to be a very simple one, one that carried the meaning "fly out and seek in the neighborhood of the hive" (73). Later, von Frisch elaborates on the bee's ability to dance more complex messages, which carry information about the quality of food and its precise location. Thus, "it is clear that the round dance and the wagging dance are two different terms in the language of bees, the former meaning a source of food near the hive and the latter a source at 100 meters or more" (73). Marking bees, observing them in the hive, and correlating them with his experimental apparatus is a way of earning the right to use the terms *message, meaning,* and *language* without apologizing or reminding the reader that they are anthropomorphic.

Jussi Parikka observes that "von Frisch and his bees stand in an interesting interzone in which different interpretations try to fix [them] as parts of different traditions and possibilities of agency."[37] Indeed, following von Frisch's first publications on the bee language during the 1950s, secondhand interpretations of the bee dance flowed from the pens of such influential human scientists as J. B. S. Haldane, Helen Spurway, Gilbert Simondon, Émile Benveniste, Roman Jakobson, Roland

Barthes, Jacques Lacan, Thomas Sebeok, and Friedrich Kittler. Parikka and Devin Fore both discuss this topic. For Fore, in the broad episteme that emerges from cybernetics and information theory, bees became "microprocessors," exemplifying an "ethological cybernetics" that imagines nature teeming with messages.[38] Since the expansion of interest in von Frisch's work coincided with the transposition of concepts such as feedback, self-regulation, and information into biology in order to explain new evidence about the chemistry of DNA, knowledge of the bee dance language came during a time when "linguistic" concerns (re)entered multiple ontological domains outside that of human language. In this respect, it is easy to understand von Frisch's work as a product of the new episteme of cybernetics and information theory, replacing the structure of organic depth that Foucault associates with the triumvirate of Nietzsche, Marx, and Freud.[39]

The problems with this interpretation are directly related to the difficulty of explaining historical continuity that the theory of epistemic breaks creates as a side effect.[40] It is easy to read terms such as *message* and *information* in relation to the ascendant episteme, but they have a longer history as well. Renaissance natural historians were content to anthropomorphize bees, and their experimental apparatus lacked the rigor of von Frisch's use of the re-mark. They did use glass hives, however, and they came to some similar conclusions about the "invisible bonds" of bee sociality.[41] While their explanations of the swarm usually depend on the logic of sovereignty, we have seen that many of these texts contain countervailing accounts of swarming as a product of decentered communication—an understanding that looks more like that of von Frisch but refers to song instead of dance. Add to this that the Austrian apiologist is concerned to show that bees use signs and to learn what their signs mean to them. His primary conflict in arguing that bees signify was with American behaviorists such as Adrian Wenner, who worked in a field closely related to cybernetics. Von Frisch does use the terms *communication, information,* and *signal*, but *signal* is at work in Renaissance texts as well, and he elsewhere refers to the dance as a "truly perfect ... language" (96). The generalizable swarm concept is closely bound up with the cybernetic episteme, but when theorists abstract it from the bee topos, the song and dance fall away.[42]

In this sense, what Parikka calls "insect media" and what Fore calls "the entomic age" are congruent with the phase of modernity that begins following World War II. In *The Order of Things*, Foucault notes that a kind of shift in exemplary life-form accompanies the break from the classical episteme to that of organic depth: plants are replaced by animals as a central topic of interest in natural history, which differentiates into biology and physiology.[43] If cybernetics and information theory characterize the next episteme, their representative is no doubt the insect, especially the social insect. Yet the role of song and dance in the bee topos forms a hole in this epistemic formation, one that leads back to an earlier period in which the "prose of the world"—a mixture of animism, analogy, and symmetry between microcosm and macrocosm—holds sway. Von Frisch rigorously studies what Renaissance natural historians had already understood as language, but his work occurs in the context of a new, anti-ontological account of such processes as system, algorithm, self-organizing swarm behavior, and code.

If this episteme is deeply modern, the bee topos is best understood in relation to what Bruno Latour calls the "nonmodern": his stopgap term for what emerges within modernity when we no longer think with the "modern constitution" and its separation of nature from society. The nonmodern need not be a Romantic formulation suggesting that we can "go back" to restore a nostalgically imagined premodern state. Rather, moving through modernity to the other side means loosening the prohibition on certain epistemologies—not least anthropomorphism and the "pathetic fallacy." Von Frisch's work is a strong example because it is a legitimate entomological advance, but one that (and this is arguably less true in fields such as chemistry and evolutionary theory) seems to advance by resonating with a premodern topos. In other words, bees have never been modern.

Life-Form Topoi

I close with an interpretation of the life-form topos as a category in literary theory. Campbell and Julian Yates provide two different definitions of topos, both writing in relation to nonhuman animals. For Campbell, the bee topos is a topos insofar as it embraces a "very large story . . . as long a story as that of so-called Western literature" and a certain consistency across periods; for example, the bee and the hive form "the ideal *civitas* itself as either a naturalized concept or a 'natural' model," one often concerned with the value "*multum in parvo*."[44] *Topos* refers to nodes of meaning that persist across longer timescales than the epistemes described by Foucault, which often serve as the theoretical backbone for New Historicist arguments insisting that the proper discursive context of a text exists within a relatively narrow range of years. Yates seems to agree when he turns to the topos in his recent *Of Sheep, Oranges, and Yeast*, which also offers a compelling survey of recent theories of posthumanism. Though the study stays focused on Renaissance texts, Yates seems to argue in several places against what the authors of the *V21 Manifesto* call "positivist historicism."[45] To address in advance the kind of concerns about historical specificity that his claims could provoke, he argues that "travel by trope or by figure means that distances accentuated by chronologies tied to human finitude (politics, economics, epistemic categories, sexuality, and more) are calibrated differently for sheep, oranges, and yeast. Historically, the difference between points may seem immense. Fold things differently, however . . . and that difference disappears."[46]

Yates's claim for the figure—its capacity for time travel, as it were—overlaps with one of Campbell's two points, but his second point concerns nonhuman species rather than the persistent kernel of meaning at work in a given topos: "Figures . . . , as a category, still matter. But they count for more than the bodying forth of absent things in media (representations) or even the effects of that bodying forth on a reader or viewer (a memory, an affective response). They designate privileged material-semiotic zones (topoi), scenes of writing or marking, from which forms of life issue. They produce time effects. But those effects are keyed more to questions of performance or the timing of their activation than to fidelity to a historical period."[47] Yates associates *topoi* not only with rhetorical commonplaces at work in the literary tradition and with what Donna Haraway calls the material-semiotic node. Not only do different species require different modes of historicization—engaging with meaning at variable speeds, perhaps—but also life-forms *emerge from material-semiotic topoi* that include both meaning and nonhuman species such as bees. That is, the meaning of the bee topos cannot be fully arbitrary because of the way bees condition its existence.

The dance language complicates this point. Different from the life-form topos of a species that does not communicate—the rose, for example—for the bee topos, writing about bees has also been writing about bee communication. Assumed to be song but shown to be dance, this language involves the use of signs. Could it be that scenes of writing or marking in this topos involve the linkage of human signs with bee signs?[48] As a system of danced signs, the bee language may be a necessary condition for the swarm concept itself, and thus for the sizable archive that accrues to it—which is not to say that this relationship with language beyond the human leads to a representationally accurate account of bees. Perhaps the question we should be asking is not whether we can understand nonhuman experience without anthropomorphizing it, but whether we can mix sign systems in a way that makes them depend on and trace one another.

This could be one way in which *life-forms* come into being as material-semiotic entities that occupy a level of partial abstraction between concrete species and individuals, on the one hand, and metaphysical distinctions such as human/animal, on the other. It makes sense that life-form topoi would be a source of formal, deep time (not to say universal) unity, because the species from which life-forms abstract into iterable meaning change at a speed slower than most human historical phenomena. They do not occupy an unchanging nature outside history. The character of the abstraction changes over time, as with *The Black Mirror*'s digital bees. The fates of the swarm concept show that substantial discontinuity accompanies the continuity of the bee topos. Even so, from the perspective of literary theory and animal studies, it could be that life-form topoi will be an expansive subject for those interested in studying the longer historical timescales of literature and culture.[49] The fact that we now have so little language for these shows the need for new theory geared to continuity. The point is not to return to the Frygean archetype or the new critical canon, which sacrifice cultural breadth for temporal depth. Life-form topoi are one way the scholarly focus on the nonhuman in the humanities can add its voice to the chorus demanding new ways of understanding the relation among timeframe, period, and form.

Notes

1. The Linnaean name of the honeybee is *Apis mellifera*. According to Constance Meinwald, in this story "bees deposit honey in the mouth of the infant Plato" (*Plato*, 11–12). In this "stock report about poets in antiquity ... the honey in the baby's mouth prefigures and symbolizes the sweetness of his verses. Transferring the story to a philosopher appropriates for him this traditional recognition of eloquence."

2. See, for example, Wilson, *Social Conquest of Earth*.

3. Henri Michaux, *Miserable Miracle (Mescaline)*, 9
4. Borges, *Labyrinths*, 28.
5. For wide-ranging examples, see Vehlken, "Zootechnologies." For examples from the intellectual history of the Enlightenment, see Sheehan and Wahram, *Invisible Hands*, 177–82.
6. Johnston, *Allure of Machinic Life*, 375–84.
7. For example, Stefan Helmreich and Sophia Roosth discuss life-form as a keyword in *Sounding the Limits of Life*, 19–35. Eugene Thacker addresses pitfalls with the concept of life in *After Life*. For problems with a unified concept of the animal, see Derrida, *Animal*. For problems with using the unified concept of the animal for the study of the Renaissance, see Campana, "Bee and the Sovereign?," 94–95.
8. See also Derek Woods, "Accelerated Reading" and "The Fungal Kingdom."
9. Foucault describes the prose of the world as an analogical mode of thinking and situates it in the Renaissance in his *Order of Things*, 17–25.
10. We find arguments that cybernetics and information theory result in a Foucauldian episteme in which multiple fields use elements of these conceptual frameworks in an (often) unconscious way in Geohegan, "Information Theory"; and Pias, introduction to *Cybernetics*; Kay, *Who Wrote*, chap. 2.
11. Thacker, "Swarm Life," 182–85.
12. Aristotle, *Complete Works*, 971.
13. Purchas, *Theatre of Politicall Flying-Insects*, 16. Perhaps Purchas alludes to Lucretius's *On the Nature of Things* in this passage, since Lucretius offers "swarming" atoms as the explanation for fierce weather in book 6 of the poem.
14. Michael Hardt and Antonio Negri use the word *multitude* to characterize anarchic self-organization from below in *Multitude*.
15. Thacker and Galloway, *Exploit*, 66.
16. Bergson, *Creative Evolution*, 183.
17. Wheeler, "Ant Colony as Organism," 310.
18. Parikka, *Insect Media*, 126. Ants are also an important example for Wiener in *Human Use*, 51–57.
19. Johnston, *Allure of Machinic Life*, 377. Saul Bass's film *Phase IV* is an example of the cybernetic swarm played out in the medium of a science-fiction film.
20. Kennedy and Eberhardt quoted in Johnston, *Allure of Machinic Life*, 379.
21. Thacker, *Biomedia*, 143. John Arquila and David Ronfeldt suggest an ominous new swarm strategy to replace the blitzkrieg-like tactics that emerged from World War II in their report *Swarming* (22, 49). They discuss the need for what they call synoptic observation or "topsight" on the part of the higher command. Topsight suggests the possibility of intervening and controlling swarming, even though swarm units normally operate with a high degree of independence. The requirement for topsight evokes the paradox whereby using the swarm technologically and embracing its principle of order seem incompatible—or point to a new modality of power. The same pattern holds in Ernst Jünger's prescient novel *The Glass Bees* (129–45). There, a Steve Jobs / Willy Wonka–like postindustrial manufacturer designs artificial bees. The protagonist becomes a swarm observer: "The way they radiated from the hives . . . then darted back, stopped short, hovered in a compact swarm. . . . I cannot say what astonished me more—the ingenious invention of each single unit or the interplay among them. . . . Zapparoni's glass collectives resembled less a hive than a telephone exchange. . . . Although scores of units were involved, the whole process was

conducted with perfect precision; no doubt, some central control or principle regulated it . . . [but he contradicts himself, and this is the paradox]. Considered as organization, this activity could be interpreted in several ways. One could hardly assume the existence of a central control panel. . . . I imagined instead a system of distributors."
22. Campana, "Bee and the Sovereign?," 97.
23. Campbell, "Busy Bees," 621.
24. Marx, *Capital*, 284.
25. Moffett, *Theater of Insects*, 895; my emphasis.
26. Ibid., 893.
27. Bergson, *Creative Evolution*, 183.
28. Rudsen, *Further Discovery*, 12; my emphasis.
29. Butler, *Feminine Monarchie*, C.50 F.
30. Frisch, *Bees*, 82. Subsequent references to *Bees* appear parenthetically by page number.
31. Munz, *Dancing Bees*, 213–16.
32. For more on observation hives, see Botelho, "Thinking with Hives," 17–24.
33. Such multidirectional ambience confronts the narrator of Jünger's *Glass Bees*, who experiences a "particularly narcotic effect . . . couldn't keep up with the task of interpretation . . . saw changes of color as in optical signals" (148).
34. Von Frisch and Lindauer, "'Language,'" 540.
35. As Devin Fore describes this phenomenon, "the swarm intelligence of the hive arrives at a collective decision using the dance-system in a manner comparable to human voting" ("Entomic Age," 44).

36. Morton, *Ecology Without Nature*, 49.
37. Parikka, *Insect Media*, 136.
38. Fore, "Entomic Age," 45.
39. Thacker, "Swarm Life," 182–85.
40. For an account of this difficulty, see Winthrop-Young, "Drill and Distraction," 841–46. See also Thomas Sheehan and Dror Wahram's critique of Foucault in *Invisible Hands*, and compare to John H. Zammito on Foucault's account of biology in *Gestation of German Biology*.
41. Bergson, *Creative Evolution*, 183.
42. For Mark Goble writing on modernism and media in *Beautiful Circuits, communication* becomes a new twentieth-century keyword, with a changed and generalized meaning, during the period that precedes and becomes contemporaneous with von Frisch's work on the bee dance.
43. Foucault, *Order of Things*, 149–50.
44. Campbell, "Busy Bees," 623.
45. Adams et al., *V21 Manifesto*.
46. Yates, *Of Sheep*, 28.
47. Ibid., 14.
48. The advantage of this ecological grammatology for Yates is that it expands the notion of "cultural graphology to inquire into the kinds of relays that form between differently animated beings and how those relays make possible certain kinds of worlds" (ibid., 85).
49. For example, see Dimock, "Deep Time." See also the exchange between Dimock and Mark McGurl in *Critical Inquiry*.

Bibliography

Adams, Maeve, et al. *The V21 Manifesto*. Accessed February 15, 2017, http://v21collective.org/manifesto-of-the-v21-collective-ten-theses/.

Aristotle. *The Complete Works of Aristotle*. Edited by Jonathan Barnes. Princeton: Princeton University Press, 1995.

Arquila, John, and David Ronfeldt. *Swarming and the Future of Conflict*. Santa Monica, CA: RAND, 2000.

Bergson, Henri. *Creative Evolution*. Translated by Robert Mitchell. New York: Random House, 1944.

Borges, Jorge Luis. *Labyrinths*. Edited by Donald A. Yates and James E. Irby. New York: New Directions, 1964.

Botelho, Keith. "Thinking with Hives." In *Object Oriented Environs*, edited by Jeffrey Jerome Cohen and Julian Yates. New York: Putnam, 2016.

Brooker, Charlie, creator. *The Black Mirror*. Season 3, episode 6, directed by James Hawes. Released October 21, 2016. https://www.netflix.com/ca/title/70264888.

Butler, Charles. *Feminine Monarchie*. Oxford, UK: Joseph Barnes, 1609.

Campana, Joseph. "The Bee and the Sovereign? Political Entomology and the Problem of Scale." *Shakespeare Studies* 41 (2013): 94–113.

Campbell, Mary Baine. "Busy Bees: Utopia, Dystopia, and the Very Small." *Journal of Medieval and Early Modern Studies* 36, no. 3 (Fall 2006): 619–42.

Derrida, Jacques. *The Animal That Therefore I Am*. Translated by David Wills. New York: Fordham University Press, 2008.

Dimock, Wai Chee. "Deep Time: American Literature and World History." *American Literary History* 13, no. 4 (2001): 755–75.

———. *Through Other Continents: American Literature Across Deep Time*. Princeton: Princeton University Press, 2006.

Fore, Devin. "The Entomic Age." *Grey Room* 33 (2008): 26–55.

Foucault, Michel. *The Order of Things: An Archaeology of the Human Sciences*. New York: Vintage, 1970.

Geohegan, Bernard Dionysius. "From Information Theory to French Theory: Jakobson, Lévi-Strauss, and the Cybernetic Apparatus." *Critical Inquiry* 38, no. 1 (Autumn 2011): 96–126.

Goble, Mark. *Beautiful Circuits: Modernism and the Mediated Life*. New York: Columbia University Press, 2010.

Hardt, Michael, and Antonio Negri. *Multitude*. New York: Penguin, 2005.

Helmreich, Stefan, and Sophia Roosth. *Sounding the Limits of Life: Essays in the Anthropology of Biology and Beyond*. Princeton: Princeton University Press, 2016.

Johnston, John. *The Allure of Machinic Life*. Cambridge, MA: MIT Press, 2008.

Jünger, Ernst. *The Glass Bees*. Translated by Louise Bogan and Elizabeth Mayer. New York: New York Review of Books, 2000.

Kay, Lily E. *Who Wrote the Book of Life? A History of the Genetic Code*. Stanford: Stanford University Press, 2000.

Latour, Bruno. *We Have Never Been Modern*. Translated by Catherine Porter. Cambridge, MA: Harvard University Press, 1993.

Marx, Karl. *Capital, Volume 1*. New York: Penguin, 1992.

Meinwald, Constance. *Plato*. New York: Routledge, 2016.

Michaux, Henri. *Miserable Miracle (Mescaline)*. Translated by Louis Varèse. San Francisco: City Lights Books, 1963.

Moffett, Thomas. *The Theater of Insects: or, Lesser Living Creatures*. In *The History of Four-Footed Beasts and Serpents*, by Edward Topsell. London, 1658.

Morton, Timothy. *Ecology Without Nature*. Cambridge, MA: Harvard University Press, 2007.

Munz, Tania. *The Dancing Bees: Karl von Frisch and the Discovery of the Honeybee Language*. Chicago: University of Chicago Press, 2016.

Parikka, Jussi. *Insect Media: An Archaeology of Animals and Technology*. Minneapolis: University of Minnesota Press, 2010.

Pias, Claus. Introduction to *Cybernetics: The Macy Conferences, 1946–1953*, edited by Pias. Chicago: University of Chicago Press, 2016.

Purchas, Samuel. *A Theatre of Politicall Flying-Insects*. London, 1657.

Rudsen, Moses. *A Further Discovery of Bees*. London: Henry Million, 1679.

Sheehan, Jonathan, and Dror Wahram. *Invisible Hands: Self-Organization and the Eighteenth Century*. Chicago: University of Chicago Press, 2015.

Thacker, Eugene. *After Life*. Chicago: University of Chicago Press, 2010.

———. *Biomedia*. Minneapolis: University of Minnesota Press, 2004.

———. "Swarm Life." In *Theory After "Theory*," edited by Jane Elliot and Derek Attridge. New York: Routledge, 2011.

Thacker, Eugene, and Alexander Galloway. *The Exploit: A Theory of Networks*. Minneapolis: University of Minnesota Press, 2007.

Vehlken, Sebastian. "Zootechnologies: Swarming as a Cultural Technique." *Theory, Culture, and Society* 30, no. 6 (2013): 110–31.

von Frisch, Karl. *Bees: Their Vision, Chemical Senses, and Language*. Ithaca, NY: Cornell University Press, 1950.

von Frisch, Karl, and Martin Lindauer. "The 'Language' and Orientation of the Honey Bee." In *Foundations of Animal Behavior*, edited by L. D. Houck and L. C. Drickamer. Chicago: University of Chicago Press, 1996.

Wheeler, William Morton. "The Ant Colony as an Organism." *Journal of Morphology* 22, no. 2 (1911): 307–25.

Wiener, Norbert. *The Human Use of Human Beings*. Boston: Da Capo, 1988.

Wilson, Edward O. *The Social Conquest of Earth*. New York: Liveright, 2012.

Winthrop-Young, Geoffrey. "Drill and Distraction in the Yellow Submarine." *Critical Inquiry* 28, no. 4 (Summer 2002): 825–54.

Woods, Derek. "Accelerated Reading: Fossil Fuels, Infowhelm, and Archival Life." In *Anthropocene Reading: Literary History in Geologic Times*, edited by Tobias Menely and Jesse Oak Taylor. University Park: Penn State University Press, 2017.

———. "The Fungal Kingdom." *Alienocene: Journal of the First Outernational*. Stratum 8. December 4, 2020. https://alienocene.com/2020/12/04/stratum-8/.

Yates, Julian. *Of Sheep, Oranges, and Yeast: A Multispecies Impression*. Minneapolis: University of Minnesota Press, 2017.

Zammito, John H. *The Gestation of German Biology: Philosophy and Physiology from Stahl to Schelling*. Chicago: University of Chicago Press, 2017.

CHAPTER 11
ILLUMINATION
"Living Lamps"

Jessica Lynn Wolfe

"Wondrous things are promised from the Glow-worm."[1] So writes Thomas Browne in a section of his *Pseudodoxia Epidemica* first added in 1650, the second edition of that work. Browne delivers a lyrical panegyric to one of the most marvelous of nature's creatures while at the same time skeptically deflating the various myths that attached to the glowworm, a catchall term for the various groups of insect larva and adult larviform females that glimmer through bioluminscence, including Spanish fly (*Cantharides*), the firefly (*Lampyridae*), and the common European glowworm (*Lampyris noctiluca*).

Bioluminscence was poorly understood during the Renaissance, but no less compelling for its mysteriousness. Particularly after Francis Bacon observed in his *Sylva Sylvarum* (1627) that the "Nature of the Glo-wormes is hitherto not well observed," thus identifying a better comprehension of the insect's enigmatic radiance as a scientific desideratum, the marvel attracted the attention of some of the era's most sophisticated naturalists, including Ulisse Aldrovandi, Robert Boyle, Robert Plot, and Thomas Bartholin, whose 1647 *De Luce Animalium* (*On the Light of Animals*) is the era's most systematic treatment of substances that emit light, a category that to the early modern imagination might include the Medusa jellyfish, the firefly, rotting wood (or rather the mycelium fungus that lives upon it), clammy sweat on bed clothes, phosphorus, and the radiant red carbuncle gem, as well as—at least for some naturalists—the eyes of hyenas and nocturnal birds, the *Ignis lambens* or "luminous mutton" examined at Montpellier in 1640–1641, and the shining face of Moses as described at Exodus 34:29–30.[2] Seventeenth-century investigations into this rather haphazard amalgamation of organisms and minerals, united solely by their shared capacity for luminescence, reveal how the study of the glowworm and its luminous humor were central to contemporary debates about the nature and behavior of light, the relationship between light and heat, and the boundary between life and death, in particular the question of what components, such as air or water, might be essential to the continuance of life.

The seventeenth-century interest in glowworms was almost certainly sparked by various reports of luminous insects and plants in the New World, some of them so fulsome, according to accounts by Conrad Gesner, Thomas Moffett, Juan Eusebio Nieremberg, and Gonzalo Fernández de Oviedo, that English explorers to the Indies mistook the insects for Spaniards approaching with their torches.[3] In addition to using the insects as lamps, an image that may have been in Andrew Marvell's mind when he imagined glowworms as "courteous lights" showing the way to those "that in the night have lost their aim," the Native Americans also stained their hands and faces with a paste concocted from the luminous juice of glowworms.[4] Yet in spite of the purportedly uncanny brightness of these "great American Glowworms," Browne, for one, asserts that their "light declineth as the luminous humour dryeth."[5] Most of the luminescent organisms studied by seventeenth-century naturalists were, however, native to Europe and in evidence across various landscapes, their diversity all the more puzzling since it was not at all clear whether the glow emitted from insects, fish, and plants derived from the same optical or biological causes as the radiance of gems and metals or from different causes entirely. Upon encountering the spectacle of an ocean shimmering with bioluminescent plankton, René Descartes believed that he was witnessing the combustion of flammable crystals of sea salt, which emit sparks "similar to those which pieces of flint give off when we strike them together," while Bartholin believed that the glow of seawater was evidence for the existence of light in all things.[6]

Yet bioluminscence, as other seventeenth-century naturalists rightly suspected, is created not by heat but rather by a chemical reaction. As early as 1605, in his *Topica Inquisitionis de Luce et Lumine*, Bacon observes that glowworms are "not hot to the touch" as are other glowing substances such as a red-hot iron, and he concludes from this observation that "it is not the property of fire alone to give light . . . small drops of the [sea] water, struck off by the motion of the oars in rowing, seem sparkling and luminous," a theory later explored in further depth by Plot.[7] Ever suspicious of misleading resemblances and analogies, Bacon warns that while "flame and ignited bodies" may appear to have an affinity with glowworms, the Indian fly (*Pyrophorus*), "the eyes of certaine living Creatures in the dark," or the "sweat of a horse hard ridden," it is not at all evident that there exists any common bond among all "Lucid Bodies," which differ in dignity according to Bacon as well as in the form and origin of their light, as unlike as "the Sun and rotten wood, or the putrid scales of Fish."[8]

Browne singles out two "wondrous" characteristics that he claims to have been erroneously credited to the glowworm: the belief that its light survives the death of the insect and the related belief that this light may be "translated" out of the insect's body and turned into "waters . . . which afford a lustre in the night," a substance often referred to as *liquor lucidus* or *liquor cicindelarum*.[9] This liquor was believed to have fueled lamps that purportedly burned everlastingly inside tombs, an ancient but subsequently defunct practice discussed by Fortunio Liceti and by Girolamo Cardano, whose *De Subtilitate* posits that the liquid extracted from the glowworm may light a lamp in such a manner that "it seems you can impose the light that has been brought down from heaven into matter, like a captive rower into a trireme, and hold it in chains."[10]

Browne's *Pseudodoxia* discredits both myths with the single counterargument that "the light made by this animal depends much upon its life. For when they are dead they shine not."[11] For Browne, belief in the possibility of creating perpetual light out of the bodily fluids of a bioluminescent insect is controverted by experimentation: glowworms preserved in fresh grass survive and shine for up to eighteen days, he notes, but "as they declined, and the luminous humour dryed, their light grew languid, and at last went out with their lives."[12] Browne's conviction that the insect's capacity to emit light is contiguous with and contingent on its life is supported by his related observation that snake venom and similarly "destructive compositions" discharged by other animals similarly "omit their efficacy in the death of the individual, and act but dependantly on their forms," a theory confirmed through experiments conducted by naturalists and physicians ranging from Galen to the sixteenth-century Montpellier naturalist Guillaume Rondelet.[13]

The glowworm offers a case study in the seventeenth-century scientific fascination with what Browne calls "vivency," the conditions and requisites for the maintenance of life. The insect was central to the challenge of determining the physiological boundaries between life and death, as well as to related investigations into the question of what conditions or substances are essential for the perpetuation of life. If glowworms appear to emit a "faint light" after death, according to Browne, the conclusion that they continue to glow when life abates is a "mistake in the compute of death, and term of disanimation," since, he reasons, it is "no easie matter to determine the point of death in Insects and Creatures who have not their vitalities radically confined unto one part," a problem only partially solved by the advent of microscopy, since many insects mistakenly appear dead to the observer when they simply "cease to move or afford the visible evidences of life."[14] This may account for why, even among the most exacting seventeenth-century observers of the insect world, there was no firm consensus about whether the glowworm continued to glow after death. Fabio Colonna, for instance, an Italian naturalist whose exactitude was much admired by Browne and early members of England's Royal Society, maintained that "even after death, as long as there is still moisture, the buttocks of the dead body shine in the dark, but once they have become dry, the light goes out" (*Post mortem etiam lucent in obscuro cadaveris nates qua[n]diu[m] adsit humor, exiccato quidem illo lumen deperditur*).[15] The question of whether the glowworm's light extinguished with his life was vociferously contested—and the subject of very frequent experimentation—during the late sixteenth and seventeenth centuries, and the various trials yielded diverse and often unreliable conclusions. When Bartholin set out to disprove Scaliger's assertion that the glowworm's light died with it, he "tried to check on the truthfulness of this experiment" but was unable to do so when his specimen, a "wingless Noctiluca ... cleverly escaped and with itself took away its light" (*Noctilucam Apteron ... astu elapsa se cum luce surripuit*), one of several reasons that experimentation on insects could prove a tricky endeavor.[16]

Throughout his writings, Browne is captivated by the problem that the appearance of death, particularly in the miniature, bloodless, and quasi-organic realms of the insect and plant worlds, is deceptive. Flies that may seem to the observer "desperate and quite forsaken of their forms" may nonetheless "by vertue of the Sun or warm ashes . . . be revoked unto life"; caterpillars that appear to die in fact undergo a "transplantation" or "transfiguration," while plants consumed by fire may appear "utterly destroyed," yet to the "sensible Artist the formes are not perished," theories that are tested through experimentation with palingenesis, the process of reanimating an organic substance that is, or at least appears to be, dead.[17] Seventeenth-century experiments on and microscopic observations of glowworms, focusing as they did on the question of what forces or circumstances extinguish their light and what the extinction of that light signifies, seek to resolve some fundamental questions about the nature of life: which vital forces—air, or water, or nutriment—are essential to the preservation of life, and which of these forces, if removed, are the cause of disanimation? This is perhaps why a 1685 article in the *Philosophical Transactions of the Royal Society* juxtaposes the underside of a dead glowworm as viewed through the microscope with the depiction of a mechanical device that approximates the rings of the insect's tail, where its light (now spent) was formerly stored (figure 2.11.1).

Browne's repudiation of the theory that the glowworm's light might be extracted and preserved after the death of the insect is partly a reaction against the many legends that circulated in works of medieval and Renaissance natural philosophy about the possibility of distilling the juice from the glowworm's tail into medicinal extracts or fluids that permit nocturnal reading. These accounts were endorsed, with varying degrees of certitude and experimental legitimacy, by Albertus Magnus, Cardano, Aldrovandi, and Giambattista Della Porta but roundly rejected by Browne's forerunner, Moffett, who scoffs that "Vainly . . . do some boast of compositions" made from the glowworm, "with which they will keep perpetual light," and testifies "from experience" that when the insects are placed into a "clear Crystal glass, so that the air may freely come at them, with a little grass" for sustenance, they continue to glow for twelve days, at which point "they languish and faint away, so the light by little and little is remitted and slackned, and in the end . . . it is totally extinguished."[18]

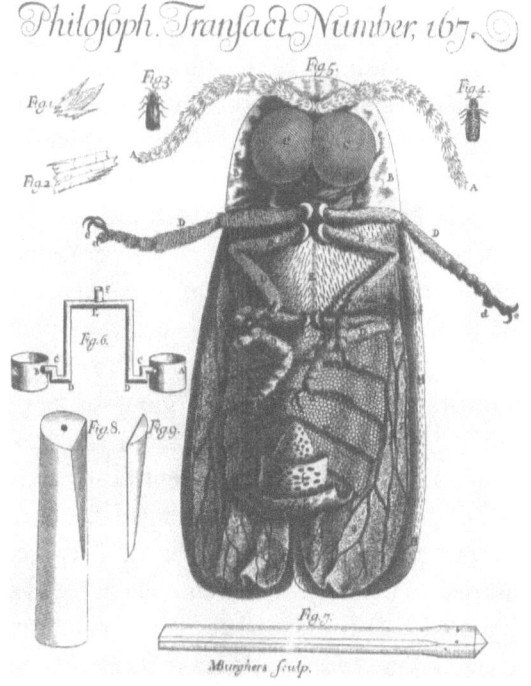

Figure 2.11.1 Richard Waller, "Observations on the Cicindela Volans, or Flying Glow-Worm," *Philosophical Transactions* 15, no. 167 (1685): 841–45; image before p. 841. Google Books.

Whereas Browne rejects as physiologically nonsensical the idea that the glowworm's juices might be extracted and conserved outside the insect's body, remaining efficacious beyond its death, Moffett objects to the hypothesis on theological as much as practical grounds, condemning attempts to "counterfeit" the glowworm's light as an "impious presumption" akin to stealing the "true heavenly fire" of God himself.[19] The vehemence of Moffett's censure against this Promethean transgression is less surprising in view of the fact that creaturely bioluminescence was frequently understood during the Renaissance as the product of an affinity with the light of the sun or the moon, an idea that in turn fostered the common belief that glowworms are "earthly stars" whose radiance, as Moffett explains, not only resembles but even originates from a "divine light" and thus encourages us to fix our eyes and mind on "Christ the lasting, true, and the chiefest light of the world," as well as on "that holy Spirit which doth illuminate our spirits in the most obscure darkness of our understandings."[20] Browne is tentative at best in his own endorsement of the principle that the light of the glowworm and that of cosmic bodies are analogous, if not also derived from the same original source. In his discussion of the insect, Browne entertains the possibility that the "refulgent humor" of the glowworm "may not have some original in the seed and spirit analogous unto the Element of Stars," but he hesitates at the corollary that the "Sun and Stars [are] living creatures" whose "lustre depend[s] on their lives," a theory rejected by Browne two books earlier in *Pseudodoxia*, and finally leaves open to future inquiry whether "the light of animals, which do not occasionally shine from contingent causes, be of Kin to the light of Heaven," thus making visible, or rendering in corporeal form, what Browne calls the "invisible flame of life."[21]

There was a twofold resistance to the belief that glowworms were "earthly stars" whose light emanated from celestial bodies, a theory that proved at once theologically disturbing and scientifically untenable. Centuries earlier, Albertus Magnus had challenged the theory that the glowworm's light springs from a "coelestiall body," because, as he reasoned, "a coelestiall nature comes not into composition of bodies generative and corruptible," a distinction that, if not maintained, would allow the sun and the moon life spans no more lasting or resilient than that of an insect.[22] Such arguments took on added urgency when considered from a theological vantage. In a 1631 meditation, Joseph Hall invites his readers to contemplate the "cold Candle" of this "sorry worm" that emits light but no heat—a characteristic that makes the glowworm a common Renaissance metaphor for the false light of religious zealots or the faint embers of faith among the lukewarm or spiritually tepid.[23] For Hall, whereas the most devout Christians, like the sun, "shine ever alike" and "shine fairest in the frostiest nights" much like stars in a night sky, the light of the glowworm "is for some shew, but for no use," since "any light that is attended with heat can impart it selfe to others," while by contrast, the false light of the glowworm cannot be transmitted to another body and thus fails to radiate everywhere like the divine light of God.[24] Hall's theologically charged language complicates and extends the physiological questions posed by the glowworm's bioluminescence, namely, whether its light is generated from within its body, internal and inborn, as Aldrovandi explains, or whether that light is reflected or absorbed from another, greater luminous body (figure 2.11.2).

Liber Quartus de Infectis. 495

A oblongiusculis, & trium articulorum : stans & cauda trahens dracunculi quodammodo speciem præbet. Cùm verò his pedibus anticis progreditur, caudam sub ventrem inflectens, & antrorsùm complicans postica parte arcuatìm repit. Nam & cauda pedum eorum vicem subit, qui in posteriori parte in veris Erucis existunt. Hanc enim candidam, & tricuspidem promit, qua posticam corporis partem inter serpendum sustinet, & cuilibet rei, vt aciculæ affixa adhærescit pendula. Prima & antica segmina longiora sunt, breuiora verò versus caudam vergentia, & medio latissimum corpus paulatim in caudæ penicillatum mucronem attenuatur. Aluo extrema egerit excrementum quoddam lentum, ac ceræ in modum fuluum, quod ipsum nonnunquam cauda ad os adductâ in circulum ceu vertitur, contractum ori admouet, quo tamen etiam similem liquorem vomere videtur, ac veluti filo facto retrocedit illud diducit, ac protrahit lentore sequax, deinde denuo absorbet. Parte prona modicè nigrescens diluta purpura, qualis Persici florum est, admixta variat. Qui purpureus huic est macularum color in quibusdam magis lutescit. ᵉIulius ᵉ*Exer.194.* Scaliger in Vasconia sine alis Cicindelas esse scribit, Erucæ maioris quantitate, crassiores, ventricosas, Lucrambam ibi vocari. Ex harum grege ea forte erit quam secunda tabella pronam, & supinam ostendo, vnà cum Lampyride alata.

LOCVS. ORTVS. GENERATIO.

C **M**ENSIBVS Aprilis, Maij, & Iunij vesperi per prata cernuntur Lampyrides, necnon & alijs anni temporibus, vt autumni, sed tunc rarò volant. Quo circa Plinius de Scarabæorum agens generibus, & ijs Insectis quorum alæ vagina cooperiuntur, inquit : Lucent, ignium modo noctu, laterum & clunium colore (legunt alij fulgore, alij candore) Lampyrides, non antè matura pabula, aut post dissecta conspicuæ. Hyemis autem tempore nullibi apparent : arcet namq; has iniuria frigoris, cuius vt cætera plurima Insecta, sunt impatientissimæ proptereaq; in frigidiusculis regionibus nullibi conspicuæ. Has putat ᵃIohannes Baptista Porta Neapolitanus è rore nasci, quod neutiquam arbitror. Hesychium autem, qui ait λαμπυρὶς ζωύφριν ἐν φρυγάνοις γινόμενον, id est Lampyris est animalculum ex stuppa natum, non ita intelligere oportet, quasi materialem ortus causam stuppam, aut sarmeta, aut similia quæ φρύγανα Græci dicunt, constituat, sed quòd in ijs tanquam in aliquo loco generentur. nam inter pabula plærunq; volitant. Harum autem procreationem ignotam antea sapientibus, primus omnium, quos nostrum adspexit seculum, doctissimus Iulius Scaliger, aperuit. ᵇ is enim plurimis in locis attestatur per coitum propagari, in ᵇTheophrastum Commentis, quando inquit. Insecta, quæ habentur pro imperfectissimis (animalibus) diutissimè in coitu immorantur, vt Pulex, Cicindela. & rursus ibidem: Insecta pariunt haud ita multò pòst: Cicindela postridiè. in cuius rei confirmationem hanc ᶜ alicubi historiam recitauit, docens eontra Cardanum Apes oua posse simul habere in vtero, & continuo esse ope re, Duo inquit, tibi, etiam sapientibus ignota declarabo. Primùm scito Cicindelam à me cū suo mari deprehensam in coitu. Mas ne contactus quidem abstitit. In pertula pixide conditi fuêre per totam noctem. Postridiè adhuc hærebat mas: in meridie solutus obijt. Ab ea hora sub vesperam vsq; oua multa edidit fœmella: quæ intra viginti horas viuificata abierunt. sic momento eduntur Insectorum oua, atque perficiuntur. Quod & Philosophus dicebat in primo de Generatione animalium. De Insectis loquens ait : Συμπλύνται μὲν πολλῷ χρόνῳ, διαλύσητα δὲ τίκτει ταχέως. Hæc si ita sint, vt mihi ex tanti viri autoritate persuadeo, necessarium est ex ijs ouis, quæ parit Cicindela Erucam, quandam fieri, quam impennem Cicindelam nominat Aristoteles, & ex hac tandem alatam gigni, sic enim ait ᵈPhilosophus.

ᵃ*Exot.non nasci.*
ᵇ*Phytog.6. cap.3.*

Coitu pro paganturs.
ᵇ*Lib.4. de caus. Plan.*

ᶜ*Exer.191.* *Cicindelæ historia mira.*

ᵈ*Hist.5. cap.19.*

T t 2   Iosophus,

Figure 2.11.2 Ulisse Aldrovandi, *De Animalibus Insectis Libri Septem* (Bologna, 1602), 4.8, "De Cicindela," p. 495. Google Books.

This interinanimation of theological concerns with questions of biology, optics, and chemistry is also apparent in discussions of the glowworm by natural philosophers such as Jan Baptista Van Helmont and Boyle. Helmont debates whether the "light of the Sun [is] married as a husband to the Splendour of the Glo-worm; so as that from them both, one only thing did glitter," or whether the former light is "Heavenly and constant" while the latter is "wormy or corruptible," an idiom that links the glowworm's fleeting and tenuous life and, by extension, the strong association of worms with the corruption and putrefaction of flesh, with the symbolic language of mortality and sinfulness in a manner reminiscent of *Hamlet*'s Ghost, who observes how the glowworm's "ineffectual fire" grows pale at dawn.[25] At stake in Helmont's discussion is the problem that if the glowworm's light is indeed "married" to that of the sun, the death of the insect—or even the mere extinction of its glow—necessitates a belief that the sun's light will also perish, since it "doth as it were take on the stain and tincture" of the fragile insect.[26]

Debates over the origin and nature of the glowworm's light, in particular the question of whether the glowworm possesses an intrinsic self-luminosity or whether its light derives from the sun or the moon, grow more urgent in the wake of the discovery of the so-called Bononian (or Bolognian) stone, a phosphorus first prepared in 1603 by an Italian shoemaker and alchemical dabbler named Vincenzo Cascariolo, who discovered that by calcifying a local stone, a barium sulfate native to Monte Paterno near Bologna, the stone would "imbibe" light during the day and later emit it at night.[27] Calling into question the purported capacity to "translate the light from the *Bononian* stone into another body," Browne likens the process to similar, and similarly suspect, attempts to "make a Shining water from *Glow-worms*," casting doubt on the efficacy of both experiments in a manner that implicates both in more wide-ranging debates about the behavior of light and the relationship between the earth and the moon.[28] In his 1622 *Pharmacopaea Spagirica*, one of the first printed investigations of the Bononian stone, the French iatrochemist Pierre Potier marvels at the way that the stone receives its light from the sun (or perhaps the moon) and reflects that light in the dark, a phenomenon that in turn prompts Potier to question "whether light is a body and what kind of a body; or a substance or an accident" (*num verè lumen corpus sit, & quodnam corpus an substantia, an accidens*), puzzles also posed by the glowworm, which, as Shakespeare's Pericles notes, "hath fire in darkness, none in light," an optical paradox frequently noted by Renaissance poets and playwrights.[29]

There were three chief answers to Potier's questions that animated discussions of various luminescent objects and creatures. First, light could be absorbed by an object and its energy converted to heat; second, light could be reflected by the object; or third, light could be transmitted by the object. Central to the era's experiments and investigations into the nature of light and its transmission, in particular the question of which luminescent things "shine only by the help of External illustration" and which "need not be previously illustrated by any external Lucid," the latter defined by Boyle as a "Self-shining substance," glowworms also served as poetic shorthand for the abstruseness of those investigations, or for the arcana of nature itself, as is evident in Thomas Heyrick's joco-serious poem addressing the scientific *insolubilia* that preoccupied members of London's Royal Society in its early decades:

If from the *Sun* the Beams of Light do flow,
How doth a *Candle* the same Office do?
How doth the *Glow-worm* with the *Sun* contest,
And Brandish forth her Beams, when He's at rest?
Why's Rotten Wood and Fishes Scales so Bright?
Why doth Sea-water Sparkle in the Night?[30]

If the glowworm's small size bestowed upon it a certain nugatory quality, suggested above by Heyrick's David-meets-Goliath competition between it and the sun, its littleness also endowed the insect with the capacity to elucidate, in miniature form, the macrocosmic processes at work in the sky.

Galileo was one of a number of natural philosophers who took interest in the Bononian stone as an occasion for studying the perplexing nature of lunar and solar light. He presented samples to Giulio Cesare la Galla (1576–1624), a professor of philosophy at the Collegio Romano and the author of *De Phenomenis in Orbe Limae* (1612), and he also engaged in a protacted debate with Liceti over the stone's source of light that would shape later discussions of bioluminescence in the animal and vegetable worlds. Galileo explained the light of the Bononian stone according to the same principles that explained lunar candor:

the light of the stone, like that of the moon, is caused by the reflection of the sun's rays from the Earth and onto the moon. Liceti, by contrast, maintained that the faint light of the new moon was due to its phosphorescence: porous and translucent, the moon absorbs light in a manner similar to the Bononian stone—and presumably to other luminescent organisms.[31] When he weighs in on this debate in *Pseudodoxia*, Browne hedges his bets, speculating that the "light of animals" might be "Kin unto the light of Heaven" but at the same time casting a sardonic shadow on that idea by calling glowworms "sublunary moons," a phrase whose astronomical outdatedness by the 1640s suggests its questionable validity, particularly for a writer so determined to debunk the false or imagined correspondences between the Earth and the stars.[32]

Despite his suspicion that they shared at best a distant affinity with heavenly bodies, Browne nonetheless marveled at glowworms, among other insects, as reflections of God's best craftsmanship in miniature form, "narrow Engines" that "neatly set forth the wisedome of the Maker" better than the "Colossus and Majestick pieces" of nature's hand.[33] For many seventeenth-century naturalists, the glowworm came to embody the paradoxes inherent in nature at large, illustrating the superior grandeur of the little while also turning topsy-turvy the order of things by reflecting, howsoever dimly, minutely, or mediately, a light that originated with the sun, and by extension with God: a "small and contemptible Insect," as Boyle writes, yet with a Light "in its tail" that possesses a "noble and heavenly Quality."[34] This admixture of disdain and esteem for the glowworm is apparent throughout many of Boyle's writings on the subject, in particular his *Upon a Glow-Worm That He Kept Included in a Crystal Viol*, printed in his 1665 *Occasional Reflections*. Boyle takes as his starting point the paradox that the glowworm's distinctive luminosity is at once blessing and curse: if the "unhappy Worm" were as "despicable" as the other creatures lurking in the hedge that supplied Boyle with his subjects for vivisection, he "might have deluded my search" and would not have found himself imprisoned in the "Crystalline prison" of Boyle's glass beaker.[35] The punishment is justified by the moral that Boyle then supplies. "Rare Qualities may sometimes be Prerogatives," he writes, using the legal term that Bacon had extended to unusual cases or instances in the book of nature, "without being Advantages. And though a needless Ostentation of ones Excellencies may be more glorious, a modest Concealment of them is usually more safe," a lesson especially applicable to those who flaunt "flashes of Wit."³⁶ Boyle defines the glowworm's existence according to a series of paradoxes: "unhappy in [his] excellency," the worm brings pleasure to others but only "Misery" to himself through a deprivation of a liberty that is nonetheless mitigated by the "Light that ennobles him, [which] is not thereby restrain'd from diffusing it self" beyond the creature's transparent gaol.³⁷

The experiments on glowworms documented in *Occasional Reflections* and other early works represent the beginnings of Boyle's lifelong investigation into bioluminescence, including trials with luminous fish, flesh, and wood that each aimed to demonstrate how the light emitted by these and other organisms was of a different nature from heat and that it depended on the presence of air.³⁸ Boyle was neither original nor definitive in his hunch that air was the crucial ingredient in sustaining the glowworm's light; almost a century earlier, Moffett had recognized that glowworms placed into a "clear Crystal glass, so that the air may freely come at them," will "give light for the space of some 12 daies" before their glow is "remitted and slackned," an experiment that may have encouraged Moffett to dismiss outlandish tales testifying to the protracted, or even permanent, preservation of the luminous liquor.³⁹ Boyle also recognized, as Colonna did back in 1616, that moisture was another crucial element in sustaining the glowworm's light, since "on being completely removed from the water," they ceased to shine "but returned to the water they shone as before."⁴⁰ Boyle's success in reviving the glowworm's light after removing, and then replacing, both air and water prompted him to argue against Browne's more skeptical viewpoint in *Pseudodoxia*. "Those learned men are dreaming who make the brilliance of glow-worms depend upon their life," Boyle writes in his *Experimental Notes on the Mechanical Production of Light*, "as if the insect would stop shining when it ceased to live."⁴¹

Boyle was ultimately proven wrong about the glowworm's supposedly posthumous glow. But his experimentation on these "living lamps," to use Marvell's epithet, did confirm his earlier suspicion that the glowworm's light was "of another Nature" from that of the sun and "proceedeth from different causes of illumination."⁴² Boyle's work also paved the way for some weightier advances in natural philosophy. Whether because his observations were improved by his use of an air pump that ensured the total removal of air from the insect's atmosphere, or whether because the scientific culture of the 1660s and 1670s witnessed a growing interest in anatomical systems such as circulation and respiration that attuned Boyle and his fellow Royal Society members to formerly obscured implications of the effects of air on the powers of a living organism, Boyle's experiments helped to establish the necessity of air for the perpetuation of organic life, serving as a suggestive foundation for John Mayow's 1674 discovery of the "spiritus igneo-aereus," or what we now call oxygen.[43]

Notes

1. Browne, *Pseudodoxia Epidemica*, 203.
2. Bacon, *Sylva Sylvarum*, 184. For other early modern discussions of the glowworm, see Aldrovandi, *De Animalibus Insectis*, 492–99, which promises a never-published book on "things that shine at night": Plot, "Discourse"; and Gesner, *Raris*. On Boyle, see below. On glowing sweat emitted at night, see Swan, *Speculum Mundi*, 98. On the carbuncle, see Boyle, *Mr. Clayton's Diamond*, in *Works* 4:197–201. On *Ignis lambens*, or luminous mutton, see Castro, *De Igne Lambente*; and Borel, *Historiarum*, 5–7, 307–8. On the face of Moses, see Bartholin, *De Luce Animalium*, 65–74. For ancient discussions of bioluminescence, see Aristotle, *On the Soul*, 2.7.4; and Pliny, *Natural History*, 11.28, 11.37, 18.8, 37.7. For a related discussion of seventeenth-century debates on the glowworm, see Ogilvie, "Merian."
3. Gesner, *Raris*; Moffett, *Theater*, 978. Recounting how English explorers to the Indies mistook the insects for Spaniards approaching with torches, see Nieremberg, *Historia Naturae*, 288; and Bartholin, *De Luce Animalium*, 205, which cites Oviedo, *Historia*, fol. 113v. See Oviedo, *Historia*, 15.8, on the use of glowworms for cosmetic paste in the New World.
4. Marvell, "Mower," lines 10–12. Compare Shakespeare, *Merry Wives of Windsor*, 5.5.83, where "twenty glowworms" serve as lanterns during the nocturnal festivities.
5. Browne, *Pseudodoxia*, 204.
6. Descartes, *Meteorology*, 280; and Bartholin, *De Luce Animalium*, 351–52. Compare Stubbe, "Observations."
7. Bacon, *Topica Inquisitionis*, 413; Plot, *Natural History of Staffordshire*, 115. See also Plot, "Discourse."
8. Bacon, *Proficience and Advancement*, 215–16.
9. Browne, *Pseudodoxia*, 203.
10. See Liceti, *De Lucernis Antiquorum Reconditis*, 2.3, col. 54C; Liceti, *Litheosphorus*, 67–83; Cardano, *De Subtilitate*, 284; and the responses by Scaliger, *Exotericarum*, 194.1, f. 262r, and Bartholin, *De Luce Animalium*, 2.11. On the liquor concocted from glowworm juice, see also Aldrovandi, *De Animalibus Insectis*, 496–97; and Moffett, *Theater of Insects*, 979, which cites Gaudentius Merula: "Of these Glowworms being putrefied, there is made a water, or a liquor rather, in a vessel which will wonderfully shine in the dark. Such a light doth this water or liquor give, by report, that in the darkest night any one may read and write, and do any other business as he pleaseth."
11. Browne, *Pseudodoxia*, 203.
12. Ibid., 204.
13. See Galen, *Simplicium Medicamentum*, 12:365. This is cited by Guillaume Rondelet, *Aquatilum*, 361. For Rondelet's experiment on the torpedo fish and its venom, see *Aquatilum*, 360.
14. Browne, *Pseudodoxia*, 204.
15. Colonna, *Aquatilibus*, sig. Ff2r.

16. Bartholin, *De Luce Animalium*, 206. Bartholin is responding to Scaliger, *Exotericarum*, 194.3. The *Noctiluca* to which Bartholin refers is not to be confused with the bioluminescent marine dinoflagellate that shares its name.
17. Browne, *Pseudodoxia Epidemica*, 204; Browne, *Religio Medici*, 1.48.
18. On medieval legends about the glowworm and its juice, see Jonstonus, *History*, 8.5, which provides a lengthy catalog of legends concerning the glowworm that implicates both Della Porta and Albertus. See also Moffett, *Theater of Insects*, 979.
19. Moffett, *Theater of Insects*, 980.
20. Ibid., 977, 980.
21. Browne, *Pseudodoxia*, 204–5. Browne classifies the ancient Greek belief "That the Sun, Moon, and Stars are living creatures" as an "innocent Error," albeit one that may lead to idolatry (48). On this doctrine and objections to it, see Tertullian, *Ad Nationes*, 2.2 (Migne, *PL* 1:589), discussing the doctrines of the ancient Egyptians, Democritus, Zeno, and Varro; Aristotle, *Metaphysics* 9.8 (1050b22). At *Pseudodoxia* 3.27, Browne is responding principally to Bartholin, *De Luce Animalium*, 300–11; Liceti, *Litheosphorus*, 132–49, 242–48, the latter debating Galileo on the origin of the moon's light.
22. Albertus, *De Sensu et Sensato*, in *Opera Omnia*, 9:30. This passage is cited by Aldrovandi, *De Animalibus Insectis*, 496; Merula, *Memorabilia*, 240; and Jonstonus, *History*, 248–49.
23. See, for instance, the "glow-worm zeal" mentioned by Collop, "The Presbyter," line 20; and Heath, "Unusual Cold," lines 11–12, on the "glow-worm zeal, / Whose warmth we see but cannot feel."
24. Hall, *Occasional Meditations*, meditation XLIX, "Upon a Glow-Worme," 117–19.
25. Helmont, "Knitting" (chap. 47), in *Works*, 353; and Shakespeare, *Hamlet*, 1.5.89–90.
26. Helmont, "Knitting" (chap. 47), in *Works*, 353–54.
27. Browne, *Pseudodoxia*, 204. Other contemporary accounts of the Bononian stone include Jonstonus, *History*, 8.5, in turn recounting the experience of Hadrianus Junius in Bologna; Liceti, *Litheosphorus*, 109–13; Bartholin, *De Luce Animalium*, 5–13; and Worm, *Museum Wormianum*. Evelyn, *Diary*, mentions seeing the stone during a 1645 visit to Bologna: "After dinner I inquired out a priest and Dr. Montalbano, to whom I brought recommendations from Rome: this learned person invented, or found out, the composition of the *lapis illuminabilis*, or phosphorus. He showed me their property (for he had several), being to retain the light of the sun for some competent time, by a kind of imbibition, by a particular way of calcination" (1:191).
28. Browne elaborates on the Bononian stone at *Pseudodoxia*, 99, writing that the stone glows, albeit temporarily, when it "imbibeth the light in the vaporous humidity of the air about it, and therefore maintaineth its light not long, but goes out when the vaporous vehicle is consumed."
29. Potier, *Pharmacopaea Spagirica*, 272; Shakespeare, *Pericles*, 2.3.48. On seventeenth-century attempts to produce Bononian stone or its luminescent factor, see Principe, "Chymical Exotica"; the discussion by Steno, *Chaos*, 133–34; and the two reports in *Philosophical Transactions*, "Relation of the Loss" and "Improvement of the Bononian Stone." Wurm discusses his sample of the stone (47, 88).
30. Boyle, "To My Very Learned Friend Dr. J. B.," in *Works*, 9:270–71; and Heyrick, *Sceptick, Against Mechanism*, lines 211–16, in *Miscellany Poems*, 93.

31. See Galileo, *Le Opere*, 8:512–14, for his 1640 letter to Leopoldo de' Medici attacking Liceti's *Litheosphorus*. On the debate, see also Liceti, *De Lucernis Antiquorurn Reconditis*, 4.7, and *De Lunae Subobscura*. Kircher denies that the stone's light is a celestial quality inherent in it in both *Magnes, sive de Arte Magnetica* and *Ars Magna Lucis et Umbrae*.
32. Browne thoroughly debunks the false correspondences between the Earth and the moon (*Pseudodoxia*, 3.27.12, 6.14).
33. Browne, *Religio Medici*, 1.15. Such celebrations of the intricacy of insects were commonplace. Compare Moffett, *Theater of Insects*, 980: "[We] . . . proceed rather piously, and modestly to behold the majesty, wisdom, and divine light in this little creature. For he which shall go about fully to search the majesty of the Creator in these small creatures shall soon be confounded with the glory of it."
34. Boyle, *Works*, 5:15.
35. Boyle, *Occasional Reflections*, 154–55.
36. Ibid., 154, perhaps echoing Moffett, *Theater of Insects*: "Even so the wits of these times, while they seek to extract this light, by their bold enterprize do violate the Deity, and while they would seem to adorn and set forth the glory of that his work, they rather detract from it and disgrace it" (980).
37. Boyle, *Occasional Reflections*, 155–56.
38. Boyle, "Experimental Notes," in *Works*, 14:482–88. For similar experiments on fish, compare Boyle, "An Occasional Digression," in *Works*, 9:282; and Boyle, "New Experiments." Boyle made a number of later experiments on the subject: see Boyle, "Some Observations About Shining Flesh." For other Royal Society experiments on glowworms, see Lister, "Letter Written," 2177–78; and Birch, *History of the Royal Society*, 2:483; 4:356, 358.
39. Moffett, *Theater of Insects*, 979.
40. Boyle, "Experimental Notes," in *Works*, 14:482.
41. Ibid., 14:483.
42. Marvell, "Mower," line 1; and Browne, *Pseudodoxia*, 205.
43. In the first two tracts of Mayow, *Tractatus Quinque Medico-Physici*.

Bibliography

Aldrovandi, Ulisse. *De Animalibus Insectis Libri Septem*. Bologna, 1602.
Aristotle. *The Metaphysics*. Translated by Hugh Tredennick. 2 vols. Rev. ed. Cambridge MA: Harvard University Press, 1956–1958.
———. *On the Soul*. In *On the Soul; Parva Naturalia; On Breath*. Translated by W. S. Hett. Rev. ed. Cambridge MA: Harvard University Press, 1957.
Bacon, Francis. *Of the Proficience and Advancement of Learning*. London, 1640.
———. *Sylva Sylvarum; or, A Natural History, in Ten Centuries*. London, 1627.
———. *Topica Inquisitionis de Luce et Lumine*. In *The Philosophical Works of Francis Bacon*, vol. 5. Edited by James Spedding. London, 1861.
Bartholin. *De Luce Animalium. Admirandis Historiis Rationibusque Novis Referti. Libri III*. Leiden, 1647.
Birch, Thomas. *The History of the Royal Society of London for Improving of Natural Knowledge*. 4 vols. London, 1760.
Borel, Pierre. *Historiarum et Observationum Medicophysicarum Centuriae*. Paris, 1657.
Boyle, Robert. "New Experiments Concerning the Relation Between Light and Air (in Shining Wood and Fish)." *Philosophical Transactions of the Royal Society* 2, no. 31 (December 30, 1666): 581–600. https://doi.org/10.1098/rstl.1666.0060.
———. *Occasional Reflections upon Several Subiects, Whereto Is Premis'd*

a Discourse About Such Kind of Thoughts. London, 1665.

———. "Some Observations About Shining Flesh." *Philosophical Transactions of the Royal Society* 7, no. 89 (December 31, 1672): 5108–16. https://doi.org/10.1098/rstl.1672.0054.

———. *The Works of Robert Boyle.* Edited by Michael Hunter and Edward B. Davis. 14 vols. London, 1999–2000.

Browne, Thomas. *Pseudodoxia Epidemica: or, Enquiries into Very Many Received Tenents and Commonly Presumed Truths.* London, 1672.

———. *Religio Medici.* London, 1643.

Cardano, Girolamo. *De Subtilitate Libri XXI.* Basel, 1560.

Castro, Petrus di. *De Igne Lambente.* Verona, 1642.

Collop, John. "The Presbyter." In Collop's *Poesis Rediviva, or, Poesie Reviv'd.* London, 1656.

Colonna, Fabio. *De Aquatilibus Aliisque Nonnullis Animalibus.* In *Minus Cognitarum Rariorumque.* Rome, 1616.

Descartes, René. *Meteorology.* In *Discourse on Method, Optics, Geometry, and Meteorology*, rev. ed., translated by Paul J. Olscamp. Hackett, 2001.

Evelyn, John. *Diary.* Rev. ed. Edited by William Bray. 2 vols. New York: Dent, 1966.

Galen. *De Simplicium Medicamentum.* In *Opera Omnia*, edited by Carolus Gottlob Kühn. 20 vols. Leipzig, 1821–1833.

Galileo, *Le Opere di Galileo Galilei.* Edited by Antonio Favaro. 20 vols. Florence, 1890–1909.

Gesner, Conrad. *De Raris et Admirandis Herbis, Quae Noctu Luceant.* Zurich, 1555.

Hall, Joseph. *Occasional Meditations.* London, 1631.

Heath, Robert. "On the Unusual Cold and Rainie Weather in the Summer. 1648." In *Clarastella Together with Poems Occasional, Elegies, Epigrams, Satyrs.* London, 1650.

Helmont, Jan Baptista Van. *Works.* Translated by J. C. London, 1664.

Heyrick, Thomas. *The Sceptick, Against Mechanism.* In *Miscellany Poems* by Heyrick. London, 1691.

"An Improvement of the Bononian Stone, Shining in the Dark." *Philosophical Transactions of the Royal Society* 12, no. 134 (March 25, 1677): 842. https://doi.org/10.1098/rstl.1677.0007.

Jonstonus, Joannes. *An History of the Wonderful Things of Nature Set Forth in Ten Severall Classes.* London, 1657.

Kircher, Athanasius. *Ars Magna Lucis et Umbrae.* Rome, 1646.

———. *Magnes, sive de Arte Magnetica.* Rome, 1641.

Liceti, Fortunio. *Antiquorum Reconditis.* Venice, 1621

———. *De Lucernis Antiquorum Reconditis Libri Sex.* Udine, 1653.

———. *De Lunae Subobscura. Luce Propre Conjunctiones, & in Eclipsibus Observata Libros Tres.* Udine, 1642.

———. *Litheosphorus, sive de Lapide Bononiensi.* Udine, 1640.

Lister, Martin. "A Letter Written to the Publisher for York, Jan: 10. 1670, Concerning a Kind of Fly That Is Viviparous." *Philosophical Transactions of the Royal Society* 6, no. 72 (December 31, 1671): 2170–78. https://doi.org/10.1098/rstl.1671.0022.

Magnus, Albertus. *De Sensu et Sensato.* In *Opera Omnia*, vol. 9, edited by Auguste Borgnet, 38 vols. Paris, 1890–1899.

Marvell, Andrew. "The Mower to the Glow-Worms." In *The Poems of Andrew Marvell*, edited by Nigel Smith. New York: Pearson Longman, 2007.

Mayow, John. *Tractatus Quinque Medico-Physici.* Oxford, 1674.

Merula, Gaudentius. *Memorabilia.* Lyon, 1556.

Moffett, Thomas. *The Theater of Insects: or, Lesser Living Creatures.* In *The History of Four-Footed Beasts and Serpents*, by Edward Topsell. London, 1658.

Nieremberg, Juan Eusebio. *Historia Naturae, Maxime Peregrinae, Libris XVI.* Antwerp, 1635.

Ogilvie, Brian W. "Maria Sibylla Merian et la mouche porte-lanterne de Surinam: Naissance et disparition d'un fait scientifique." In *Les savoirs-mondes: Mobilités et circulation des savoirs depuis le Moyen Âge,* edited by Pilar González-Bernaldo and Liliane Hilaire-Peréz. Rennes: Presses Universitaires de Rennes, 2014.

Oviedo, Gonzalo Fernández de. *La historia general de las Indias.* Seville. 1535.

Pliny. *Natural History.* 10 vols. Translated by H. Rackham. Cambridge MA: Harvard University Press, 1938–1963.

Plot, Robert. "A Discourse Concerning the Sepulchral Lamps of the Ancients, Shewing the Possibility of Their Being Made Divers Waies." *Philosophical Transactions of the Royal Society* 14, no. 166 (January 20, 1684): 806–11. https://doi.org/10.1098/rstl.1684.0079.

———. *The Natural History of Staffordshire.* Oxford, 1686.

Potier, Pierre. *Pharmacopœa Spagyrica.* Bologna, 1622.

Principe, Lawrence J. "Chymical Exotica in the Seventeenth Century, or How to Make the Bologna Stone." *Ambix* 63, no. 2 (2016): 118–44.

"A Relation of the Loss of the Way to Prepare the Bononian Stone for Shining." *Philosophical Transactions of the Royal Society* 1, no. 21 (May 30, 1665): 375. https://doi.org/10.1098/rstl.1665.0139

Scaliger, Julius Caesar. *Exotericarum Exercitationum Liber XV, de Subtilitate.* Paris, 1557.

Shakespeare, William. *The Merry Wives of Windsor.* In The *Norton Shakespeare,* edited by Stephen Greenblatt, Walter Cohen, Jean E. Howard, and Katharine Eisaman Maus. New York: Norton, 1997.

Steno, Nicolas [Stensen, Niels]. *Chaos: Niels Stensen's Chaos-Manuscript, Copenhagen 1659.* Edited and translated by August Ziggelaar. Copenhagen: Danish National Library of Science and Medicine, 1997.

Stubbe, Henry. "Observations Made by a Curious and Learned Person, Henry Stubbe, Sailing from England, to the Caribe-Islands." *Philosophical Transactions of the Royal Society* 2, no. 27 (December 30, 1666): 494–502. https://doi.org/10.1098/rstl.1666.0036.

Swan, John. *Speculum Mundi, or, A Glasse Representing the Face of the World.* Cambridge, 1635.

Tertullian. *Ad Nationes.* In *Patrologia Latina,* edited by J. P. Migne. Alexandria, VA: Chadwyck-Healey, 1996.

Worm, Ole. *Museum Wormianum, seu Historia Rerum Rariorum.* Leiden, 1655.

EPILOGUE
CONCEPTS

Keith Botelho

As if beekeepers didn't have enough to worry about, then came the murder hornets. The first two decades of the twenty-first century had broadcast widely the threats to honeybee populations worldwide due to disease, intensive agricultural practices, and pesticides, rallying people to "save the honeybees." Then, in spring 2020, as a pandemic stalked the globe, reports of the Asian giant hornet (*Vespa mandarinia*) on US soil rippled across news sources, with stories that they "use mandibles shaped like spiked shark fins to wipe out a honeybee hive in a matter of hours, decapitating the bees and flying away with the thoraxes to feed their young."[1] Although these hornets pose little risk to humans—in actuality, according to the World Health Organization, mosquitos are the true murder insect, accounting for more than 1 million human deaths annually worldwide—the sensationalist reporting delivered a jolt to people who understood the possible consequences of further depleting these necessary pollinators.[2]

But bees are not alone in the insect world when it comes to threats to survival. Recent reports reveal an alarming global problem. An April 2019 review of data in the journal *Biological Conservation* notes that more than 40 percent of global insect species have declined over the past decade, threatening many of the world's insect populations with extinction. The authors of the study point out that scientific and public attention "has focused on charismatic vertebrates . . . whereas insects were routinely underrepresented in biodiversity and conservation studies in spite of their paramount importance to the overall functioning and stability of ecosystems worldwide."[3] Species decline could lead to extinction within a few decades, with catastrophic consequences to the world's ecosystems. As Deborah Bird Rose has noted, "What is happening to other creatures in this era of mass anthropogenic death may be too large to think, too unprecedented to know how to imagine."[4]

Yet hope beckons. Greg Garrard writes that apocalyptic rhetoric is a necessary component of environmental discourse, "capable of galvanizing activists, converting the undecided and ultimately, perhaps, of influencing government and commercial policy."[5] In all this talk of extermination and depopulation, catastrophe and decline, the necessary keywords that emerge might be *resilience*, *recovery*, and *restoration*. To achieve such things, much relies on humans changing their ways to positively affect insect biodiversity around the globe, healing the earth and its ecosystems teeming with the tiniest of creatures. Such environmental threats thus might foster new ways of thinking about insects.

This type of insect-inspired activism was on display when I had the opportunity to be the proverbial fly on the wall for the monthly meetings of the Bartow County (Georgia) Beekeepers Association one summer. What struck me was the hive of activity at the meetings, a vibrant collective of seasoned beekeepers side-by-side with a new crop of budding apiculturists, many of them skewing considerably younger. After a presentation, discussion ensued, and on the minds of beekeepers that summer was the impending threat of the varroa mite, which was causing havoc in hives across the country. The apian-inspired camaraderie, wisdom, and problem solving on display that summer—a snapshot of the activities of beekeeping societies across the country—mirrored humanists and natural historians like Thomas Moffett some four centuries before, when the sharing of best practices and building off the work of those who came before was the norm.

The eleven chapters in this volume have begun a conversation as to how lesser living creatures enable conceptual thinking about life-forms. Of course, much remains to be explored: How are insects resilient? How do insect colonies work as a superorganism steeped in nonhierarchical activity, and what might they teach us about networks? How do webs or hives offer us ways to think about architecture and design, about creation and re-creation? And what about concepts like waste and disposal, companionship, pollination, and life cycles? These concepts offer pathways forward as animal studies embrace an insect turn, giving us potential ways to unlock connections and to think strategically across disciplines about the productive entanglements of humans and a world crawling with lesser living creatures.

Notes

1. Baker, "Murder Hornets."
2. "Forget 'Murder Hornets.'"
3. Sánchez-Bayo and Wyckhuys, "Worldwide Decline," 16.
4. Rose, "Shadow," 12.
5. Garrard, *Ecocriticism*, 113.

Bibliography

Baker, Mike. "'Murder Hornets' in the U.S.: The Rush to Stop the Asian Giant Hornet." *New York Times*, May 2, 2020. Accessed May 27, 2020. https://www.nytimes.com/2020/05/02/us/asian-giant-hornet-washington.html.

"Forget 'Murder Hornets,' Experts Say—This Is the Real 'Murder Insect.'" CBS News, May 12, 2020. https://www.cbsnews.com/news/murder-hornet-mosquito-disease-death-millions/.

Garrard, Greg. *Ecocriticism*. New York: Routledge, 2011.

Rose, Deborah Bird. "In the Shadow of All This Death." In *Animal Death*, edited by Jay Johnston and Fiona Probyn-Rapsey. Sydney: Sydney University Press, 2013.

Sánchez-Bayo, Francisco, and Kris A. G. Wyckhuys. "Worldwide Decline of the Entomofauna: A Review of Its Drivers." *Biological Conservation* 232 (April 2019): 8–27.

CONTRIBUTORS

Keith Botelho is professor of English at Kennesaw State University. He is the author of *Renaissance Earwitnesses: Rumor and Early Modern Masculinity* (Palgrave Macmillan, 2009), and he has published essays in journals including *Studies in English Literature*, *Early Modern Culture*, *Early Modern Studies Journal*, and *Comparative Drama*, and chapters in scholarly collections including *The Routledge Handbook of Shakespeare and Animals*, *MLA Approaches to Teaching Aphra Behn's Oroonoko*, *Ecological Approaches to Early Modern English Texts*, *Object Oriented Environs*, *Shakespeare and Geek Culture*, and *Ground-Work: English Renaissance Literature and Soil Science*.

Joseph Campana is William Shakespeare Professor of English and director of the Center for Environmental Studies at Rice University. He is the author of *The Pain of Reformation: Spenser, Vulnerability, and the Ethics of Masculinity* (Fordham University Press, 2012), the coeditor of *Renaissance Posthumanism* (2016), and the author of three collections of poetry—*The Book of Faces* (Graywolf, 2005); *Natural Selections* (2012), which received the Iowa Poetry Prize; and *The Book of Life* (2019). He has received the Isabel MacCaffrey Essay Prize, the MLA's Crompton-Noll Award for LGB studies, and grants from the NEA, the HAA, and the Bread Loaf Writers' Conference. Current projects include a study of children and sovereignty in the works of Shakespeare, titled *The Child's Two Bodies*, and *Living Figures*, a study of energy, ecology, and creaturely life in early modernity. He teaches at Rice University, where he is Alan Dugald McKillop Professor of English, editor of *Studies in English Literature: 1500–1900*, and the director of the Center for Environmental Studies.

Lucinda Cole, Conrad Humanities Scholar, is associate professor and affiliate professor at the Institute for Sustainability, Energy, and Environment at the University of Illinois, Urbana-Champaign. Author of *Imperfect Creatures: Vermin, Literature and the Sciences of Life, 1600–1740* (University of Michigan Press, 2016) and several articles on early modern and eighteenth-century insects, she is now working on a book-length manuscript about literature and zoonotic disease.

Frances E. Dolan is Distinguished Professor of English at the University of California, Davis. She is the author of five books, most recently *Digging the Past: How and Why to Imagine Seventeenth-Century Agriculture* (University of Pennsylvania Press, 2020), as well as numerous editions, books for students, and essays.

Lowell Duckert is associate professor of English at the University of Delaware. With Jeffrey Jerome Cohen, he is the editor of *Elemental Ecocriticism: Thinking with Earth, Air, Water, and Fire*; and *Veer Ecology: A Companion for Environmental Thinking* (nominated for the Association for the Study of Literature and Environment's Ecocriticism Book Award). His book *For All Waters: Finding Ourselves in Early Modern Wetscapes* (University of Minnesota Press, 2017) was short-listed for the Michelle Kendrick Memorial Book Prize from the Society for Literature, Science, and the Arts.

Andrew Fleck is associate professor of English at the University of Texas in El Paso. His research focuses on early modern English interest in the Dutch and in the history of science.

Rebecca Laroche is professor of English at the University of Colorado, Colorado Springs. She has published on ecofeminist theory, Shakespeare, early modern women's writing, medical history, and recipe collections. In 2009, her monograph *Medical Authority and Englishwomen's Herbal Texts, 1550–1650* was published by Ashgate, and in 2011, she was the guest curator of the exhibition "Beyond Home Remedy: Women, Medicine, and Science" at the Folger Shakespeare Library and coeditor (with Jennifer Munroe) of *Ecofeminist Approaches to Early Modernity* (Palgrave). Again with Jennifer Munroe, she has written *Shakespeare and Ecofeminist Theory* (2017) for the Arden Shakespeare and Theory series.

Jennifer Munroe is professor of English at the University of North Carolina at Charlotte. She is coauthor of *Shakespeare and Ecofeminist Theory* (Arden, 2017), author of *Gender and the Garden in Early Modern English Literature* (Ashgate, 2008), and editor of *Making Gardens of Their Own: Gardening Manuals for Women, 1550–1750* (Ashgate, 2007). She is also coeditor with Rebecca Laroche of *Ecofeminist Approaches to Early Modernity* (Palgrave, 2011) and with Lynne Bruckner and Edward J. Geisweidt of *Ecological Approaches to Early Modern Texts: A Field Guide to Reading and Teaching* (Ashgate, 2015). She has published articles in *Shakespeare Studies, Tulsa Studies for Women's Literature, Prose Studies, Early Modern Studies Journal, Renaissance Studies,* and *Pedagogy*. She is at work on another monograph, *Mothers of Science: Women, Nature, and Writing in the Seventeenth Century in England*. In addition, she is a founding member and steering committee member for Early Modern Recipes Online Collective (EMROC), a group that is developing a public access database of transcribed manuscript recipe materials from the early modern period.

Amy L. Tigner, professor of English at the University of Texas, teaches and writes about Shakespeare, food, and gardens. Her most recent books are *Literature and Food Studies* with Allison Carruth (Routledge, 2018) and *Culinary Shakespeare,* coedited with David B. Goldstein (Duquesne University Press, 2017). She is the author of *Literature and the Renaissance Garden from Elizabeth I to Charles II* (Ashgate, 2012). Tigner is also the founding editor of *Early Modern Studies Journal* and a founding member of Early Modern Recipes Online Collective (EMROC), a digital humanities project dedicated to manuscript recipe books.

Jessica Lynn Wolfe is Marcel Bataillon Professor of English and Comparative Literature, Romance Studies, and Classics at UNC Chapel Hill. She is the author of *Humanism, Machinery, and Renaissance Literature* (Cambridge University Press, 2004) and *Homer and the Question of Strife from Erasmus to Hobbes* (University of Toronto Press, 2015). Her interests include the history of classical scholarship, epic and lyric poetry, and the history of science, medicine, and technology. Her two ongoing projects are an edition of Thomas Browne's *Pseudodoxia Epidemica* and a biography of the poet and playwright George Chapman.

Derek Woods is assistant professor of communication studies and media arts at McMaster University. He is writing a book about ecotechnology, science fiction, and earth system science. His essays look at such topics as the philosophy and mediation of scale, biopolitics, and modern

Anglophone literature. With Karen Pinkus, he edited an issue of *diacritics* (47, no. 3) about terraforming. With Joshua Schuster, he published *Calamity Theory: Three Critiques of Existential Risk* (University of Minnesota Press, 2021).

Julian Yates is H. Fletcher Professor of English and Material Culture Studies at the University of Delaware. His books include *Error, Misuse, Failure: Object Lessons from the English Renaissance* (University of Minnesota Press, 2003), a finalist for the Modern Language Association's Best First Book Prize; *What's the Worst Thing You Can Do to Shakespeare?* (Palgrave Macmillan, 2013), written with Richard Burt; *Object-Oriented Environs in Early Modern England* (Punctum Books, 2016), coedited with Jeffrey J. Cohen; and *Of Sheep, Oranges, and Yeast: A Multispecies Impression* (University of Minnesota Press, 2017), winner of the Michelle Kendrick Memorial Book Prize from the Society for Literature, Science, and the Arts. *Noah's Arkive*, written with Jeffrey J. Cohen, is forthcoming from the University of Minnesota Press.

INDEX

Note: Page numbers in italics indicate illustrative material.

Accademia dei Lincei, 40, 41
Acosta, José de, 115
actors' movement, 137–38, 139n26
Addison, Lancelot, 78
Aelianus, Claudius, 38, 46n34
Aesop's fables, 93
Africanus, Leo, *Geographical Historie of Africa, A*, 65, 71
agriculture
  earthworms' role in, 123–25, 128
  sericulture, 125–28, 129n12
  soil amendment and composting, 122–23, 128
Alaimo, Stacy, 50, 56, 107, 118n11
Albala, Ken, 106
Albertus Magnus, 184, 186
Aldrovandi, Ulisse, 180, 184
  De Animalibus Insectis, 63, 186, *187*, 192n2
Alexander, Cecil Frances, 30
Alvarez, Francis, *True Relation of the Lands of Prester John of the Indies, A*, 65–66
animetaphor, 24–25, 25n25
anthropocentrism, 3, 117, 135, 142–44
anthropology. *See* ethnography
ants
  fire ants as imported pest, 57, 64
  militaristic qualities of, 52
Apiarium, 40, *40*
apocalyptic imagery, 69
Aristotle
  on the lousy disease, 76
  political animal concept, 6
  on scale, 30–31, 33
  on spiders, 84
  on spontaneous generation, 63
  on swarms, 163
  on wasps, 18
  History of Animals, The, 30–31, 163
  Metaphysics, 165
  Politics, 143
Arquil, John, 176n21
artistry, of silkworms, 127, 128
Audley, James Tuchet, Seventh Baron, 100n36

Bacon, Francis, 190
  Sylva Sylvarum, 180
  Topica Inquisitionis de Luce et Lumine, 182
Baker, Margaret, 106, 112
Barberini, Matteo, 40
Barberini family, 40–41, 43
Barthes, Roland, 171–72
Bartholin, Thomas, *De Luce Animalium*, 180, 182, 183
Bass, Saul, 176n19
beast fable, as genre, 93
beauty, of butterflies, 94, 98
Bede, 73, 80n29
beekeeping, 113, 114
bees
  Barberini association, 40, 40–41, *41*, 42, 43
  beekeeping, 113, 114
  commonwealth of, 23, 84, 85
  communication of, 152, 162–63, 166–71, 172, 173, 174–75
  honey from, 89, 112, 113, 114
  humanity's analogical fascination with, 2–3
  medicinal properties of, 104, 105, 110, 111
  murder hornets, 197
  Plato's mouth, 160, 167, 168, 175n1
  population decline, 197, 198
  sovereignty of, 15, 17, 23–24, 84, 114, 163–64, 167–69
  stings of, mechanism, 20–23, *21*

bees (*continued*)
    stings of, transferred to parchment, 13–15, 25
    as swarms *vs.* individuals, 164
Bekey, George A., 134
Beneviste, Emile, 171
Bennett, Jane, 124
Beowulf, 136
Bergson, Henri, 164, 165
biblical associations
    apocalyptic imagery, 69
    and beast fable genre, 93
    of glowworms, 181
    of locusts, 66, 67, 68, 71, 73, 78
    See also religion and spirituality
Bigelow, Allison, 127, 129n20, 129n22
bioluminescence. *See* glowworms
Black Mirror, The (television series), 161
Blount, Thomas, *Glossographia*, 78
Bodin, Jean, *Six Livres de la République*, 85, 87–88, 90–91
Boemus, Johann, *Fardle of Facions, The*, 63
Bondeson, Jan, 76, 77
Bonoeil, John
    His Majesties Gracious Letter to the Earle of South-hampton Treasurer . . ., 126
    Observations to Be Followed, for the Making of Fit Roomes, to Keepe Silk-Wormes In, 126
Bononian (Bolognian) stone, 188–90, 193nn27–28, 194n31
Borges, Jorge Luis, "Garden of Forking Paths, The," 161
Boswell, John, 100n36
Boyle, Robert, 180, 188, 189, 191–92, 194n38
    Experimental Notes on the Mechanical Production of Light, 191
    Occasional Reflections, 190–91
Briggs-Owen, Lucy, 137
Brinkley, Robert A., 101n46
Brown, Eric C., 4, 101n45, 101n49, 134, 146
Brown, Richard Danson, 101n50
Browne, Thomas, *Pseudoxia Epidemica*, 78, 180, 181, 182–83, 184, 185–86, 188, 190, 191, 193n21, 193n28
Brumwich, Anne, 56
Brusoni, Lucio Domizio, 90

Butler, Charles, 114, 164
    Feminine Monarchie, 168–69
butterflies
    beauty of, 94, 98
    conflict with spiders, 92, 94–95, 96, 97–98
    gardens of, 92, 96–98
    militaristic qualities of, 92, 100n36
    wings of, 93–94

Campana, Joseph, 101n49, 165–66
Campbell, Mary Baine, 166, 173–74
Cardano, Girolamo, 184
    De Subtilitate, 182
Carson, Rachel, *Silent Spring*, 57, 58
Cascariolo, Vincenzo, 188
Castleton, Grace, 109
Catchmay, Francis, 110
Catchmay, Grace, 55
Cavendish, Margaret, 127
Cesi, Federico, 40, *40*, *41*
Chakrabarty, Dipesh, 31
charisma, 2, 3, 4–5
Chen, Mel Y., 50
Christianity. *See* religion and spirituality
cicadas
    Brood V, 141–42
    shedding skin, 154
    singing of, 152–53, 154
    tettix etymology, 144
    See also locusts
cicadian rhythms, 144
Clark, Timothy, 31, 32, 33
class divisions, 54, 58
cochineal, 115–17
coexistence, 54–56
colonialism
    and global trade, 64, 114–15
    and glowworm encounters, 181
    and locust extermination, 66–67, 79
    and sericulture, 125–26, 129n12
Colonna, Fabio, 183, 191
coloring agents, 115, 116–17
Columella, *De Re Rustica*, 123
commonwealth
    of bees, 23, 84, 85
    customary privileges in, 87–88
    of families, 91

free *vs.* constricted movement in,
   86–87, 96–99, 100n16
  hierarchical conception of, 85
  private *vs.* public property in, 85–87
  unjust laws in, 89–90, 91, 97
communication, 141–56
  and anthropocentrism, 142–44
  and co-composition, 154–55
  compromise in, 155–56
  dance language, 169–70, 171, 172, 173,
    174–75, 177n35
  and dissection, 150–51
  epistemological structures, 162–63,
    172–73
  parasitical, 145–47, 149, 151, 153–54
  pleasure in, 152–53
  and praise, 147–49
  and re-mark, 170–71
  signal/noise distinction, 167
  singing as, 152–53, 154, 163–64, 166–68,
    172, 173
  and temporality, 167–69
  topos of bee, 162–63, 173
  and vibration, 144
  violence of, 149–50
composting and soil amendment, 122–
  23, 128
conjuration and excommunication, 66–67
consumption
  by earthworms, 123–25
  and famine, 68–71
  and food dyes, 117
  gluttonous, 83
  intimacy of, 105–6
  of lice, 53
  lice-inducing diets, 54
  of locusts, 65, 71–77, 78
  modern promotion of edible insects,
    104–5
  by parasitic worms, 108
  and transcorporeality, 107–8, 112, 116,
    149
  See also medicinal properties; receipt
    books
Corderoy, Jeremy, 89
corruption
  and disease, 53, 74–75, 76–77
  and earthworms, 124, 125

lice thriving on, 52–54
  See also decomposition
cosmetics, 110, 113, 116, 117
creeping and crawling, 132–38
  agility and stability, 132–33, 134–35, 136–
    37, 139n9
  alternative terms for, 135–36
  and fear, 133–34
  by stage actors, 137–38, 139n26
crickets, 155
  See also cicadas; locusts
Crosby, Alfred, 64
culinary properties. *See* consumption;
  receipt books
custom *vs.* laws, 87–88, 89
cybernetics, 162–63, 165, 169, 172–73, 176–
  77n19, 176n10

dance language, 169–70, 171, 172, 173, 174–
  75, 177n35
Dannenfeldt, Karl, 67
Darwin, Charles, *Formation of Vegetable Mould through the Actions of
  Worms with Observations on Their
  Habits*, 124
death
  appearance of, 183–84
  extinction and depopulation, 197–
    98
decomposition, 122–28
  earthworms as agents of, 123–24
  earthworms as threats to, 124–25
  soil amendment and composting, 122–
    23, 128
  and transcorporeality, 107–8
Dekker, Thomas, 90
Della Porta, Giambattista, 184
depopulation, 197–98
Derrida, Jacques, 90, 99n4, 99n9, 143, 168,
  170
Descartes, René, 181
Descola, Philippe, 26n4
Dessen, Alan, 137
Dicke, Marcel, 105
diet. *See* consumption
diminutive sublime, 35–38, 39, 101n49
Dimock, Wai Chee, 32
Diodorus Siculus, 74–75

disease, 53, 74–75, 76–77
    See also medicinal properties
dissection, 20, 21, 38–39, 150–51
divinity. See God
domesticated spaces, 52
Donne, John, 115, 135
dyes, 115, 116–17

earthworms
    medicinal properties of, 109–10
    work of, 123–25, 128
eating. See consumption
Eberhardt, Russell C., 165
Eedes, Richard, 90
Egerton 2608 receipt book manuscript, 104, 105, 110, 111
Elizabethan epyllia, 93
Elizabeth I, Queen of England, 68
Emmons, Paul, 31
Enterline, Lynn, 101n44
entomophagy. See consumption
environmental justice, 50, 56–59
epistemological structures, 162–63, 172–73
ethnography
    and entomology discipline, 63–64, 79–80n2
    and insect consumption, 65, 72–73, 74–77
Evans, E. P., 67
Evelyn, John, *Diary*, 193n27
Ewan, Vanessa, 138
excommunication and conjuration, 66–67
extinction, 197–98

famine, 68–71
Fanshawe, Ann, 110
farming. See agriculture
fear, 133–34
feminization, 52
Fenton, Geoffrey, 90, 91
Few, Martha, 79
Field, Catherine, 109
fire ants, 64
fireflies. See glowworms
flies, 85–88
food. See consumption
Fore, Devin, 172, 177n35
Fortescue, John, 88

Foucault, Michel, 162–63, 172, 173, 174, 176n9, 177n40
Freedberg, David, 40
Fry, Steven N., 134
Fudge, Erica, 99n3, 101n58
Fumerton, Patricia, 34, 118n24

Galen, 76, 106, 183
Galilei, Galileo, 40, 189–90
gardens
    beekeeping in, 113, 114
    butterfly, 92, 96–98
Garrard, Greg, 198
Garret, Jacob, 155
Gatens, Moira, 107–8
gender
    and domesticated space, 52
    and misogyny, 151
    and sericulture, 127, 129n22
    sexing of sovereignty, 17, 114
Gerard, John, *Herball*, 19
Gervais, Bertrand, 146
Gessner, Conrad, 16, 30, 63, 153, 181
glowworms, 180–92, *185*, *187*
    air as cause of bioluminescence, 191–92
    and the Bononian stone, 188–90, 193nn27–28, 194n31
    celestial bodies as cause of bioluminescence, 185–88, 189, 190, 194n33
    heat as cause of bioluminescence, 181–82
    juice of, extracted for lamps, 181, 182, 184–85, 192n10
    life and death related to bioluminescence, 182–84, 191
    paradoxes of, 190–91
Goble, Mark, 177n42
God
    and divine law, 90
    light of, 185, 186, 190, 194n33, 194n36
    mercy of, 71–72, 74, 75
    punishment from, 52–53, 66, 67, 70, 76
    workmanship of, 147–49
Goldsmith, Oliver, *Historie of the Earth and Animated Nature, An*, 62–63
Goldstein, David, 111
Goodman, Godfrey, *Fall of Man, The, or the Corruption of Nature*, 68
Granville, Mary, 108–9, 116, 117

grasshoppers. *See* cicadas; locusts
Green, Debbie, 138
Greene, Roland, 4
Greuter, Johann Friedrich, 41
Griffin, Donald R., 170
Gros, Elizabeth, 144
Guevara, Antonio de, *Epístolas Familiares (Golden Epistles)*, 90

habitats, 83–99
  butterfly gardens, 92, 96–98
  spider webs, 83–84, 85–88, 89–90, 91, 95, 97–99
Hadfield, Andrew, 100n36
Hakluyt, Richard, *Principal Navigations, Voiages, Traffiques, and Discoveries of the English Nation, The*, 63
Haldan, J. B. S., 171
Hall, Joseph, 186
Haraway, Donna, 174
Hardt, Michael, 176n14
Harkness, Deborah, 16, 17
Harrison, William, 91–92
Hart, Henry C., 78–79
Hart, James, *Klinike, or The Diet of the Diseased*, 75–76
Harti, Agnes Sri, 110
Hartlib, Samuel
  Rare and New Discovery, A . . . For the Feeding of Silk-worms in the Woods, 126, 127–28
  Reformed Virginian Silk-Worm, The, 128
health. *See* medicinal properties
Helmont, Jan Baptista Van, 188
Helmont, Val, 59n19
Helmreich, Stefan, 176n7
Henderson, Judith Rice, 100n14
Hentschell, Roze, 99n12
Herod, 76
Hexbug (toy bug), 132–33
Heyrick, Thomas, 189
Heywood, John, *Spider and the Flie, The*, 85–87, 88–89, 91–92, 97, 99n11
Hive (tabletop game), 1
hives. *See* bees; swarms
Hoby, Margaret, 106–7
Holland, Philemon, *Historie of the World*, 35

Holstun, James, 99n11
Homer, *Iliad*, 52
honey, 89, 112, 113, 114
honey-like speech, 160
Hooke, Robert, *Micrographia: or, some Physiological Descriptions of Minute Bodies Made by Magnifying Glasses*, 20–23, 21, 44–45
Hopper, Grace, 146
household management, 51–52
Howard, Albert, 123
Hunt, Alice, 100n13
Hunt, Simon, 118n24
Hunter, Lynnete, 113
Husserl, Edmund, 168
Hutton, Sarah, 113
hygiene, 53, 76–77

illumination. *See* glowworms
immigration, 58
infestations, 62–79
  and entomology-ethnography relationship, 63–64
  and famine, 68–71
  and insect consumption, 65, 71–77, 78–79
  ritual excommunication against, 66–67
  See also pest control
information theory, 163, 167, 172–73, 176n10
insecticide. *See* pest control
intimacy, of consumption, 105–6

Jakobson, Roman, 171
James I, King of England, 125–26, 129n12
James, Heather, 100n37
Jenerette, G. Darrek, 33
Johnston, John, 165
John the Baptist, 72, 73, 78, 79
Jonson, Ben
  Poetaster, 143
  Timber: or, Discoveries, 143
  Volpone, 89
Jonstonus, Joannes, *History of the Wonderful Things of Nature, An*, 193n18, 193n27
Junger, Ernst, *Glass Bees, The*, 176–77n21, 177n33
jurisdiction. *See* laws

Kellhoffer, James A., 73
Kennedy, James, 165
kermes, 115–16
keywords, 3–4
Kircher, Athanasius
   Ars Magna Lucis et Umbrae, 194n31
   Magnes, Sive de Arte Magnetica, 194n31
Kittler, Friedrich, 172
Korda, Natasha, 50
Kumar, Krishan, 30

labor exploitation, 58
Lacan, Jacques, 172
La Fontaine, Jean de, 146
La Galla, Giulio Cesare, 185
language. *See* communication
Laroche, Rebecca, 105, 118n11
Las Casas, Bartolemé de, 64
Latour, Bruno, 142, 173
Lauck, Joanne Elizabeth, 157n12
laws
   vs. custom, 87–88, 89
   divine, 90
   on free *vs.* constricted movement, 86–88, 96–99, 100n16
   on private *vs.* public property, 85–87, 88
   unjust, 89–90, 91, 97
Lawson, William, *New Orchard and Garden, A*, 113
Leahy, John Patrick, 4
Leong, Elaine, 107
liberty. *See* laws
lice
   coexistence with, 54–55
   and corruption, 52–54
   internal infestations of, 74–75, 76–77
   remedies for, 55–56, 57
Liceti, Fortunio, 182, 189, 190
life, and bioluminescence, 182–84, 191
life-form, as concept, 162, 176n7
life-form topoi, 162, 173–75
light. *See* glowworms
Lime Street, natural history community on, 16
Lindauer, Martin, 170
Lippit, Akira Mizuta, 25n25
Lockwood, Jeffrey A., 134, 141, 156
locomotion. *See* creeping and crawling

locusts
   biblical associations, 66, 67, 68, 71, 73, 78
   consumption of, 65, 71–77, 78
   eradication strategies, 66–67, 70–71
   fruit/vegetable interpretation, 73, 78–79
   geographical origins, 62–63
   militaristic qualities of, 68–70
   ritual excommunication of, 66–67
   See also cicadas
Lorimer, Jamie, 157n14
Lucretius, *De Rerum Natura*, 154, 176n13
Lycosthenes, Conrad, 90

MacInnes, Ian, 124
Maisano, Scott, 45
Mandelstam, Osip, 144
Mandeville, Bernard, *Fable of the Bees*, 166
Mann, Charles C., 64
Maplet, John, 125
Markham, Gervase
   Farewell to Husbandry, 125
   Inrichment of the Weald of Kent, The, 122–23
   Second Book of the English Husbandman, The, 51–52
Marlowe, Christopher
   Doctor Faustus, 139n20
   Edward the Second, 135
Marvell, Andrew, 181
Marx, Karl, *Capital*, 166
Mary, Queen of England, 85, 99n11
Mascall, Leonard, *Countrymans Recreation, The*, 125
Matthews, Janice, 134–35, 139n9
Matthews, Robert, 134–35, 139n9
Mayerne, Theodore de, "Epistle Dedicatory," 38–39, 150, 153, 155
Mayow, John, 192
medicinal properties
   of bees, 104, 105, 110, 111
   culinary connections, 106–7
   remedies for lice, 55–56, 57
   remedies for stings, 19, 26n16
   remedies for worms, 108–9
   of scale insects, 116
   of snails and earthworms, 109–10
Meinwald, Constance, 175n1

Melissographia, 40, 41, *41*
men. *See* gender; women
Menely, Tobias, 155
Merula, Gaudentius, 192n10
Mexía, Pedro, *Foreste*, 84, 87
Michaux, Henri, 161
microscopes, 20, 37, 38–40, 41, 42, 45, 184
Middleton, Thomas, 90
migrant workers, 58
Mildmay, Grace, 111
militaristic qualities
    of ants, 52
    of bees, 21–23
    of butterflies, 92, 100n36
    in household management, 51, 52
    of locusts, 68–70
Miller, Daphne, 129n8
Milton, John, *Paradise Lost*, 40–41
Mirror for Magistrates, 100n36
Mishan, Ligaya, 105
Moffett, Thomas
    fieldwork approach to natural history, 16–20
    Silkewormes, and their Flies, The, 126
    See also *Theater of Insects, The*
Montgomery, David, 123–24
moonlight and sunlight, 185–90, 193n21
Moretti, Franco, 32
Morgan, C. Lloyd, 164
Morton, Timothy, 170
mosquitos, 197
movement. *See* creeping and crawling
mummy/mummia, 111–12
Munroe, Jennifer, 118n11
murder hornets, 197
Murharyati, Atiek, 110
music. *See* singing

nationalist discourse, 50, 51, 57, 75–77
Negri, Antonio, 176n14
Nicostratus, 38
Nieremberg, Juan Eusebio, 181
Noble, Louise, 111
Nunn, Trevor, 137

Ogilvie, Brian, 63, 79n2
Oktariani, Meri, 110
original sin, 53

Orlemanski, Julie, 32
Orosius, Paulus, *History Against the Pagans*, 65–66
Ovid, *Metamorphoses*, 52, 95
Ovidian etiologies, 92, 93, 94–96
Oviedo, Gonzalo Fernández de, 181

paradoxes of measure, 34–37, 42, 44
parasitical communication, 145–47, 149, 151, 153–54
parasitic worms, 108–9, 129n8
Paré, Ambrose, *Anatomie Universelle*, 26n16
Parikka, Jussi, 171, 172
Paster, Gail Kern, 99n4
pastoral imagery, 24
Patterson, Annabel, 101n43
Patterson, Robert, *Natural History of the Insects Mentioned in Shakspeare's Plays*, 78
Penny, Thomas, 16–20, 30, 63, 153, 156
Pepys, Samuel, 55
perception, human, 36, 38
Persio, 41, *41*, 42, *42*–43, *43*
pest control, 49–59
    binary discourses on, 50–54
    and coexistence, 54–56
    and earthworms, 125
    environmental justice framing of, 50, 56–59
    See also infestations
Pharamacopoea Belgica, 116
Phase IV (film), 176n19
Phipson, Emma, 78
Plato, 160, 167, 168, 175n1
Pliny, 35, 71
    Natural History, 19
Plot, Robert, 180, 182
Plumwood, Val, 56
Plutarch, 76, 84, 99n3
poison. *See* venom
political, the
    and nationalist discourse, 50, 51, 57, 75–77
    and scale, 40–43
    See also colonialism; commonwealth; laws; militaristic qualities; sovereignty

population decline, 197–98
Pory, John, 65–66, 67
positivist historicism, 174
Potier, Pierre, *Pharmacopaea Spagirica*, 188–89
Purchas, Samuel
    Purchas His Pilgrimage, 63
    Theatre of Politicall Flying-Insects, A, 2–3, 37–38, 70, 164, 176n13
purity concerns, 52–54, 73, 77
putrefaction. *See* corruption

racial discourse, 50, 53–54, 58
    See also ethnography
Raffles, Hugh, 156
Ramachandran, Ayesha, 101n46
Rao, Namratha, 100n39, 101n50
Rasmussen, Mark David, 100n38
receipt books, 104–18
    and beekeeping, 113, 114
    bees as ingredients, 104, 105, 110, 111
    dual culinary-medicinal purposes, 106–7
    human bodies and bodily fluids as ingredients, 111–12
    remedies for lice, 55–56, 57
    remedies for stings, 19, 26n16
    remedies for worms, 108–9
    scale insects as ingredients, 116–17
    snails and earthworms as ingredients, 109–10
    violence in, 110–12, 118n24
red dyes, 115, 116–17
relationality
    and coexistence, 54–56
    of parasites, 145
    and transcorporeality, 56, 107–8, 112, 116, 149
    See also scale
religion and spirituality
    conjuration and excommunication, 66–67
    lice associated with, 52–53
    and light sources, 185, 186, 188, 190
    See also God
re-mark, 170–71
remedies. *See* medicinal properties
reproduction, 63, 124
ritual excommunication, 66–67

Rondelet, Guillaume, 183
Ronfeldt, David, 176n21
Roosth, Sophia, 176n7
Rose, Deborah Bird, 198
Ross, Alexander, *Arcana Microcosmi, or the Hid Secrets of Man's Body*, 76–77
Rudsen, Moses, *Further Discovery of Bees, A*, 164, 167
Ruth (biblical figure), 83

Sahagún, Bernardino de, *Historia General de las Cosas de Nueva España (Florentine Codex)*, 115
scala naturae, 30–31
scale, 29–45
    critical theories and models of, 30–34
    and the diminutive sublime, 35–38, 39, 101n49
    and human prerogative, 44–45
    and microscopes, 37, 38–40, 41, 42, 45
    and paradoxes of measure, 34–37, 42, 44
    and politics, 40–43
    in print culture, 29–30
scale insects, 64, 114–17
Sebeok, Thomas, 172
sericulture, 125–28, 129n12
Serres, Michel, 145, 146
sex and gender. *See* gender
Shakespeare, William
    As You Like It, 136
    Coriolanus, 101n49
    Hamlet, 108, 112, 136, 137–38, 188
    Henry V, 85
    Henry VI, Part 2, 13–14, 17, 136
    King Lear, 94, 98–99, 114
    Measure for Measure, 136
    Merchant of Venice, The, 54, 136
    Merry Wives of Windsor, The, 111, 137, 192n4
    Midsummer Night's Dream, A, 136, 137
    Much Ado About Nothing, 139n19
    Othello, 78–79, 138
    Pericles, 189
    Romeo and Juliet, 136
    Tempest, The, 137
    Titus Andronicus, 137
Shannon, Laurie, 98, 100n41, 133, 143
Shi, Yuhui, 165
Shurgot, Michael, 138

Sidney, Mary, 126
Sidney, Philip, *Old Arcadia*, 89, 93
silkworms, 125–28, 129n12
Simondon, Gilbert, 171
sin
 original, 53
 punishment for, 52–53, 66, 67, 70, 76
singing
 of bees, 162–63, 166–68, 172, 173
 of cicadas, 152–53, 154
slime
 of silkworms, 127
 of snails, 110
Smith, Courtney Weiss, 20, 22
Smith, Lisa, 112
snails, 109–10
Snow, Jackie, 138, 139n26
soil amendment and composting, 122–23, 128
Solomon (biblical figure), 84
sovereignty
 of bees, 15, 17, 23–24, 84, 114, 163–64, 167–69
 customary privileges, 87–88
 and divine law, 90
 and scale, 42
 sexing of, 17, 114
 and swarms, 163–64, 166, 167–69
 See also commonwealth
Spanish trade, 115
species decline, 197–98
speech. *See* communication
Spenser, Edmund
 Faerie Queene, The, 34–35
 Mother Hubberds Tale, 93, 101n43
 Muiopotomos, 85, 92–98
 Shepheardes Calender, The, 93
 Virgils Gnat, 89
spiders
 conflict with butterflies, 92, 94–95, 96, 97–98
 webs of, as encroaching and constricting, 85–88, 89, 92, 97–99
 webs of, as fragile, 83–84, 89–90, 91
 webs of, skill in crafting, 95
Spinoza, Baruch, 107
spirituality. *See* religion and spirituality
spontaneous generation, 63, 124
Spurway, Helen, 171

stage actors, 137–38, 139n26
Stelluti, Francesco, 40, 41, *41*, 42, 42–43, *43*
Stewart, Susan, 34
stings, 13–25
 of bees, mechanism of, 20–23, *21*
 of bees, sovereignty dynamics, 23–24
 of bees, transferred to parchment, 13–15, 25
 remedies for, 19, 26n16
 of wasps, fieldwork on, 18–19
Strabo, 74
Sugg, Richard, 118n28
Sulisetyawati, Dwi, 110
Sulla, 76
Sullivan, Garrett, 31
Sully, Justin, 33
sunlight and moonlight, 185–90, 193n21
Suzman, Janet, 137
swarms, 160–75
 as concept, 161–62
 cybernetic swarm concept, 165, 176–77n21
 and dance language, 169–70, 171, 172, 173, 174–75, 177n35
 epistemological structures, 162–63, 172–73
 and life-form topoi, 162, 173–75
 paradox of, 161, 167
 relation between subject and, 166–67, 170
 as single organism and collective whole, 164–65, 166–67, 168
 and sovereignty, 163–64, 166, 167–69
 and topos of bee communication, 162–63, 173
 See also infestations

Talpin, Jean, *Christian Pollicie*, 91
Tanoukhi, Nirvana, 32
Tennant, David, 137–38
tettix, 144
Thacker, Eugene, 163–64, 176n7
Theater of Insects, The: or, Lesser Living Creatures (Moffett), 148
 on ants, 52
 on bees, communication of, 152, 166–67
 on bees, sovereignty of, 17, 23–24, 114
 on bees, superiority of, 112, 166
 on butterflies, 94, 98

Theater of Insects, The: or, Lesser Living Creatures (Moffett) *(continued)*
   on cicadas/grasshoppers/crickets, 150–51, 152–53, 155
   as co-composition, 154–55
   on earthworms, 125
   on glowworms, 181, 184–85, 191, 194n33, 194n36
   on lice, 52–54
   on locusts, and famine, 68–69, 70–71
   on locusts, consumption of, 71–74
   on paradoxes of measure, 36, 37, 38
   on poison, 149–50
   preface, 147–49
   publication and editions, 16, 29–30, 63, 153–54
   on spiders, 84
   on wasps, sting of, 18–19
theatrical movement, 137–38, 139n26
theology. *See* biblical associations; religion and spirituality
Thirsk, Joan, 123
Thompson, D'Arcy Wentworth, 33
Topsell, Edward, 83, 101n58
   Historie of Four-Footed Beasts and Serpents, The, 16, 29, 63, 151
transcorporeality, 56, 107–8, 112, 116, 149
Trump, Donald, 58
Tucker, Herbert, 30

universal history, 63, 64
Urban VIII, Pope, 40

venom
   of bee/wasp stings, 19, 21, 22
   communication hampered by, 149–50
vermilion, 115
vibration, and communication, 144
violence
   of communication, 149–50
   of dissection, 39, 150–51
   of murder insects, 197
   in receipt books, 110–12, 118n24
   See also militaristic qualities; pest control; stings
Virgil, 52
Virgilian epic, 92
Virginia silk cultivation, 126, 128, 129n12

Von Frisch, Karl, 157n7
   Bees, 169–71, 172, 173

Wall, Wendy, 111
warfare. *See* militaristic qualities
wasps. *See* bees
W.b. 653 receipt book manuscript, 117
weapon imagery, 20–23
webs. *See under* spiders
Wecker, John, *Secrets of Nature*, 118n24
Wenner, Adrian, 172
Werth, Tiffany Jo, 31, 32–33
Wheeler, William Morton, 164–65
White, Martin, 137
Whitehead, Alfred North, 164
Wiener, Norbert, 165
Williams, Edward, 127
Williams, Raymond, *Keywords*, 3
Wilson, Catherine, 139n13
Winche, Rebeckah, 108–9, 111, 116
Wither, George, *Britain's Remembrancer*, 68–70
women
   and cosmetics, 110, 113, 116, 117
   culinary and medicinal work of, 106–7, 109, 113, 114 (*see also* receipt books)
   and hygiene, 53
   sexing of sovereignty, 17, 114
   silence of, 151
Wood, Robert, 134
Woods, Derek, 31–32, 35
Woolley, Hannah, *Supplement to the Queen-Like Closet*, 55, 117
work
   of earthworms, 123–25, 128
   of silkworms, 125–28
worms
   creeping and crawling, 135, 139n13
   parasitic, 108–9, 129n8
   silkworms, 125–28, 129n12
   See also earthworms; glowworms
wormwood (*Chenopodium ambrosioides*), 109
Wotton, Edward, 30, 63, 153
Wu, Jiango, 33

Yates, Julian, 173, 174, 177n48